D1151157

FOREWORD

Tom Buncle,
Former Scottish Tourist Board Chief Executive

'Resilient', energetic, diplomatic and discreet. Part of the job description of a Scottish Tourist Board Quality Advisor which hardly did justice to the true demands of the role.

Reta has lifted the lid on life behind the wheel and beneath the sheets in pursuit of making Scotland a great place to visit. She explodes the myths of endless four course dinners and five-star luxury (although she's had her share) and takes us through the roller coaster of her day job with humour and a keen eye for the good, the bad, and the downright bonkers. Laced with jaw-dropping anecdotes, this book tells it as it was, through the lens of a sharp eyed, observer. All the while her professionalism, dedication and compassion shine through.

It's easy to forget today how important the role of a Quality Advisor was in the pre-TripAdvisor era. As impartial and skilled assessors, their judgement was one of the most useful sources of information, before peer-to-peer social media channels offered everyone the opportunity to have their subjective say. Travelling mostly incognito, with the constant threat of having their cover blown by an over-inquisitive proprietor, came with the territory. They had to sit with the wise and sup with the disgruntled, treating both with equal respect and professional detachment, in pursuit of a better Scotland.

This book is more than just a fascinating read it is a tribute to Reta and the other unsung heroes of the road, her fellow Scottish Tourist Board Quality Advisors, who played such an important part in helping Scotland become the great place to visit that it is today.

Willie Macleod
Former Director of Industry Services, VisitScotland

The role of a Quality Advisor at the Scottish Tourist Board (VisitScotland) sounds idyllic – the ideal job! And, in many respects, that's true. Travelling the length and breadth of the land, visiting far-flung places, wining and dining at some of Scotland's best watering holes and being paid for it!

But that's only part of the job. There was isolation, the solitary existence of travelling alone, especially in the middle of winter. There were schedules to be kept, unpalatable meals to be consumed, some nights endured in cold and uncomfortable beds, feedback to be delivered to some inattentive or obdurate hosts and the relentless discipline of objective report writing.

Reta played a significant part in training and managing those *professional guests* who were dedicated to ensuring that the visitor to Scotland was provided with independent and objective guidance on what to expect in quality of food, where to eat, visit and stay in the days before TripAdviser and other user-generated on-line reviews existed.

The QAs in Reta's book all came from different career backgrounds, were individuals, mavericks even! What they did share was a true commitment to their job and to each other (as do the current QAs) as well as a sense of 'dark' humour and an energetic ability to party when they got together after meetings!

Reta tells the tale like it was in the 1990s and the new millennium. The experiences are all true and real page-turners and I know there are others, not told here, that are best left unmentioned. It was my privilege for eight years, to get to know this extraordinary band of people who gave so much to tourism in Scotland and did so with great passion and insight.

TRAVELLING
SCOTLAND
WITH
ONE YELLOW WELLY

TRAVELLING SCOTLAND WITH ONE YELLOW WELLY

And a Boot Load of Stories

Reta MacLennan

For
John, Douglas and Steven

All my stories are based on actual experiences.
I have been creative with some incidents, names and locations
which have been fictionalised to give anonymity.
I am grateful to those who gave their permission to be included
in this book and have shown my appreciation in the
Acknowledgments.

Table of Contents

ACKNOWLEDGEMENTS

I wish to thank the following people:

Iain Morrison, of Ideam, for his creativity, enthusiasm and patience with my changes in producing a cover for this book.

My Quality Assurance friends and ex-colleagues, especially Colin Houston for his invaluable archive of STB documents.
Laura Alexander, Neil Borthwick, Sheila Cowan, Tracie Denoon, Ranald Duff, Naomi McMahon, Margaret Morrison, Alan Norris, Richard Pinn, Kim Ross, Marie Smith, Malcolm Smith, Dave Thom, Lorraine Thomson, and Margaret Wearmouth, for allowing me to include them in this book.
I would also all like to acknowledge with appreciation, the shared memories with my late colleagues: Ronnie Pearcy in 1998, Diana Carroll in 2004, Mike Elwis and Mary Stewart in 2008, Mark Sherwin in 2011 and Tony Mercer in 2019. They were good friends and we miss them.

To the following people for allowing me to tell their stories: Conrad Hodgkinson for Christine Barton; Struan and Frances Erskine, of Cambo Estate; Iain Morrison of Turusmara; Mary Robinson of Doune Bay Lodge; Christine Sloan of Crathie Opportunity Holidays; Phillip Southcott of Duke of Gordon Hotel.

My *Otago Tartan Bunnet* friends; Hamish and Mary Banford, David and Isobel Halliday, Jock and Wendy Latham, Carol and Ivor Menzies, Frances Plews, Joe and Betty Twaddle, for their encouragement to write this book.

Betty Twaddle, Conrad Hodgkinson and Barbara Darling for reading specific parts of this book. Walter Beveridge and Dorothy Baird who were generous with their time and final reading, editing and support.

Jamie Drummond for his help with knowledge of wines.

The tutors and fellow students of ARVON and the Edinburgh Stranger Than Fiction group who gave their candid opinions, encouragement and feedback.

Our two sons Douglas, for his IT input and suggestions and Steven for his IT input and publishing.

My husband John for his endless patience, many hours of listening, reading my rewrites, encouraging me and cooking for us.

PROLOGUE

We'd arrived in Kirkwall. I'd been looking forward to this visit which the guidebook told me had been the capital of Orkney since Norse days. As John parked the car, an ominous bank of charcoal cloud was building columns of water just offshore. It advanced with a shift of air, the first heavy drops making spit-holes on the surface of the Wide Firth, so we hurried with our cases making it to the hotel just before the deluge reached the town.

The receptionist gave us the key for room 5 and when John opened the door before entering the bedroom proper I hurried to the ensuite.

I jumped with fright. A man and woman were waist high in the bath water, shoulders hunched, one behind the other as if in a sinking boat with no oars. They got a fright too.

The young lady whimpered, with her hand crossed over her breasts. 'We asked for a late check-out.'

The young man said 'That's right' with as much command as a naked man in a bath can have in front of a female stranger.

My 'Sorry' could not have sounded genuine as I held onto my laughter and my need to find another loo.

I could hear John in the bedroom saying, 'What the ….'

Though it was still daylight, the curtains were closed, but when John opened them, they'd slid right off the ends of the rail landing in two slithering heaps on the floor. We then spotted their clothes thrown over a chair so left assuring them we'd ask for another room.

Trundling our cases back to reception, I whispered. 'Late check-out! It's after 4 o'clock. That's stretching it a bit and how come there was a key available for us anyway? Security's a bit lax.'

John clacked the key back on the high counter with a smile. 'Excuse me!'

'Yeh?' The receptionist, with a flying-swallow tattoo just above her left breast, turned her head a little with her eyes still fixed on the TV screen as was her bottom to her chair. She laughed at some rivetingly entertaining programme; her attention to us on pause.

'You gave us the key to room 5. There's a couple *in* Room 5.'

A gentleman in shirt and V-necked pullover who was rushing past the desk obviously overheard: he stopped dead. 'What! They're still in there?'

'Yes, in the bath actually.' I added.

'In the bath?' He screeched. And with that, grabbed the key and picked up speed to a run.

I caught John's eye and wondered if he was thinking *Fawlty Towers* as well. Meanwhile, the receptionist had swivelled her chair to be back with us. She made a *phfew* sound, checking the registration book. 'MacLennan. Says here that's you in room 5.'

'Yes, we are MacLennan.' I said.

'And you requested a late check-out?'

'No, the people who are *in* room 5 already, *they* wanted a late check-out and are still there. And I have to tell you the curtains came off the rail when I opened them.' John, as usual, dealt with the situation very calmly.

Moving her chewing gum around a bit she finally understood. 'Ah. Got it now.' I'd rubbed out the pencilled-in late checkout.' She looked down the list in the well-thumbed register again for another room, saying 'No worries, that sometimes happens. Sorry about that. Try this one.'

She handed us another key from the rank of pigeon-holes behind her. 'It's to the front street. Could be a wild Friday night in Kirkwall you know.' she giggled, raising her eyes to the ceiling. 'Just warning you!'

Little did they know I was there incognito, to assess the food and services at this small hotel on behalf of Taste of Scotland, a small Scottish foody booklet. My husband John, was on Orkney on business, so it was a convenient coincidence that we were there together. He'd stayed in this hotel before and had been surprised that the owner thought his restaurant belonged in the pages of that prestigious little publication.

We were first in the dining room at 7.00pm, soon followed by a young couple with their little girl in a pink-sequined party frock and glittering shoes. Her father carried an armful of her toys as she clung onto her mother's hand, not looking around, stroking her cheek with a corner of her security-blanket; a stuffed rabbit.

'She's just wakened.' They explained as they passed and settled themselves at a table by a window, wiping the condensation off to have a better view of the storm.

The gentleman who'd run off to turf the guests out of room 5 took our food order. When he was out of earshot John whispered, 'That must be him. The owner. The one I heard about. The distillery manager told me about him.'

John recalled the story he'd heard of how a crew of yachties having completed their sail from Norway to Kirkwall were celebrating at this hotel. They had to be drunk to imagine they could sneak a bag-squeezing, chanter-blowing piper back in after the owner had thrown him out, but they did.

Interrupted only by his own quiet wheezing laughter, John could hardly continue. 'The owner had come thundering back downstairs, saw the piper shouldering the bagpipes, marching and skirling back and fore in his dining room again.' John paused to wipe his eyes. 'Oh, ho. He must have been in such a rage. He grabbed the bagpipes and hurled them out of an open window.'

Apparently, they died on the street below, the last squeals from the drones squeezed out under the wheels of a passing car. It turned out that those bagpipes were the piper's grandfather's most valuable and prized possessions and the yachties had to pull the piper off the hotelier before the life was squeezed out of him as well.

A teenage waitress with Halloween-hair and Goth-black lipstick delivered our food. 'Fish? Steak?' She checked before sliding the plates in front of us with hands hampered by chipped black-lacquered nails.

The little girl in her pink party frock, recovering from her initial shyness ventured over to our table. She was Rebecca and now at ease with her surroundings, showed us her toys. However, they were soon abandoned when she spotted the breakfast table-settings at floor level under the sideboard; tablemats already topped with cutlery and a folded paper napkin. These were real professional toys and at just the right height for her.

After a while, as other diners arrived, she was well into her make-believe game of being a waitress. She skipped and bustled around with an all-consuming keenness, following guests to their tables, bringing them additional cutlery and napkins from her under-the-sideboard stock; her smiling parents watching, now and again smiling 'Awe. Bless.'

Encouraged by praise from amused diners her fun upped a gear to mimic the twitchy owner. She had 'Now, what can I get for you?' spot on, pretending she had a pad and pencil.

As she skipped into the hallway shouting 'Two steak pies please.' the owner appeared from the kitchen, stopped her in her tracks and pinned her arms by her side. Crouching down till they were eye to eye, he stretched his neck until their noses were almost touching. We could see his teeth side-on as he snarled a whisper like a Brothers Grimm character who might eat children.

Whatever our landlord spat out had an immediate effect: she appeared to stop breathing then let out a scream of astonishing decibels for such a wee poppet. All heads turned but from our table, we were the only ones who could see what had caused her trauma.

He had to think fast then before her parents arrived, so lifting her he attempted to pat her arched back as she kicked and wriggled to be free. 'There, there, you're okay.' He handed her over, shaking his head as if he had no knowledge of the cause.

She curled up on her father's lap cuddling her rabbit, her fun over and the frightening experience bringing on aftershocks of sobs.

I collected Rebecca's scattered toys and returned them to her. Making no attempt to whisper, I said 'Hope you're okay. Did that man scare you?'

She nodded.

'Never mind, you were doing a great job. Do you know, very good waitresses get a tip? Here is one for your piggy-bank.'

She lifted her brimming eyes and her mother thanked us.

If the receptionist's warning of a wild night did occur, we didn't notice; we slept soundly, no doubt from the effect of our journey, the good food and wine.

After breakfast the next morning while John settled our bill, I completed my report for Taste of Scotland. I managed to leave my business card on the unattended reception desk as we left.

Taste of Scotland required their inspectors to remain incognito, but this didn't give business owners an opportunity to explain or gain from feedback which could doubtless cause some frustration or even angst. However, remembering this owner's history with the bagpipes and the Rebecca incident the night before, on this occasion I was glad of this approach and even happier to just disappear.

John had gone ahead to our car with the cases and took off even before I'd buckled myself in, knowing I wanted to be away quickly. We accelerated past the hotel entrance and without needing to turn our heads saw the owner standing outside on the pavement with a small white card in his hand, scanning the street looking ready to kill.

In the car, glad to have left unscathed, I thought about that visit. 'I wouldn't choose to stay there again. Would you?'

John shook his head, smiling to himself.

I thought out loud. 'The kitchen staff had produced well-cooked fresh Scottish produce, all-be-it unimaginatively, but clearly, that was not the whole story. Other areas, mainly services, needed fixing, starting with this hotelier's behaviour. I couldn't recommend his hotel for inclusion in the Taste of Scotland booklet on my experience of this stay. But it would have taken courage to have a face-to-face with him. I might have been thrown out the window like the bagpipes.'

John had been listening and nodded.

WINTER 1992 - 1994

Scottish Tourist Board News Bulletin, January 1992

Membership of STB's Quality Accommodation Scheme has increased by 300%. Eight new Grading and Classification Officers will join the team in February 1992

It was after three summer seasons working for Taste of Scotland that I saw the advertisement in the Scotsman. A job with the opportunity to travel around Scotland assessing hotels, guest houses, B&Bs and self-catering establishments. Not just the food, but the whole experience from check-in to check-out, giving feedback on my stay and issuing awards. I desperately wanted that job.

The advert read 'Only those with relevant experience are invited to apply.' Having had hands-on experience of running my own catering business for seven years, feeding the directors and guests of blue-chip companies in Edinburgh, inspecting for Taste of Scotland and having good listening skills from my current training as a relationship counsellor, I wondered if that was relevant enough for me to be considered.

They wanted people with a strong constitution, whatever that meant; I was fit and well and could eat everything except stewed tripe. Travel throughout Scotland? I could read maps, enjoyed driving and had a clean driving licence.

Was it Really Luck?

I got the job and the third of February 1992 marked the start of a new lifestyle for me and my seven new colleagues. I'd never worked away from home four nights a week before and although I had very fleeting periods of a guilty conscience about leaving John to fend for himself, I was really feeling useful and exhilarated by the fact that this job had become reality. Working in small villages, towns and cities, among mountains and moorlands, passing lochs fed by streams and waterfalls. In sunshine or thunderstorms, it didn't matter: this was my dream job.

It was Friday and I was heading home at the end of a busy week feeling a satisfied tiredness: the work felt worthwhile. I had completed one of the first few weeks working on my own since training and work-shadowing in this new job.

There was fresh snow on the road from Fort William and I joined a line of cars following a snowplough until it turned into a layby. The mesmerising rhythm of the windscreen wipers and the snowflakes in the headlights appeared like white rivets driving at my windscreen. As darkness fell, I was staring, wide-eyed to stay awake and not really seeing so took a break at Callander. This made the journey three hours to the Edinburgh office instead of five.

It was 8.00 in the evening when I arrived there. Rock music was belting out from one of the offices and girl I hadn't met before pointed at me then pulled me in to have a drink. This was her leaving party.

She slurred. 'You're one of them? Aren't you?'

'One of who?' I asked.

She hesitated. 'Whatever you're called.'

I helped her out. 'Grading and Classification Officers?'

'Yeh. You know. You were damned lucky to get that job and I know why.' She threw her head back emptying her glass, reached for a bottle of red, refilled her own and handed one to me, just managing to miss my brand-new-to-me Hobb's coat I'd bought from the Cancer Care shop, the original price tag still attached.

'I was told there were more than 240 applicants, so maybe I was a bit lucky.' I replied but had a feeling she had more to tell me.

With her glass held well out of the way at the end of an outstretched arm and her mouth inches from my ear, perhaps she thought she was whispering against the background music but bellowed, 'I applied for that job you know.' Then narrowing her eyes, she pouted, shouting just as loudly. 'That bitch of a boss probably blocked my advancement because she couldn't do her job without me. Time will tell now. I'm off. Without me, she'll be exposed. Totally exposed.'

Pulling me by the arm, she headed for two chairs. Looking at me as if I was slightly out of focus, her speech slurring, she continued. 'I didn't tell you this okay. Someone, who shall remain nameless, "was assisting" (she made exclamation marks with her fingers) with the selection process for that job. She shouldn't have told me, but she can't keep her mouth shut. She took the pile of applications home. It was raining hard. A windy night too apparently. Right?' She paused to take a drink of wine. 'The pavements were wet. Right? She was balancing all the applications in her arms. Probably with an umbrella and a handbag too. Dropped them. Dropped the lot. You understand?'

I imagined the scene. 'Goodness. What ...?'

She hung her head, slowly shaking it in disbelief. 'And there's more. Wait. They scattered everywhere, got blown about.' She needed another slurp. 'So, then. Into the house. Sort, sort, wipe, wipe. Very wet ones? Chuck! Out they went.'

'Really?'

'Yep. So then. Wait for it. You couldn't make it up. She spread them out on the carpet in front of the fire. Took a break. Put the kettle on and when she returned, her wet cat came in. Wet paws. Right? Walked all over them to get to the fire. So, she ditched those ones. So, I tell you. Lady Feckin-Luck had a hand in the lot of you getting that job.' She tightened her lips, looked straight at me, giving me one big nod of confirmation. 'Lucky.'

'Oh Gosh!' I laughed. 'If I'd known, I would have gone around and kissed her cat.'

Her eyelids moving like heavy shutters, her face crumpled then her shoulders shook. Tears of self-pity ran freely down her cheeks. They might have been alcohol induced but I felt sorry for her. Poor girl, looking in a mirror, she'd wish she'd worn waterproof mascara.

I apologised, regretting my insensitivity, handed her a tissue and asked her about her new job: but she was now out of it. The music had quietened, two girls were collecting the glasses and I was glad to see one of her colleagues arrive with her coat. Between us, we managed to get her onto her feet and into it, then out to his car. I never saw her again. What a story to tell my colleagues on Monday. Pity I didn't get her name though.

On the journey home that Friday evening I reflected on my good luck in getting that job. Loving the work as I did, I had good reason to be grateful to that mucky-pawed cat, but it wasn't all luck. Since ever I can remember I'd had wobbly confidence but a can-do attitude which made me nervous of the targets I set myself, just to prove I could achieve them. I'd honed that application to make me seem as good a fit for the job as possible, even hand-delivering it to the office in case it might have been missed lying in the bottom of a Royal Mail bag.

I had started a part-time training course as a relationship counsellor a year before I had secured this nine months Tourist Board contract. The timing was not perfect but I hoped I could manage both. I certainly wanted to.

Instant Experts

We were to encourage our membership to raise the standards of guest accommodation and services. Out with the practice of charging for a bath plug, needing to feed a coin-meter to get heat in your bedroom, the only breakfast choice being bacon, egg, sausage and beans with white toasted bread, or needing to be tucked up in bed by 10.00 pm because that is when the landlady locks the front door. Guests being issued with a key? What a thought indeed! We were on a mission to rid Scotland of those unimaginative and limiting practices and encourage better service, more ensuite rooms, lounges for guest use. Suggest higher quality everything really.

People we visited expected us to have a wide knowledge of the quality of furniture, decor, carpets, heating, lighting, service standards and food. I'd felt competent with some of those; with others, I felt I was masquerading as a proper GCO. No sooner was I comfortable on a visit than a new challenge would crop up and stall me. A bit like when I learned to windsurf, fine in a steady force 4 but in an unexpected gust I could have the board whipped from under me and be tossed in the water with the sail over my head.

In the office

Every few months the week started with an all-GCO meeting in which we'd present and discuss any problems encountered. Driving the twenty minutes to our head office at 23 Ravelston Terrace, I was wavering between enthusiasm and trepidation at the thought of exposing my work for scrutiny in front of my colleagues at the meeting. My stomach felt as if I'd swallowed a swarm of bees. Having to fit into a slick team of apparently confident people, I sometimes felt slow to learn and memorise all that was involved.

I sat at traffic lights taking deep breaths, I gave myself positive messages; you've been well trained to do this job, you're a very good communicator, your visits have gone well. Nevertheless, doubts in my ability crept in and nibbled at the edges until I told myself, lighten up, girl, get a grip on reality It is just a job in tourism, you're not a surgeon having to perform a life-saving operation.

Our tiny office, an annexe to the admin team's room, held ten desks, two lots of fours pushed together in primary-school fashion. Richard, our Chief and Neil, Assistant Chief faced each other across another two desks with no privacy to discuss management issues. It was crowded with even half the team there but hardly enough personal space when all 17 of us were gathering, as we would be today to learn from our recent experiences.

Brian, who had been work-shadowing Cynthia, a more experienced colleague arrived keen to tell us about one of their overnight visits to a B&B. He'd been awakened around 2.00 am by loud drum-thumping music. Downstairs, he'd found the landlady passionately locked together with a gentleman guest, swaying to Abba's Waterloo. Brian had to shout *excuse me* a few times and wave his arms about to be noticed above the music in the dimmed lighting.

When he complained about the volume the bold woman had staggered out of the lounge, climbed the stairs and flopped onto his bed. In drunken laughter, she'd announced between hiccups, 'I can't hear it from here!'

Next morning, waiting for any sign of breakfast activity and failing to find even a cornflake, Cynthia and he had given up, packed up and gone looking for the lady owner. She appeared at the door of her dancing guest's bedroom in the previous night's melting makeup and a towel. When they asked her to sign the visit form accepting that she had no award, having failed to provide breakfast, they had at least expected an apology, but were further disappointed when she just told them to 'fuck off'.

Richard recalled one from his early days. Whilst staying in a town centre guest house in Dumfries and Galloway, he'd slept in a bedroom with no door. The previous occupant had heaved it off its hinges! The owner, who had been sunbathing all day and was still clad in a somewhat revealing bikini had thoughtfully pinned up a blanket with drawing pins instead.

Neil remembered one of his very first visits. The B&B landlady's dog left a hole in his trousers and teeth marks in his ankle. 'Were you carrying a suitcase?' She'd asked. He was, of course, so she just shrugged. 'Ah well'.

Diana had difficulty convincing a B&B lady who imagined that her plain unadorned white-emulsion walls should get an excellent score for decor, claiming it was a minimalist approach. Diana's argument was 'Since the Stone Age, man has been decorating the walls of his cave. Would you consider minimalist pieces of artwork?'

I told them the drunken story I'd heard at the leaving party and how lucky we'd been that a cat with wet paws had avoided padding over our application forms. We unanimously agreed, he must be an offspring of Mr Mistoffelees, that magical cat; very intelligent, eliminating the riffraff.

In our cramped space, sharing and comparing our experiences, the energy and hilarity among my gregarious new colleagues rose, (especially after the lovely spirited Ronnie's arrival). Next door in the spacious bright-and-light-filled office, the exclusive domain of our admin team, the atmosphere was subdued. With our exuberance it would be easy for them to believe we just played around Scotland, dining at the Tourist Board's expense while they were desk-bound. In contrast, their work seemed perhaps boring and repetitive.

As each GCO arrived they deposited their three-weeks of visit reports onto the growing stacks in the admin team's in-trays. Those trays soon disappeared under the mountain of paperwork which dimmed any glimmer of their already lukewarm Monday-morning dynamism lasting beyond coffee time.

In the admin office, Liz would set the tempo of the staff's work pace by slowly assembling her breakfast and consuming it at her desk. While appearing detached from the chatter she was alert and listening. Snippets overheard or shared innocently would find their way to our director Tim Oliphant's ear when it felt like an advantageous moment for her. I learned to keep my mouth shut in her presence.

When I'd been running between visits in Edinburgh one day I'd been gasping for a cup of tea. I happened to say that unusually, I hadn't been offered one on any of my visits. Her response, issued with a false sympathetic smile was 'Maybe they didn't like you.'

Alistair, one of the clerks, kept a black book where he recorded what he considered to be our misdemeanours.

Jack, another clerk, couldn't conceal his glee one-time, braying donkey-style when he'd called to tell me I'd left my suitcase standing in the driveway of the last house I'd visited. He'd enjoyed that.

Thankfully Pat, Tim's secretary was cheerful and helpful.

That Monday morning, Jack pushed his way through the chatter of voices in our room and thumped a stack of concertinaed computer printouts onto Neil's desk.

'Good morning Jack. Had a good weekend?'

'Morning Neil. Wonderful thank you, time away from you lot is always good,' he threw back over his shoulder.

Neil, with an amused smile set about flipping the pages of the thick stack of computer printouts, using his geographical grasp of Scotland to rip off wads and pass them to us as areas in which to book our visits. There were very few roads in Scotland which Richard, Neil and our experienced colleagues hadn't driven on and given a name, location and description of a frontage, they could recall with extraordinary detail, much of the experience of being there.

Once those who'd driven from some distance away had arrived, we relocated to the top floor for our all-GCO meeting.

Over the next couple of hours, we sat around the extended boardroom table with Richard and Neil in charge and presented any problems we'd encountered on visits. We discussed what might seem to an outsider very boring detail but was important to ensure consistency of opinion across the team. Problems were teased out with a light but focused degree of banter.

Was a bone-china dinner service higher quality than a Highland Stoneware one, it being hand-painted? What about hand-painted stoneware as opposed to Villeroy and Boch fine china? And, was that fine bone-china dinner service scuffed, scratched and worn or still as new? It was only when the question 'Can this be improved on?' was answered with a resolute 'No', could the top grading mark be justified.

Lunchtime was an entertaining break. We heard of a previous meeting when Mike had reached into his briefcase and unwrapped a tiny parcel revealing a crusty brown-edged fried egg, demonstrating that its strength and rigidity resembled a frisbee.

My own lunchtime was cut short, however. Quite rightly, random checks were carried out on expenses claims and I'd been summoned by the Finance Department to account for mine. I was confident my claims had been accurately recorded but felt a tiny shudder of assumed guilt in my stomach.

Without introducing himself (and I didn't ask in case I ought to have known who he was) the man in the chair on the other side of the desk leaned back, looking at the ceiling in contemplation, which felt like an uncomfortably long time.

He eventually glanced at the top of my expenses form. 'Reta isn't it?

I nodded.

'Well, Reta. After a big breakfast you seemed to need,' he paused, 'a morning coffee and a scone. Then you went back to the same cafe for a bowl of soup and a sandwich. Then tea and a Kit-Kat in the afternoon. Then a steak pie and apple crumble in the evening with wine' He narrowed his eyes. 'That seems excessive in one day.'

'Ah, yes. You will see I was on the Isle of Arran. Regarding the wine, I was staying in a pub with rooms so was assessing the bar service. The sleet and rain never stopped that week ...'

He interrupted me. 'But you GCOs get given tea and scones etc. everywhere you go!'

I was assessing self-catering properties. They were unoccupied and cold. There was no-one around to offer me a cup of tea. I had to get into a cafe and was glad to find one open in winter. I wrote my reports there, trying to get warm.'

Without looking at me he said. 'Why are all your phone calls home either 20p or exactly £1?'

I felt my cheeks burning. He didn't know me yet and I really was *not* trusted. 'Our allowance is £1 a day for a call home. Yes?'

He nodded.

'I keep two of those plastic pouches you can get from the bank. One has 20 pence pieces and the other 50s. I use them for parking and phone calls. If I get the answering machine at home, it's 20p by the time I've left a message. If my husband answers, £1 is enough. He doesn't do long phone calls.' I laughed. He didn't. I asked, 'Is there anything else?'

'No, that's all, thank you.' He then lifted the phone to move on to his next task.

'Okay, I'll tell Richard there was no problem with my expenses.'

He nodded. He was just doing his job, but I hurried back to the boardroom with an image of him as Chief Inspector Clouseau jumping out from behind a potted palm, dipping his finger into my glass of mineral water in case the lemon slice might be floating in a gin and tonic, when the job didn't require me to have one.

The Long Reaching Shadow of Guilt

After lunch, Richard announced 'We've had a few complaints, since our last meeting, but we can all learn from them.'

He started reading the first one. I drifted into listening to my own internal dialogue; guilt stirring again.

The headmaster stood with a note in his hand. 'Would whoever spilt liquid soap all over the Janitor's floor, come to the front now.' I was quaking inside. My eight-year-old self, walked forward. My right foot squelching in a pink carbolic-soaked sock and sandal, dried blood on my grazed shin. I'd stepped up on top of the drum-shaped container to reach for my confiscated tennis ball. I was relieved when I saw the corners of his mouth trying not to smile. The embarrassment had been punishment enough and I was still to face Grandma. This is the Grandma who, when young and vigorous had been up in court and fined 10 shillings and sixpence for battering her neighbour!

I did hear. '... a B&B ... a croft on Arran ... a problem parking the car beside the house. The owner says it was suggested he build a car park with flood-lighting.' Richard then looked out at the view to avoid making eye contact with anyone. 'It might not have been quite as he claims, people sometimes don't really hear what is said. I would just ask you to be clear and think about the appropriateness of your advice, in such an environment.'

Having missed some of what he said, I remained quiet, my school-girl face throbbing. I wanted to say, 'It was me. I didn't say 'floodlights' or 'car park'.' There were no streetlights and it was dark. I remembered opening their field gate to an acre of grazing ground driving through clumps of reeds in the middle of the track and stepping out of the car onto the mushy ground with cow pats close to the croft house. I'd asked them to consider clearing an area for cars beside the house and perhaps install a light above the front door.

I'd tell Richard my version later. Maybe. Once the heat had gone from my face and my stomach had stopped churning.

After the meeting, my colleague Colin took a phone call. We heard 'Really. Well, well. I see. Yes indeed. I will. Thank you.' Then he put the phone down. Some of us lifted our heads from our paperwork.

'Right. I'm just going to pop out to revisit a guest house on the Corstorphine Road. I saw it last week and it seems a neighbour has shopped them; turned informer. With his hand on the door handle, he said. 'I'll be back and will reveal all.'

He returned with the story. When her husband saw his wife return from the front door with Colin, he choked on the mouthful of cake he was having with his tea.

The lounge Colin had seen on his pre-arranged day-visit the previous week, was now a bedroom. They'd removed that bedroom furniture and replaced it with their own lounge furniture.

They needed a guest lounge to get one more crown on their plaque so had created a pop-up lounge purely for Colin's day visit. It had obviously been important to be one crown better than the neighbour. Unfortunately, the one who'd shopped them.

Driving home that evening I thought overall it had been a good day. I'd learned a lot more about the fine-tuning of grading, I'd felt tense and a bit vulnerable at times, but I'd managed in the busy atmosphere to get well on the way with my bookings for the next three weeks. Goodness. I hadn't yet given a thought to what we were to have for dinner.

The next morning, I beat the crawl of commuter traffic and was at my desk by 8.00 am before the phones started ringing. I would be able to plan things more clearly before the others arrived, line up possible visits on a route plan so that around 10.30ish when breakfasts and check-outs might be over, I could hit my list of phone calls and complete my bookings.

Comparing Richard and Neil's fingertip knowledge of the country to my own, searching the pages of the computer print-out with all the members' details, some of it in code and acronyms, I felt slow. Warnings were clouding my progress: check, check, check that the business is not up for sale, that they have paid, that they are open for winter business, that they haven't been visited in the last six months. Don't book an overnight when they only need a day visit and vice versa.

To complicate things, there could be two villages with the same name. Check the postcodes but don't rely on them for directions: check the roadmap. Postcodes can stretch over a road-free mountain. Make sure journey planning makes the most economical use of time and money.

As the desks filled and my colleagues were booking too, my concentration was waning. I got slower and slower and felt the pressure of having to complete this in time to leave the office that afternoon.

Scottish Tourist Board News Bulletin 1992

'Extensive research has shown the need to further recognise excellence and the highest-level award will now be Deluxe. At the start of the new scheme year visits will take account of this and the new awards will appear in brochures in 1993.'

Deluxe Awards

The introduction of the Deluxe grade was a result of a general feeling that the Commended band had within it too wide a range of qualities.

In moving the entry-point of each grade to accommodate this new Deluxe Award, we could foresee more tricky situations. There would be downgrades and upgrades, disappointments or celebrations or even downright outrage.

In smaller establishments; B&Bs and Guest Houses, owners could understandably react very personally to our findings, whereas in larger establishments run my managers, the reaction could be less so. We discussed ways of focusing on small details, simple changes to appease disappointments and keep the standards rising.

Expect the unexpected

At the end of that Tuesday I was heading for the Kingdom of Fife in a conga-line of cars exiting the city centre and crossing the Forth Road Bridge. I was feeling euphoric, playing an Elton John CD loudly, relieved to have the next three weeks' bookings organised.

By 6.00 pm I was soaking in a bath in a B&B in Dunfermline, finally feeling relaxed. I lay there, my eyelids heavy, watching the bubbles popping around me as I soaked in the hot water. A key turned in the bedroom lock and the door opened. I heard my landlady say. 'I'd like you to start here. This room will be free after breakfast tomorrow for three days.'

A gentleman in paint-stained white overalls and a head of curly hair passed the bathroom door. I slid low in the water and coughed. 'Hello, I'm still here. In the bath actually.'

She gasped. 'I'm so sorry Mrs MacLennan, I thought I heard you go out. Oh, my goodness, I'm terribly sorry. I am showing the decorator around the bedrooms.'

'It's okay. I'll stay here.' I answered, remembering I'd been warned to be prepared for the unexpected.

I then heard the man say. 'It's okay I've seen enough anyway.'

I guessed that would have included my discarded clothes, bras and pants lying on the bed. They were a matching set at least.

The East Neuk of Fife

One weekend in my first summer in the job, John and I were walking on the Fife Coastal Path. I was now able to point out to him, houses I'd visited, recalling some of the details as we walked around Crail.

This is the oldest of the East Neuk villages in the Kingdom of Fife and dates back to its 12th-century castle and harbour. It draws families who return year after year for its slow-moving pace and coastal-village tranquillity, its award-winning beaches and its rich local history.

There are sympathetically restored 16th to 18th century whitewashed cottages with crow-stepped gables, their red-pantile roofs warming the greyest of skies and front doors with low lintels perched at the top of fore-stairs with shallow treads. Those sandstone steps which now hold locally thrown pots of cascading geraniums and petunias in summer and have visitors clicking their camera shutters at every corner were once worn down by fisher folk's clogs.

We bought freshly cooked crab at the harbour, picking at it for lunch. Strolling around, looking over the shoulder of a group of artists, we watched how they captured a scene with their brushes and palette knives, attempting to catch the changing light and shadows on the water or in its steep narrow wynds with their cobbled twists and turns.

We'd seen silver-haired tourists with the guidebook in their hands and a keen eye delighted to find the stone-carved marriage lintels above the low doors of the old terraced houses.

Finishing our walk, we had been more than ready for cool beers and had managed to get two seats at a table outside the Ship Tavern in Anstruther. We faced the sheltered marina with the sound of the rigging clinking against the masts, amused by the customers who sat in their cars, waiting for opening time at the award-winning Anstruther Fish Bar. They strolled towards it, resisting the urge to make a dash for the growing queue. We knew they would enjoy the best fresh-caught haddock supper there very soon.

But that was a happy memory of one-weekend last summer. It was now a bitter January day in 1993 and I was delighted to have had my nine-months contract made permanent.

I'd returned to Fife. The North East gales were whipping up the sand, howling around the houses and rattling the pantiles, ripping the stark stems of the climbing rose and clematis off their trellises. East-coast absentee owners had battened down anything which might fly and the East Neuk had shuttered itself into dormancy.

I'd visited three unheated self-catering properties that day, fumbled with keys, reluctant to remove my gloves and my fingers had difficulty holding a pen.

I had one more cottage to see so turned off the A915, driving downhill on that familiar road into Lower Largo past the Crusoe Hotel at the harbour and continued along Main Street. The village didn't seem to have changed much since I had holidays there with my family in the 1950s, except there were now new houses where sea views had been. The shop after the bend where my cousin and I had bought fishing lines with lead sinkers was now a house, but there was still the statue of Alexander Selkirk looking out to sea, between numbers 103 and 105. I remembered reading Robinson Crusoe by Daniel Defoe that summer, one of my cherished collection of picture-book Classic Tales.

The cottage I was to visit was just a few yards further along on the shore side of the road and had been left unlocked for me by a neighbour. It was a recent purchase and the absentee owners had requested an advisory visit before tackling the upgrade.

They wished to preserve the character of this little place, retaining the old doors and windows, even the low ceiling. However, the council planners may have had stipulations regarding the lack of height.

This cottage had black scart-marks across the very low, distempered ceiling-boards just inside the front door; probably from the sacks of coal being carried to the bunker in the scullery.

There was a recess in the living room/kitchen. It held the same smell of dampness as the one my family had rented for two weeks when I was around age 10. I'd slept in a sofa bed in a space like that. This damp smell was even in my pillow.

In the garden, the grass was cut but the borders were wild. Fuchsias and hydrangeas grow well there by the sea, but those ones needed deadwood pruned out and reshaped. Otherwise, it was a good south-facing space.

I noticed the remains of a hen house with broken fencing Then I spotted something: the carved plaque with a thistle and rose design at the apex above the door of the hen house. It had been painted blue and red then. Now the wood was silver with age. This was the actual hen house so possibly the actual cottage. The one I had stayed in all those years ago. *I used to mimic the noises the hens had made as I pushed bread through the wires.*

I wrenched open the rotting wooden gate to the beach; the steps were also rotten now, too badly damaged and needed to be replaced. I stood in the biting wind looking at the beach for a minute, wondering if there would still be crabs and lobsters under those rocks.

A sunny, early morning walk while the tide was out. The cold, hard ridges of the wet-rippled sand hurt my bare feet. Where the tide had left a pool of water under the rocks, I watched my uncle push a hooked rod under a barnacled one. He felt a tug on his hook and pulled firmly. One claw came out with a rush. I felt horrified, panicky and scared. He tried again and this time the rest of a lobster appeared slowly its legs finding no grip on the sandy bottom. It must have been in pain.

I wanted to cry. I felt so sorry for it. He told me that lobsters can grow another claw, but this one wouldn't. It didn't have time before it was to be cooked. It was scratching to get out of the boiling water and screeching noises came from the pot. I covered my ears. I couldn't eat it.

That night my family were awakened by my cries. Crabs and lobsters were under my bedclothes crawling up the bed, their huge claws trying to find my toes.

About as Bad as it Gets

My next stop was in Leven which lies south of the East Neuk and I was heading to a pub with rooms, once again, in need of warmth. I was hoping to thaw out in front of an open fire, have hot food and a cosy bedroom. No such luck.

It was dusk by the time I arrived in the car park. My headlights panned across a heap of bin bags, a rusting radiator, a mattress with a growth of moss and a rusting industrial extractor fan. The black peeling paintwork on the windows was lifting, but my spirits were sinking. As they'd joined the tourist board scheme and would be expecting a visit, albeit incognito, they could have made a bit of an effort surely.

I made a tight manoeuvre and drove out to park under a streetlamp. Unimpressed, I reminded myself that most of the things I worry about never actually happen. I was right in this case. I would not be staying here.

The swing doors gave an un-oiled screech and I entered bringing a chilly draft with me. I scissored my way over to the bar in my high heels, well-cut navy suit and bright multi-coloured scarf, my trench coat over my arm, wheeling my suitcase behind me. I felt as out of place as an air hostess in a building-site bothy.

Three men were hunched at the bar in high-vis anoraks and cement-stained jeans. their clarty, hard-toed boots on the steel foot-rail. Misted pint glasses sat in front of them, their eyes fixed on the football match on an old TV on a shelf above the spirits.

One of them turned his head to see who had arrived. Coughing with a smoker's wheeze, he made a fist, thumped his bicep, jerked his arm up and nodding towards the barman said, so that I could hear, 'Ye'll be awe right the night then Alex, eh?' Alex didn't respond but his mates glanced at me and chuckled.

Alex, the young man behind the bar, looking smart in a striped shirt and tie asked, 'Can I help you?'

'I have a room booked for tonight. MacLennan.'

He ran his finger down the page of a tattered registration book to today's date and took a key from the rack. I read the registration book upside down. *MacLemon - single - female.*

'If you'd like to follow me, please? The accommodation is just next door. We've no single rooms I'm afraid.'

The door squeaked again, and Alex left the responsibility of the bar to lead me to the adjoining house which had the same peeling exterior paintwork. Its front door was right on the pavement and once inside he put the key into the lock of a ground-floor room to the front street with the noise of a bus grinding uphill.

The walls were covered in woodchip, the decorative finish reminding me of mixing leftover paint from part used tins. Like a toddler's first attempt at mixing colours, the finished effect was shit-brindle. A similar darker brown colour, covered the doors, skirting boards and the only bedside table.

I pointed to the old cathode-tube TV with a reshaped dry-cleaner's hanger pushed into the indoor aerial socket. 'Does that work?'

'I'll check it for you.' He tried. Surprisingly the TV did work but only whilst he held the makeshift aerial in place, otherwise it reverted to a snowstorm. I could see him realising he'd have to stand there all night to keep it working. He blushed but was keen to please. 'I could maybe swap it for the one from the bar?'

I imagined the workmen trying to find the football in a white-out. 'It's okay. Thanks for trying anyway.' I smiled.

The thin curtains which hung by a few remaining hooks, were probably never used as the passing traffic had created a very effective, thick opaque finish to the bottom half of the high windows anyway.

The floor space was taken up with four single beds with just enough room to edge between them. There was a leg missing from one bed base: an upturned beer crate topped with layers of torn cardboard made the bed stable. Each bed had very pilled floral or striped polyester bed linen but none, not even one item, matched another. I threw back a duvet cover. Shining through the very thin bed sheet were the words. KIRKCALDY DISTRICT COUNCIL. They

They'd sellotaped bin bags together as mattress protectors.

The bulb in the one bedside lamp didn't work, a cluster of wire hangers hung in the wardrobe and this was the worst bedroom I'd ever seen.

Along the hallway, I found the door to the shared shower and toilet facilities. Some prankster had removed a stick-on letter. It now read *SHOWER AND TO LET*. The shower curtain refused to close because black mould, fading to pink as it rose, had stuck the folds together. Blue mould in my cheese I like, but pink and black on a shower curtain? No thanks. The WC had one sound hinge to the seat, the other was repaired with wire.

This was wonderful material to share with my colleagues. I photographed those excellent examples of poor quality items. We had never seen this standard ever in training: a genuine doss house.

I put my suitcase back in the car, returned to the bar and handed back the key.

Alex coloured up again. 'I didn't think you would stay. I know my mother wouldn't. I feel so embarrassed.'

I felt sympathy for him and murmured 'Is the owner here?'

'No, sorry, he comes in around 10.00 in the morning and leaves around 4.00 for his tea, but he might be back later.'

'Well, would you take my card for him, please? I'm from the Scottish Tourist Board. I could call back tomorrow morning around 11-ish. Would you give him a message saying I will drop in then? If it is not suitable, he could call me, and I will visit another time.'

'I can do that for you, of course.' I offered my hand and we shook on it as he leaned forward with an apologetic whisper. 'I'm so sorry, I don't know quite what to say. Our business is these guys. They're on a contract, working at the Methil construction yard building the oil rigs. I'm just here till I can get another job, I'm a student and need the money. I'm really sorry about this.'

I whispered too. 'No worries. He's lucky to have you. I hope you find another job soon. Many thanks anyway.'

As I turned to leave, I heard one of the guys call out 'Awe, has your luck run oot Alex? Ye'll just hae tae snog me instead.' It could have been worse I suppose, I might have had those guys snoring in the other beds.

It was now dark. I'd nowhere to stay and that didn't feel comfortable. I was just a little concerned. If I couldn't find somewhere from my list, I'd have to drive home, that would put my mileage up and would mean my strike rate of visits for that week would be down.

I got clear of the traffic and drove along Leven promenade passing its neat bungalows and well-tended gardens in winter mode. I parked and had to smile to myself at that owner's audacity to imagine that guests would willingly part with their money to stay at such a dump.

Listening to the sound of the incoming surf on the long sandy beach for a few minutes I was wishing some comfortable accommodation would just pop up in the area for me.

The moonshine reflected off the watery sand. This was the beach in Leven which Jack Vettriano chose as the setting for his painting *The Singing Butler*. He placed his upper-class couple, dancing in evening dress, with attendant butler and a maid holding umbrellas against the weather. I remembered one of my counselling client's stories; he'd told me they'd been so poor; he'd collected coal from this very beach as a four-year-old together with his older brother. What struck me most then, about that painting was the gallus incongruity.

Having no bed for the night was a real problem and frustrating. In the town centre, I scanned the streets I passed, searching for a phone box. Then I spotted one and fortunately, it was under a streetlight too.

With the car heater running, I scrolled through the printout list of members who still required a visit, hunting for somewhere to stay. I found one in Glenrothes, some seven miles away and hoped it would be an easy visit; a one-bedroom B&B but as yet untested, a new member like the last one, but hopefully much better.

I dialled the number and waited. The regeneration of this area as a holiday destination was happening. But in winter they relied on business from Cameron Bridge, one of the largest distilleries in the world and Diageo's huge bottling plant, together with other large industries which brought blue and white-collar workers. Some of them would be searching for accommodation, just as I was now, among the limited winter choice available.

A man's voice answered. 'He-e-ell-o.'

'Hello, I'm sorry to call you at such short notice, but I'm just over in Leven now making my way to Glenrothes and wonder if you have a room for tonight?'

'Is it just for yourself?'

'Yes please.'

'Hud oan, please.' I heard a bit of fumbling. 'Daisy, dae ye want tae let the room the night?'

Back came a whisper, loud and clear. 'The room's no' ready.'

'It'll be fine hen, dinnae worry. 'Ah'll check if she's had her dinner and that'll gie us time tae sort the room oot.'

I could hear every word clearly. Perhaps he thought that covering the speaker with his fingers instead of his palm gave him privacy.

Then he said. 'Would £25 be okay, breakfast included?'

Of course, it was, but I wondered what to expect at that low price. Was I lined-up for shock number two?

'Did you say you were in Leven?' he added.

'Yes. Near the promenade.'

'Well, there's a guid Indian restaurant there, if ye'd like tae get yersel something tae eat before ye arrive that would be fine.'

I did need to eat and get out of the cold night somewhere. 'Thanks for that, it is good to have a recommendation. I'll go there.'

'What's your name hen?'

'Reta MacLennan. Reta with an e instead of an i.'

'Lovely Reta, Meta-Maid.' He sang it, then gave me very clear directions saying. 'We'll see ye later then.'

At least he was caring.

I put 20p in the coin box and called home as I did every evening but heard my own voice on the answering machine. 'Hi, it's me. You're not there?'

John lifted the phone then. We updated each other on our day, his much more stressful than mine and I had yet another pang of guilt about being away every week. Since I got this job, our two sons had left home to go to university and our two Jack Russell dogs, which used to give such a warm welcome, had both died the previous year. I felt sorry for John left in the house on his own all week. But he called it freedom.

A large glass of merlot and a Lamb Rogan Josh later, the guilt had gone, and I felt warmer and optimistic.

Chick Murray Lives On

Driving slowly in one of the Glenrothes 1950s council schemes looking for the right house number, I was reminded of the one I lived in as a child in Balerno: all the houses were the same style with pinkish-beige harled walls.

In my childhood, those two-bedroom houses had an open fire in the lounge with vents in the chimney stack to carry the warmed air into the upstairs bedrooms. They had simple well-tended gardens and there was no provision needed for garages or car parking.

Since then, Maggie Thatcher had encouraged the tenants to purchase their homes and local authorities offered very good deals to those who'd lived there for many years. Porches, extensions and conservatories, UPVC windows and B&Q front doors now proliferated and residents now parked their cars where grass and shrubs once grew. Others parked bumper to bumper along the streets. I found the B&B by its house number.

The front garden was populated by a working-party of gnomes, one wheeling a barrow of dead bedding plants, another digging and yet another one watching, as workmen do. Despite the freezing temperature they all appeared by the light of the streetlamp to be happy at their work.

A Chick Murray doppelganger opened the door and stood looking down at me, a cap on his head and hands thrust into the pockets of his fawn cardigan. I had an immediate flashback to my childhood. *Rothesay Pavilion his side-splitting comic lines: his wife Maisie, tiny in comparison, standing in front of him playing the accordion. She turned to smile up at him, he smiled back until she turned away then he grimaced. We all laughed. They sang together at the end of his act.*

'He-llo Reta with an 'e'. Ye're lucky we still have yer room. A woman came tae the door a wee while ago and said: "I'd like to stay here please." So, I just said, politely you know, 'Well stay there then.' and shut the door.

'Oh.' with a giggle, was all I could manage as I stepped inside, astounded that this look-alike was also acting the part.

We shook hands then and he smiled in the restrained Chick Murray way, lifting one eyebrow 'Welcome, I'm Jock, aka Chick. Ah've seen that look afore. It's shock. A wee cup o' sweet tea's what ye need on a night like this. Eh?'

I found my voice. 'Oh, I'd like that Jock. Thank you.' I was thinking hard, but a witty response just wouldn't come fast enough. 'Yes. It's a cold night.'

He lifted my suitcase and led me upstairs to my room then left me saying 'Jist come doon when ye're ready, Ah'll go and put the kettle oan.'

Knowing the layout of the house and seeing cans of deodorant and hairspray, noticing a couple of Kirby grips also on the dressing table, I knew immediately that this was their room. Also, there was no lock on the bedroom door.

On a closer look, I was amused to find that their own personal items of clothing filled the wardrobe. I opened one drawer, it was too personal; lady's underwear. I imagined that because I was a last-minute one-night booking, they didn't think I'd use the wardrobe or drawers. There was clean, well-ironed bed linen and a thick bath towel folded on the bed, topped with a sprig of plastic white heather tied with a tartan bow.

The only bathroom had their preferences in toiletries and a spare toilet roll waiting under the crocheted crinoline-skirt of a Barbie doll. She had moving eyelids with long lashes and her stiletto shoes and long legs were stuffed down the cardboard hole.

Feeling refreshed but tired, I went downstairs and met his wife. 'And you must be Maisie?'

Almost. She laughed. She was Daisy, and like Maisie, was also tiny. Her neck was wrinkled and tortoise-like, but her face showed contentment and she had smiling eyes. Their home was polished and gleaming, even having antimacassars on the backs of the settee and chairs. She clearly had a fondness for frills and lace trimmings too.

As she trotted briskly between the kitchen and the coffee table bringing crockery, homemade pancakes and raspberry jam, shortbread and ginger nuts, I noticed her hands were rough from hard work.

She'd hear him, not in an unkindly way, use her as the brunt of one-liners about 'the wife' and laugh as if she was hearing them for the first time. She poured our tea then settled into her chair again taking up her knitting, smiling and tutting at him, enjoying the fun and so was I: It was an entertaining and relaxing time with them.

I learned Jock had a retirement job as a part-time traffic warden, he was a kind-hearted one. He knew lots of local people and their cars. He'd tell them to leave their phone number on the dashboard so that he could call them if they were about to run over on the meter time.

One of his stories was about a lady who rushed to the door of the hairdressers with her head full of curlers, called him over and gave him a pound coin and her car keys. She asked him to put a ticket on her windscreen and bring the keys back, telling him that she would be under the second drier from the door. 'The coonsil's no makin' much oot o' ma patch, Ah'll tell ye.' He laughed and winked.

'Have you always been a traffic warden Jock?'

'Ah wis a miner afore that,' he said. 'Aye a hard job, but we had a great crack, an' we awe looked oot fir each ither. Then Ah worked in a bar in Kirkcaldy for a while. Aye, Ah did. Met loads o' they famous Fifers. Gordon Brown, the Prime Minister ye ken, he liked a pint. The Reid brothers, The Proclaimers? Ye'll huv heard o' thaim. Ah' will walk one hundred miles and ah will walk one hundred mo-ar. (It was 500 miles, but I didn't want to correct him.) They used tae play on the live-music nights. Val McDermid and Ian Rankin, they're famous writers ye ken, they're frae here tae, but I've no met thaim.'

As he was telling me all this, a grey cat staggered into the room, struggling to stay upright. It moved its mouth as if to meow, but nothing came out.

He looked down at it and sighed. 'Ouch she's on the way oot, she's 15. Might no' be here in the mornin' Pare thing.'

I gathered up my plate, cup and saucer, glad that I hadn't had a dessert at the restaurant, and Daisy rose to take them from me. 'Well, thank you for the wonderful home-baking and the tea Daisy, it was just what I needed. I'll be off to bed now.'

Jock held up a finger. 'Afore ye go then, just tae let you know, there's a gentleman guest, Archie he's called, in the ither room. Just in case, you're wonderin'. Now, what time wid you like yer breakfast? Ah forgot tae ask yin couple, so I went up and knocked. The wumin opened the door in her nighty. Ah thoucht, whit a funny place tae keep a door.' He laughed again. 'Guid yin eh?'

I laughed too and said 'Eight o'clock. Would that suit you?'

Up in the peace of my room, I kicked off my shoes and lay for a few moments on top of the bed thinking how friendly they were. There were only three doors off the upper landing, their bedroom, the other guest bedroom and the bathroom. They had given up their room and were sleeping in the lounge; the sofa was a bed-settee.

Feeling stiff and tired I ran a bath and added a little of Daisy's scented bath oil. It felt uncanny, luxuriating in the hot water in a bath in a house which was the identical layout to the one I'd lived in through my childhood and into my twenties.

Grandma, who had used a tin bath in front of the fire for the family for most of her life, polished it till it gleamed as if it was a valuable ornament. Friday nights were bath nights. Fifteen minutes only. She believed any longer and I would faint with the heat.

Next morning Archie had got to the bathroom before me. I wriggled cross-legged on the edge of the bed waiting for him to vacate. When things went quiet, I'd tried the door handle, but he didn't seem to get the message. The splashing of water and taps being turned off and on continued.

Eventually, I heard the snib on the door pulled back and him closing his own door. Every centimetre of the bathroom was sparkling clean and dry, as if unused. This was surprising.

There was no sign of Archie at breakfast though, and no place setting for him. The table was set with china from their glass showcase, a shiny white polyester tablecloth and napkin, a polished Pico-ware teapot, sugar and cream set. There were small individual dishes of Daisy's excellent home-made marmalade and strawberry jam.

Jock arrived from the kitchen with a bit of an act. Looking proud, he held a Tiptree's one-portion jar of honey between his thumb and first finger, pinkie extended and said. 'Ye'll see we keep a bee.' He had such a cheerful and happy-go-lucky personality, guests might enjoy this, but they didn't have to live with him.

While I ate, I watched the TV with the sound turned right down. Jock interpreted the news programme for me, putting his own slant on it, it would have been at least the second time around for him that morning.

The cat sat motionless during all this, her eyes closed and her head dropping to one side. I was concerned about her and said so.

Jock lifted the phone and dialled a number. 'It's Jock here again Jim. She's still wae us. Aye. Right then. See you.' He replaced he receiver. 'That's it sorted. She's had enough.' He turned to Daisy. 'Ah'll take her to the vet noo. She goin' when the Chinese git their teeth pulled.' He looked at each of us. 'Tooth hurty.' He laughed.

We sat together after breakfast and they found it hilarious that I was an incognito Tourist Board 'wumin' and they hadn't guessed. They listened to my feedback and agreed that sharing their bedroom facilities was not great. They were uncomfortable with it.

Jock explained how they had coped in busy times so far. 'Ye see, tae be personal for a minute, Archie's got a potty and usually lets the guests go first. That's what he does if there's anybody else in, maistly just fir a few weeks in the summer ye ken.'

'We'll tell ye aboot him in a minute. You dae your paperwork and Ah'll pit the kettle oan again. You carry on hen. Your dae'in fine, we know yer just dae'in yer job.'

They took time to ask questions and were sensitive to my need to apply the rules while wanting to show my appreciation for what they did offer.

I completed a form, a to-do list which they had to return to us when some simple things were changed, remove their own personal items from the room or lock them away and fit a lock to the bedroom door. Jock returned with fresh coffee while Daisy told me Archie's story.

Apparently, he had OCD and cleanliness and checking that everything was clean was one of the symptoms he had to cope with. This meant, of course, he was a very tidy guest. Almost three years before, he'd arrived for a two-week holiday and had stayed on ever since.

'Well he'd nae hame,' Daisy explained, 'Ye canny pit a budy oot whae disnay hae a hame tae go tae.'

Archie's wife had said she could put up with him while he was working but not for 24 hours a day when he retired, so when he did retire, that was it. He'd stayed on, finding a home with Jock and Daisy, sharing their bathroom but otherwise keeping himself to himself. They'd given him a combination microwave oven, a portable electric ring and a TV in his room and the potty of course. He washed his own dishes and pans when the kitchen was free, Daisy washed his clothes and ironed them for him and he lived there, contented and undisturbed in their back bedroom.

Not only that, he had been a librarian and was an avid reader. Jock had put shelves up right around the room for his books. Archie could not have found a better home with kinder people.

While Daisy had been telling me all this, Jock had looked preoccupied. When she'd finished, he slapped his knees and said 'I've got it. That's it, Daisy. Let's just git oan wae it. We were goin' to add oan a big conservatory oot the back, but we could change that, build a bedroom wae an ensuite for the guests, the plumbin's jist through the wa' in the kitchen already. And we could hae a sitooterie further doon the garden, A've seen them at Dobbie's. In the summer, we'd go upstairs wae himsel'.' Turning to me he beamed. 'Consider the job done hen.'

Daisy looked surprised but giggled. 'Whit a man ye are, it wid be grand and we could be there oorsels in the winter. An ensuite? That wid be fair posh.'

I buckled myself into the car and waved to them as they both stood in their doorway smiling. My ease and contentment diminished as I drove back to Leven. I was soon thinking about the pub I'd left the night before. I was not looking forward to that visit.

Puffing and Blowing

When I returned to meet the owner of the dreary pub it was 11.15am and as Radio One blared out rock music I raised my voice above the DJ's.

'Hello. Mr MacManish? I'm Mrs MacLennan.'

He nodded.

'I came to stay last night. I'm from the Tourist Board.'

He was sitting at a table, a baker's tray of rolls balanced conveniently on two chairs beside him. Unshaven, greasy-haired, his tight black-lycra T-shirt hugging his man-boobs, he lifted his lit cigarette waiting in the ashtray, placed it in the side of his mouth and with one eye closed against the smoke, continued: opening a bread roll with his thumbs, spreading it with Stork margarine, adding a slice of plastic ham, blowing a plastic bag open till it ballooned, shoving the roll in, swinging it by the corners, then knotting it. I waited.

'Aye, ah' ken.' He said eventually, then he put his cigarette back in the ashtray, took a drink from his mug, a bite from his own roll and continued, two thumbs opening another roll, spreading, filling, blowing it open it, shoving, swinging and knotting.

'Did you know there may be an improvement grant available if you want to upgrade your establishment?'

'Aye, ah ken.'

'Well, I'm sorry I can't give you an award on the strength of my visit last night. There is a lot that needs attending to first. Would you be interested in talking about it?'

He looked at me with an ill-concealed wry smile. 'Naw hen. Ah'm no' fussed.'

I was irritated by his rudeness but tried again. 'Are you busy enough with the business you have?'

'Aye, enough. I might sell up though. Tesco might make me an offer Ah can't refuse. Eh? You never know.' He grinned.

'Okay.' I shrugged, just wanting to make sure he heard me out. 'But even just better paintwork, better bed linen, fixing the broken toilet seat and having a clean shower curtain would make things much better for your guests. If you change your mind, you have my card and know how to reach me. Okay?'

'Cheers hen.' He lifted his hand in acknowledgement and put the cigarette back in his mouth.

We had no legislative right to make registration of hospitality businesses compulsory. His pub seemed to serve the market he had but I don't suppose his guests would have minded a good TV reception and at least some of my recommendations. It felt right to be removing places like this from the tourist radar. He would have no award from us, so could not advertise with us, but I wasn't finished.

Back at the shopping centre I phoned the office and got details of the local Environmental Health Office. They could check out his kitchen, might even know of this publican already, but maybe not and it might take Tesco a while to close a deal with him.

Hell, Hath no Fury

We made our bookings in three-week batches but trusting a three-week weather forecast for the Highlands and Scottish Borders could mean cancelled visits. Heavy snowfalls and drifting conditions could make driving hazardous or impossible. This made finding enough work difficult when many places also closed in winter. It made sense for us to work in the lower snow-risk areas.

However, in February 1994 I did manage to find enough work and an enjoyable routine developed for a while. I visited around 20 or 30 establishments of all sizes and types, left believing they were sound businesses run by good people and I'd been useful. Then a challenging one popped up.

It was scary. My shortest visit ever. Five minutes in total. I never got over the doorstep. I'd booked a non-incognito day visit, but she must have forgotten.

I heard a bolt drawn back, a key turning. The door was yanked open and there she stood, a lady larger than nature intended, eyes full of fury, breathing through clenched teeth, one hand on the handle of a large suitcase, getting ready to throw it.

She was taken aback when she saw me there. I was taken aback when I saw her. She was perhaps 40ish, her short-sleeved T-shirt stretched over bulging worked-out biceps. That might well have been her Hell's-Angels type monster-bike which stood in the carport.

I wanted to run. My business card was my only defence. I offered it to her and babbled something automatically.

'I can't have you here now.' She blustered.

'This seems like a bad time. Shall I come back later? Make another appointment?' I asked feeling more composed.

'No. There's no point.' She made to close the door.

What was with the suitcase? Something personal? Was she throwing a guest out?

I had to tell her as gently as I could, not wanting to fuel her wrath, that as she'd not cancelled my visit and I was already here, she wouldn't get a refund. But I was nosey and the counsellor in me (forgetting my boundaries) had a really stupid idea, I added feeling concerned. 'But as I'm here, is there anything you'd like to talk about?'

With lips pursed and chin up she took a firm stance, feet apart, filling the doorway. She stared at me, giving herself time to think, then took a deep breath. Her voice was quiet, controlled, heavy with threat but soon built up to a crescendo, a match for any Wagnerian diva. 'My fornicating husband is next door. If you'd like to knock on *her* door you can tell her she's a lying cow and I'll have her for this. And tell *him* I've packed his case and he is toast, that would give you something to do and would suit me just fine. Now otherwise, disappear.'

She needed another long breath and with a thrusting arm and pointed finger directed me to the door on the left.

I had a vision of this woman wearing fur skins, a Viking hat with horns and long blond pigtails, hatchet in hand, her husband running next door for his own safety. Caught in that long second of concerned listening, professionalism and shock, what I regrettably said was 'Oh dear, *hit shappens* doesn't it.' The Rev. Spooner might even have tutted at that one.

She screwed up her eyes, threw an arm across them and backed away, closing the door and that is why I turned up at the Cambo Estate at Kingsbarns just south of St. Andrews, earlier than expected.

Cambo Estate

The sky was clear blue and although it was cold, where the sun had moved across the canopy of bare trees it had melted pockets of the light covering of snow. The air was still, and sounds travelled. I had time on my hands to fit in a bit of exercise before the next visit and get that last disturbing experience out of my mind.

I leaned against the back of my car finishing a sandwich while changing into my walking boots and was enchanted by a group of under-fives. Holding hands in twos, led by their nursery nurses, they were singing as they toddled on the pathways through the woodland. It was annual Scottish Snowdrop Festival time held every February and March.

The leaflet informed me that there were seventy acres of snowdrops forming the national collection of around 350 different varieties which carpeted the woodland floor. I had never considered snowdrops to have a perfume but walking among them the air was sweet with the scent of newness and like a fine wine I thought I could detect fresh washing drying in a light breeze and sunshine, rich moist earthy notes, even overtones of honey.

Families would travel from some distance and make it an annual event to visit Cambo Estate at this time of year; they'd dine in the cafe, join a free workshop, admire the antics of the piglets and take home a souvenir of a good day out.

I took up an aerobic but comfortable pace on the path down to the beach at Kingsbarns to pick up yet another tiny shell or a piece of tumbled seaglass from yet another Scottish beach. The tinier and more varied the better to fit into my small stoneware dish which sits on our kitchen windowsill. They were a reminder of places I'd visited and now and again I'd lift them into my palm and enjoy the memory.

Cambo Estate self-catering apartments are in the main house and I was left to assess the vacant ones on my own. It was like stepping back into Victorian times; walking along the stone-floored servants' corridor to the old gated lift, the names of the apartments, such as Upper Servants and Lower Servants summoning images of hard work and a division between the above and below stairs classes. The apartments had loose-covered chesterfields, antique four-poster beds and mahogany cabinets and wardrobes with a consideration for comfort which would have amazed the original occupants.

I flicked through one guestbook and found years of appreciative comments from guests who'd enjoyed the period character of this old house and estate with the comfort of today's modern conveniences. Their comments and stories also conveyed an atmosphere of relaxation from being in the woodlands, walking to the beach, hearing the birdsong and enjoying the tranquillity.

I was very pleased and happy to tell the owners that I had only praise for the quality and condition of everything and would be able to reconfirm their award.

St. Andrews the Golfing Mecca

Driving on to St. Andrews on the coast road from the East Neuk, a grit-brown crust covered old snow which had been thrown under bare hawthorn hedgerows. They cast long shadows from the late afternoon sun. I loved this view over the town so pulled in at a field gate just before the Kinkell Braes Caravan Park to complete my report on Cambo Estate apartments.

St. Andrews, once the ecclesiastical capital of Scotland lay in the distance below and I caught glimpses of the Old Course and the long sweeping sandy stretch of the West Bay which borders it. In the background, conifers of the Tentsmuir Forest created a dark band on the North side of the Eden estuary and two RAF jets rose silently from Leuchars airfield before their roar reached me. This pulled my eyes away from the three remaining 12th-century towers of what still remained of Scotland's largest and most magnificent Cathedral.

I checked in at the Rusacks Hotel, which overlooks the 18th hole on the Old Course, looking forward to a luxurious room, a hot bath, excellent food and a comfortable evening. As I relaxed in the lounge with a good view of the room in order to assess the bar area and services. I folded the Scotsman newspaper to the crossword section: this was where I could openly make notes to prompt my memory when writing my report.

My pre-dinner drink was delivered to my table in the lounge with a tray of nibbles and I tuned into a conversation close by. This had become a habit and my husband John thinks I will eventually develop the ability to swivel my ears like horses. In a quiet room, I can listen to guests' and staff's conversations while appearing to pay attention to him. He finds it very irritating and rude, but for GCOs and spooks, it is actually very useful.

That evening, what I heard made me smile. A young man in a trendy pastel-range of Golfino wear, leaning towards his golfing friends seated around a coffee table was fused with energy as he told them. 'When I was at high school, I made this life decision, it would be golf, golf, golf and man, I got that scholarship.' After a good five minutes of self-praise he continued, making gentle chopping hand movements onto his palm, 'Today I played par par birdie birdie birdie eagle then a double bogie but man, I focused, put it behind me.'

The older gentleman at his elbow, listening and nodding approval added 'He sure did, and his game is improving so fast since we got him a personal coach. I think he's goin' places and his mom and I are so proud. It has been worth every penny.'

I guessed from the silence and the dropped heads of two of their golfing companions, that they'd heard similar before. I didn't catch his name though.

Golfers from all over the world are pulled to St. Andrews like iron filings to a magnet, hoping to play a round on the world-famous Old Course where clubs have been swung for 600 years.

Even non-golfers want to record the experience of being there. Like the oriental tourists, the barman told me about, being handed a club each by their hired chauffeur as they alighted from their people carrier.

He'd checked that they knew how to address the ball, then waited with them, carrying their cameras. When the paying golfers on the 18th green finished putting, shook hands at the end of their game and left, those gentlemen in their black shoes, ankle length trousers and white socks trotted straight onto the green for a photograph. They then did the same by the Swilken Burn Bridge, making sure the background included a view of the Royal and Ancient Clubhouse; just for authenticity of course. The ladies looked on from the roadside.

It is a pity their tour company couldn't have scheduled them to be there on a Sunday when the Old Course is closed for golfing. Then an ancient tradition is upheld where the public may stroll on it, enjoy the sea air and the views.

Enthusiasts, perhaps like those who were listening to the budding American professional player in the bar, could have had their rounds guaranteed as part of a very expensive golf package holiday. Those less fortunate have to enter a draw held every morning and the lucky winners are given their tee-off times for the day. I've heard of keen single golfers who queued, stamping their feet to keep warm from around 5.00 am to maybe have the chance of making up a three-ball or foursome, but many have had to put the clubs back in the boot by 8.00 am and thaw out their disappointment.

Arnie's Story

Becoming a Member of the Royal and Ancient Golf Club is a complex and protracted process; but not so for Arnie Maran who was one of John's very entertaining curling friends.

There were normally several levels of scrutiny and a measure of luck involved before being considered for acceptance. A prospective member had to be male, be at least a reasonable golfer, produce well-connected references and have unsolicited recommendations from members who were not supporting any other applicant. Those waiting for a vacancy to occur would be wise to have shown a benevolent nature: volunteered at events, willingly have accepted tasks such as carrying the board which said Quiet Please and seven years later, they may have been offered membership.

Women had to wait until February 2015 before this all-male establishment even considered accepting females, then they could expect the seven-year filtering system; unlike Her Royal Highness Princess Anne who was among the first women to be offered honorary membership.

Arnie was an orthopaedic surgeon. He'd had a patient with a tumour, who was an important member of the R&A. The operation had gone well and the gentleman in an 'aristocratic gravelly voice' had inquired if he was a member. When Arnie told him that he was not, the grateful gentleman informed him that he would see to it. One morning, a year later Arnie lifted from his doormat a letter telling him he was now a member.

A Student's Life

Next morning, I looked out onto the contours of the Old Course sculpted by the rising sun's rays: a pristine-white covering of glittering frost with snow-pockets still lying in the shade of some bunkers.

I breakfasted on Eggs Benedict, savouring both the food and the scenery, knowing that my days and immediate weeks ahead would likely deteriorate from this point onwards.

I recalled the pleasure of last summer. I had discovered the hard-to-find parking places in the crowded streets and enjoyed the buzz of the crowds. Cafes and bars had sprouted window boxes and hanging baskets, even more golfers trundled trolleys, tourists wandered the castle and cathedral ruins and parents built sandcastles with their children. The more energetic jogged on the beaches and windsurfed in the waves, browsers trawled the shelves in the bookshops and raked among the summer clothing on the rails in its many charity shops. The hungry and thirsty filled the tables at restaurants, cafes and wine bars and the tourist pound had the tills ringing and the credit card machines munching through the paper rolls.

But this was still winter. I had enjoyed one Sunday, watching students gather in St. Salvator's Quad, chattering and enveloping themselves in their red gowns. I was initially puzzled by their style but was told that their robes are worn as tradition dictates; full on the shoulders in the first year, off the shoulders a little in second, in the third year off the left shoulder for the Arts Faculty, right for the Sciences. Fourth-year students trail it behind them falling off their backs, the hems showing tidemarks of vintage mud.

I followed on the opposite pavement with my camera as they paraded out along the Old Pier. On reaching the end, those in stiletto heels and pelvic-pelmets, their modesty protected by their red wrap-around gown, were helped to climb the ladder to the higher level, then they paraded back to the Quad.

St. Andrews has two seasons which affect the self-catering industry: term time followed by tourist time. In term time the university halls of residence, apartments and cottages are the temporary homes of some 7,000 students, then those places are refreshed for the high season swell of summer visitors.

It was day one on the start of a few weeks' touring those student self-catering properties. There were too many of them to visit in the small window of time when the changeover period happens after exams, so we agreed to view them in winter with students in residence.

The letting agent Jim, brought along a small suitcase of keys all fastened on hooks into their allotted space and escorted me, his case clinking, around the properties he managed. Jim informed me that those bright young things may have had outstanding academic abilities, however, housekeeping held no interest for them. 'We see the properties when they are due to arrive, and they can reduce a house to a slum in weeks. I hope you are ready to be shocked.' He had warned me on the phone when I booked with him and so had my smiling colleague who'd visited the previous year.

He continued. 'Our office will get calls like "Sorry to trouble you, but we have a problem with the vacuum cleaner.".'

'Can you tell me what the problem is?'

'Well, it seems to have broken. It doesn't suck up anything now, in fact, it is dropping more than it collects.'

'Have you replaced the bag?'

'What bag?'

Those baffling vacuum cleaners could stand abandoned at the back of hall cupboards for the duration.

Someone had to do those visits and they were on my patch this year. I saw the result of mixing Coca-Cola and flour and throwing it at a ceiling. It did create stalactites, but the inevitable resulting stalagmites were trampled into the carpets. Those and also curry stains would mean those carpets would need ripped up and replaced. I saw greasy baths and shower trays where the only porcelain visible amongst the grey gunge was an area where two feet could stand. Greasy sinks and cookers which would almost require sandblasting to remove the varnish of cooking oil and fat actually became numbingly boring, as were burnt worktops, but fortunately, in most properties, a very deep-clean and a fresh coat of paint would restore them back to a good standard.

I liked to think our own two student sons, although disinterested when I showed them at the time, how to clean a bathroom and kitchen, use a vacuum cleaner and duster had remembered my tuition. But I now wondered how often they changed their sheets and towels: what were the chances?

I issued detailed candid reports and recommendations based on the turmoil I saw; however, we had an agreement with the owners to mark the housekeeping standard as *Good*. The motivated ones would return their properties to a normal habitable state once the students had left and we knew the system worked: the level of complaints from tourists was negligible.

The third and final week progressed, the last Friday arrived, I thanked Jim for his company and time and my jingling-keys tinnitus stopped.

At the end of each day, I ate in bistros where the students gathered, absorbing their vibrancy, energy and youthful banter; an antidote to the dreariness of those visits. Their robes in a jumbled pile on chairs, that freedom to just be themselves away from parental influence was palpable. Although I was now also a part-time student, albeit a mature one with my counselling studies, I still carried a slight resentment about having to leave school just after my 15th birthday, being deprived of that independence to just be myself. Here, however, I could dress down, take counselling studies work with me and in a surrogate way, feel as if I was one of them.

Vintage Ball Gown

Before leaving the town centre to visit my last self-catering apartment of the week, I had some dress-shopping to do.

Every main charity in the UK seems to have a shop in St. Andrews and I liked dropping in now and again. Some wealthy people lived in and around the town and I became quite adept at spotting the famous-label new clothes with their original swing-tags still attached which shared the packed rails with student-priced clothes.

I'd spotted an interesting shop on North Street. It sold nothing but ball gowns, gently used ones and I promised myself the reward of looking for a dress there when I'd completed those student visits.

John and I had an invitation to a charity ball sitting on the mantelpiece. I possessed a couple of cocktail frocks, but no ball gown so popped in. All the clothes had been dry cleaned and were in almost-as-new condition. I tried on several, but even allowing myself a unsafe margin of teetering-moments on the highest of heels, I was still not tall enough to carry those hemlines above the floor and their rigid-boned supports dug into my armpits.

Just when I was leaving the changing room feeling disappointed, I spotted sheeted hangers in behind a screen. I felt nosey, was desperate not to leave without a dress, so I pulled one of the sheets aside and saw it.

The label read, 'By Appointment to the Late King George, Jenners Limited.' My mother had worked in the accounts department of Jenners shop on Princes Street, Edinburgh in the 1940-50s and I remember her saying that their rich clients bought bespoke ball gowns; no design was ever repeated, and they were hand-finished. During the Ball Season, customers who held accounts were allowed fur coats and capes out on approval. They were sometimes returned as not suitable a few weeks after the season finished, with cloakroom tickets still in the pockets. Possibly this is when Edinburgh upper-class ladies were described as having 'fur coats and nae knickers.

'Is this dress for sale?' I asked.

'Yes, it has just come in and I've not had time to check it over or price it yet, but you can try it on.'

I looked in the mirror and remembered. It was my twelfth birthday *Doris Day's dress had the sheen of satin and had sequined patterns strewn across it. The off-the-shoulder low necklines showed off her smooth shoulders and rising breasts atop a fitted bodice which enhanced her small waist. The soft folds in the full panelled skirt flowed gently and swayed as she walked. She wore it with long evening gloves as she looked at the moon and sang something endearing, looking happy and in love. I hoped to have breasts and cleavage like hers one day, fill a dress just like that one and fall in love.*

This dress was certainly a 1950s close copy. It was silver satin, with emerald green and silver sequins sewn in swirls onto the bodice and skirt. My sister-in-law Mary had no problem pinning up the hem for me. A quick run around the new hem with my sewing machine and it was as if it was made for me and was the best £25, I ever spent.

It's Good Enough for Tourists

Now onto the last visit of the week with the dress carefully packed in the boot. I imagined, judging by the address, this would be an up-market contrast to the student ones. I drove due West on the A939 out of St. Andrews, shielding my eyes from the sinking sun, to visit a new member with a self-catering property. This was an area of mature trees, large properties with extensive grounds and expensive cars parked in gated driveways.

I arrived at a country house which sat well back from the road behind a high granite wall. I stopped outside the heavy oak gate on rollers, climbed out of the car, pressed the buzzer and waited. No response.

I pressed again; a woman answered. 'Lady Ruthingsham-Clarkson is expecting you. She is in the garden and will see you arriving. I'll open the gate now.'

The gate rolled back revealing a fine grade, grey pebble driveway, bordered by an immaculately clipped mature yew hedge sweeping alongside. I drove slowly trying not to disturb the raked surface. A broad archway in the hedge gave a glimpse of formal plantings. A rock garden with a variety of winter-flowering Erica in bud, some white tips already in full bloom. A lawn opened out on the left of the driveway with a stand of white-barked birches. They were underplanted with Winter Aconites giving a splash of bright yellow through the remains of melting snow, their green leaves frilling them like open-fingered palms.

This was a socially superior garden, definitely a Yew type as in the journalist, James Bartholomew's Yew & Non-Yew gardening book. Not a hint of coloured lights, gnomes or pampas grass.

In front of the house, a life-size bronze stag looked out from his rocky plinth towards me. Behind him was a cover of mature rhododendrons, the long leaves having folded themselves back against the cold, the fat buds already promising large blooms.

The driveway widened to an in-out system and I kept to the left driving around to the front entrance. A high class and excellent property indeed. I was looking forward to this visit, imagining it would be easy. I was wrong.

I parked outside the front door under the wide portico, not seeing an alternative. At the far end of the front lawn, I noticed a man and woman in discussion. He had been working on the herbaceous border and had a full wheelbarrow beside the long curved empty bed. It was in full sun and the soil would be warmer and workable. He touched his cap as she left him to join me. Not his lordship then.

The woman in her mid-60s I would guess strode towards me. She was dressed in a navy quilted jacket, Burberry box-pleated skirt, green wellingtons and judging by the amount of yellow-gold and bold classic colours, a Hermes silk headscarf, covering her silver hair rolling back from her forehead, just like the Queen's. 'You must be Mrs MacLennan, lovely to meet you.' We shook hands.

'I'm pleased to meet you, Lady Ruthingsham-Clarkson.' *What a mouthful.* 'What a ... beautiful garden. Have you lived here for some time?'

'This is my husband's family home. So convenient for town yet so quiet. One can enjoy the birdsong, it is so private and secluded, just like in our lodge in Ross-shire. Now I'm sure you must have a tight schedule, so why don't you go around to the side of the house there? (A rhetorical question me thinks!) You will see the door to the apartment. If you'll excuse me, I'll meet you there. Hmm?'

I heard footsteps advance on the other side of the apartment door. Her ladyship unlocked it for me. 'When you are finished, please ring the copper bell on the corner of the house. Hmm?' With that, she turned and left, pulling the connecting door behind her and I heard the click of a bolt.

Another unheated apartment; so cold my fingers would soon stiffen holding the pen. I decided to use the Dictaphone, so returned to the car to collect it then quickly proceeded to list everything I saw, together with the quality and condition.

What a disappointment. *Click on.* A smell of pine-scented cleaning materials ... underlying musty smell ... linoleum surrounds and threadbare carpets in traffic areas ... two-bar electric fire heating ... old gas range ... a jumble of well-used dishes, pans and utensils. *Click off.*

When I reached the bathroom, I was surprised. *Click on.* Bathroom, real potential ... original watery-green Vitrolite panels to dado height ... green porcelain bathroom suite, WC with a high cistern … original chrome taps, a bit pitted but could be restored. *Click off.*

This apartment could be a stunning period restoration; keeping the bathroom, the door furniture, the service bells to call the staff, the mahogany-lined butler's pantry, the tiny decorative fireplaces. I felt excited about the prospect of them perhaps being interested in an extensive upgrade. Nothing to lose in trying.

I found the copper bell outside. It was huge. So high on the corner of the wall that when I swung the rope to the clapper it hardly moved. I put down my briefcase and with both hands gave it a good belt. I felt the clang reverberate in the fillings in my teeth and wondered if it could crack crystal glasses in the town centre. She appeared in a few minutes, calling me from the door of the letting apartment.

'I've had a good look around now Lady Ruthingsham-Clarkson. Could we sit somewhere and discuss my findings?'

She drew in her brows. 'Doesn't one just receive a report or a certificate or something?'

'Yes, but I will need some information from you first please.'

'Regarding?' she added with a hint of irritation in her voice.

'Booking procedures, what other services you offer, what arrangements you have in place for welcoming guests. I'd also like to discuss my findings and give you the opportunity to ask questions.'

'My housekeeper takes care of all that, but I think I might know a little. She checked her watch. 'Very well, I can give you half an hour. Come this way.'

She turned and walked briskly back through a doorway to the main part of the house, a short corridor and another doorway and we were in the main hallway. Oak panelling, grandfather clock.

She led me to their drawing room. Wilton quality carpet the colour of face powder … large mahogany circular table polished to a reflective shine ... Scottish Field, Country Life and a National Trust quarterly issue, fanned just so and in the centre a copper bowl of bright Tete-a-tete Narcissi. There was of course no need to assess this, but I'd formed a habit hard to break.

'Please take a seat.' She said as she opened the double French doors to the conservatory to talk to the gardener waiting outside.

I sat on one of the sofas in the drawing room and thought for a moment about my strategy but was feeling tense. Conservatory rebuilt ... secondary glazed and sitting on the footprint of the original tiled floor ... large, deep stone sink and tap in the corner ... white antique wrought iron chairs ... expensive tapestry plumped-up cushions set around the edges.

She perched stiffly opposite me on one of the upright chairs and my efforts to establish a rapport seemed more tolerated than welcomed, but given she had only half an hour, I went ahead with as great a degree of sensitivity as I could manage regarding the low standard next door. I assumed that she would not want the award I was about to offer; our lowest one. I finished with 'One Crown and Approved, as it stands today,' however, ...

She cut me short. 'What does that mean? One Crown and Approved.'

'It means that most of the items are utility quality, acceptable but very well used now. A higher award is possible, it just depends on what market you are aiming at and how much you want to invest in upgrading. But I have to say, the bathroom is a valuable period piece and is very worthwhile restoring.' *Important to stay positive.*

She straightened her back. I watched her eyebrows rise and corrugate her forehead. She pinned me with a stare; one of superiority mixed with disbelief. Seconds of silence ticked on the mantelpiece clock. *Hold it. Hold it.* I curled my toes inside my shoes.

She broke it with 'Do you know who my husband is?'

'No, I'm sorry I don't'. *Was that now a look of astonishment at my ignorance? Oh heavens, should I have known? Will she ask me to leave? I won't go without her signature. Or will I have to?*

'Hmm. Well. That award is incredibly insulting. Speaking for my husband, I know he will find this unacceptable. He will want to write to your Chairman. He may well know him.' At this, she gripped the arms of her chair and made to stand.

I remained seated. 'A letter to our Chairman would be passed down to me asking for an explanation, which I can give you now. It is important that you think this is a fair assessment. If not, I'm happy to go back to the apartment with you and explain my decisions or return another time if that is more convenient.'

She remained seated, so I continued. 'I'll be as quick as I can. When I compare the apartment to what I see in your own part of the house, it is easy to see that you appreciate and know high quality, so I am sure you understand the difference.' *Goodness. Was that cheeky?*

She sniffed and cleared her throat. 'Hmm, but those who've stayed didn't complain really. One is only providing a holiday apartment.'

'Can you tell me what you mean by really?'

'One can't hope to please everyone, but we charge a very modest price and I think, give very good value.'

'You might be losing out on a very lucrative market Lady Ruthingsham-Clarkson.' *Would she be imagining I thought they needed the money? Was my assumption insulting?* 'In these beautiful grounds, attached to this impressive house, with the Old Course just 5 minutes away, travel agents are looking for high-quality accommodation as part of elite golf packages. It can be a very lucrative market. There are not many top-of-the-range self-catering properties, which many prefer rather than staying in a hotel; it gives them more privacy and space. I think your apartment has incredible potential to be in that category. I'd be happy to supply you with names of travel agencies who might be interested in marketing it, but I am not able to recommend any one in particular.'

I got lucky. She was interested in hearing more and the half hour passed quickly. I wrote to her later with suggestions and after 4 months, received a request to return.

When I did, there were vans and cars parked at the apartment entrance and two large skips which looked full.

'Mrs MacLennan, nice to meet you again and thank you for coming so soon. I imagine you will want to see the improvements to our apartment. Shall we go straight there?'

This was a friendlier welcome. 'Nice to be back. Yes indeed, I have been looking forward to it.'

'Do follow me. Come along. We'll go this way. Hmm?'

She walked ahead via their main hall, enthusiasm in every stride, talking as we went. 'The marketing agency wouldn't consider taking this on without photographs, so we decided to go right ahead with the renovations. We hope to get business from them this summer of course.'

As we walked from room to room her eyes were creased into a smile. Pride? Joy at least. She informed me of the changes and progress, and I was amazed to see such a transformation in such a short time. The investment must have been considerable. I scribbled like mad, taking notes.

Bedroom numbers reduced to form four with ensuite shower rooms … central heating … Anta tartan-like woven fabric carpeting, fastened with brass studs … thick underlay. I thought it worth mentioning; 'The last time I saw woven fabric as carpeting like this was in a hunting lodge on the Balnagowan estate owned by Al Fayed of Harrods' She smiled with a throaty little laugh.

Oak country-house style furnishings throughout ... inset ceiling lighting, modern minimalist task and mood lighting from free-standing lamps … piped music system … soft furnishings in soft pastel tones coordinated to carpeting.

I complimented their choices. 'Those Anta soft furnishings are such high quality and they marry well with the Highland Stoneware pieces placed here and there.'

'Yes indeed.' she added. 'The building contractor managed to get the room alterations approval quickly and meanwhile our interior designer, who was recommended by a dear friend was working on the furnishing and decor. We are very pleased with his work. Now for the old bathroom. Let me show you. We created a master bedroom and knocked through to make it ensuite.' She surprised me. She clapped her hands.

Vintage pieces … now with a contemporary look. Black and white chequered polished tiled flooring with underfloor heating … original fittings restored … fixed two-metre-long glass screen … variety of shower options … a gentle slope in the floor allowing drainage. The effect was so unobtrusive in the overall space that I had to look twice to see it.

Heavy floor-length lined and interlined curtains … an armchair in Anta tartan-effect fabric … delivery of thick bathrobes ready to unwrap … a stack of luxury bath sheets and hand towels piled on a marble-topped side table.

'Isn't this amazing. I have asked the interior designers to have a look at our own facilities. I rather like this.' She smiled and led the way to the kitchen. The kitchen installers were unpacking more oak units to examine them, and the head fitter showed me a CAD drawing, computerised images and a sample mood-board of finishes.

'As you can see the installation is progressing well, and they think they will be finishing here by the end of next week. Amazing. I think we are in the way; shall we return to the house now?'

She held her hand out to indicate the way back and strode off chatting as we went. 'Our housekeeper was happy to shop for the kitchen equipment on your inventory list and she tells me that everything is there. We added a few extra items ourselves, an espresso machine and a toastie maker I believe. The dinner service is not new and might not be dishwasher proof but not to worry, it is replaceable. We found quite a surplus in the old butler's pantry and we have an excess of silverware too, so we are happy to give them a new home. Our housekeeper is also going to take care of the apartment and she has the name of a cook who is willing to cater for guests should one so wish.'

For someone who took little to do with the old apartment, this was a real turnaround.

'Lady Ruthingsham-Clarkson, I am so pleased to see the transformation and it has been achieved in such a short time. I can see you are happy with the result.

She gave a modest glance down at her lap. 'It has been disruptive, but such fun. I can't take any credit for the decisions, Mimi, my husband's PA acquired the brochure for the lodges at Gleneagles and we visited them. Our son, who is an accountant, believes that we should recoup our investment in just a few years. He is also happy to look after the business side for us. It has all worked out rather well really.'

I was now seated at their kitchen table. She opened one of the wall cupboards, reached in and with her hand on a bottle of Tio Pep, asked me, 'I usually enjoy an aperitif about now before I start cooking. Will you join me? One could say we are celebrating.

SPRING 1994 – 1997

One Yellow Welly

Mid-March 1994 was still roaring like the proverbial lion. The night-time temperature had dipped well below zero and a biting storm blowing down from the Arctic had ripped ivy off our wall, blown garden furniture over and snapped off the dead wood from our old copper beech. The branches were left stacked against the garden wall; at least that saved us some clearance work.

I poured John's coffee and he joined me at the kitchen window waiting to hear the weather forecast at 6.30 am. The anger of the storm had gone now. The sky appeared blameless in the first streaks of daylight, softening and feathering the vapour trials turning them pink.

As we stood there, we spotted a roe deer standing, chewing away at the foot of the garden. He must have come down from the higher woodlands and was looking around. We now knew what had been nibbling the bark of our young eucalyptus. That was such a wonderful and rare sighting, we just watched and let it be. I warmed both hands around my cup waiting for the weather forecast.

Black ice, further high winds with heavy snowfalls were forecast for the next few days, but not in the milder west of Scotland. I was heading there, to Argyllshire but decided to leave my winter survival kit in the car just in case; extra warm clothing and walking boots, a small shovel, a torch and a flask for hot water, tea bags and chocolate digestive biscuits. I usually ate those regardless of the weather.

With sleety rain slowly sliding down the windscreen, the engine running and the heater on full blast John closed my car door saying. 'Drive safely. Stay safe Reet. Take care now.' I was in my new-to-me car, an Opel Manta.

I nodded. 'You too.' with a smile. It was not the right time to tell him I once trudged knee-high through drifting snow blowing off a field to visit a remote and yet another empty unheated cottage.

I discovered my well-loved Ford Capri was going to bring a hefty bill in order to pass its MOT, so I decided it was time to find a replacement. Shopping for one was nowhere near the top of my list of pleasant ways to spend a Saturday lunchtime after seeing counselling clients, but I now needed one in my modest price range. It had to have fairly low mileage, be comfortable, have a good-sized boot; that was all.

After a few boring strolls back and fore along lines of well-polished shiny bonnets and windscreen price-displays, I couldn't believe my luck when I spotted our close friend Walter's White Opel Manta. He was indeed 'One Careful Owner'. I hadn't expected to be excited about a car but had always thought it was such a cool one. I sat in the very comfortable Ricard bucket seats and had good all-around visibility. It was in excellent condition of course; the back seats looking as new as if only well-behaved shopping bags had sat there. It was white with a black interior (wouldn't show marks). Job done. Next time we visited Walter and Margaret we'd drive there in the Manta and surprise them.

However, it wasn't until after the first few weeks I noticed it had developed an idiosyncrasy. In heavy rain, it started to leak a steady drip onto the accelerator pedal if I drove above 50 mph. I had my bright yellow, spot-them-in-the-dark wellingtons in the boot and had no option but to wear the one for my right foot, my court shoe on the left and lay my Scotsman, the newspaper that is, in the foot-well to soak up the puddle.

John had tried applying shower sealant from where we thought the leak might start, then tried a watering-can test but it just wouldn't perform that trick when parked. I had a vision of him hanging onto the roof, the can in his hand, pouring water down the windscreen at various points while I drove at speed; but was sure he would not agree to that.

Babysitting

Babies and B&Bs can be a difficult mix and it was, on that Monday morning in Dumbarton. My colleague Margaret M, who was a real people person and inspiring, had stayed overnight with Jennilee the previous year. She'd enjoyed her stay and described her as a young and enthusiastic American owner.

Since then she'd become a new mother, she had dark shadows under her eyes. Her husband worked away from home and she was not coping with their three-month-old colicky baby Sara-Jane. There had been little sleep for either of them for the last three nights and Jennilee had six guests in three double rooms.

I heard the baby's painful cries when I arrived and shortly after, Jennilee, totally defeated, sobbed into a wad of paper hankies. 'Rooms not cleaned yet … Sara-Jane cries for hours at a time… I just can't do this any longer … my poor baby girl … chemist …Co-op … Mom not flying over to help now. She's ducked out.'

The screaming continued as Jennilee looked at herself in the mirror over the fireplace, dabbing her red swollen eyes and seeing the spread of red blotches she sobbed. 'I can't go out looking like this and' … she flopped back onto the sofa 'I … just … am not coping. I need my mom.'

She picked up Sara-Jane cuddled her, and they cried together. I had a vague memory of a yoga exercise for releasing wind and with her agreement, we had a go. Sara-Jane had both knees pulled up to her tummy as if in cramp. I gently massaged her tiny tummy until she uncurled her left leg and let me straighten it and helped her keep her right knee to her tummy. The screaming continued. Then both knees pulled up, I rocked her from side to side. We then repeated the exercise with the other leg. After a good few tries, rat-a-tat sputtering of gas escaped. It was working. Jennilee took over, massaged her baby's tummy and the crying lessened to after-sobs then ceased. The wee darling smiled at us with tear filled eyes.

I could see the rooms serviced or not, that didn't matter but I found myself offering to take Sara-Jane out to the chemist and Co-op. *This is not my job; do I have time to do this?'*

I made a phone call to check with my next visit and it actually suited them that I'd be with them half an hour or so later.

Jennilee got a start made on clearing up after breakfast and tended to the guest rooms while I headed off with Sara-Jane in the pram. The trundling of the pram and the rain pelting the plastic cover seemed to do the trick; she was sleeping before I reached the chemist's shop.

They had no Gripe Water, which was the standby cure when my sons were babies 20-and-more years before and he had nothing else to suggest.

As I was leaving, a lady was arriving. She looked in the pram then looked at me without smiling.

Then on to the Co-op and as I waited for Jennilee's order, there the same lady was again, hanging around the magazine area, glancing at me. She approached and with a stern expression asked me 'Is that wee Sara-Jane in that pram?'

'Em ...' *I mustn't tell her I'm with the Tourist Board. That was not the GCO image I wanted going around the area.* '... Well.' I nodded. 'I'm just visiting.'

The timely interruption of 'Order for Whittingstone? saved me from further explanation. There you are, will you get it all under the pram on her tray?' The mystery lady backed off, turning away to use her phone. I wondered if she was cancelling a 999 call before the cop-cars came blue-flashing down the street.

I needed to make no changes to Jennilee's Commended award and over a cup of tea, she managed to see the funny side of her holding Sara-Jane against her shoulder with one hand while basting fried eggs or filling a teapot or dishwasher with the other. We decided it would be better to phone some friends to see if any one of them, or a few to spread the commitment, could help out during breakfast or take little Sara-Jane away during that difficult time; a temporary arrangement of course.

Kindness Itself

Later that same day the rain had stopped but the sky had fallen, hiding the hilltops. As I parked at the B&B in Helensburgh, I had a view of the Clyde river traffic, a few yachts tacking away from the sailing club and a pleasure boat just manoeuvring into the pier, its bunting flapping in the breeze.

Although that was not a match for my nostalgic memories of holidays in the 1950s, sailing on the paddle steamer the Waverley; her red, black and white twin funnels and the churning wake from her paddling sides.

I held my grandpa's hand tightly in the heat and noise of the engine room, watching her polished gleaming pistons and feeling the terrifying force of them. The accordion, fiddle and saxophone band played on her deck, people were dancing, opening their flasks and eating their sandwiches. The voice of Kenneth McKellar sang out The Song of the Clyde from the megaphone on Rothesay Pier as she docked.

It would be six decades before I'd sail in her again in her restored condition.

George and Isa Simpson, a gentle elderly couple, stood with me on their doorstep and pointed out a small group of women waving to them, their brightly coloured saris billowing below their anoraks, with their menfolk and children waiting on the pier. They were about to board the pleasure boat to take them on a day trip to Rothesay and Dunoon.

'They're lovely people. Some of them are staying with us.' George smiled. 'They came for one night and are still here, three days later. A really nice wee family.'

The Guptas from Mumbai, with two children, had turned up looking for a family room. They were very fortunate to knock on George and Isa's door. They told me their story.

Once the Simpsons had got their guests settled in, they'd strolled out to buy more breakfast provisions. Returning home, they'd turned the corner at their house and were met with six children running about in their front garden. When George put his hand on the garden gate, the children froze then ran into the house. There was a people-carrier parked just around the corner.

The smell of curry had wafted towards them as soon as they entered. George was sent to investigate and could hear a babble of voices from behind the bedroom door. He knocked; heard hurried whispering before the door was opened. There were four more adults and the children; some sitting on the beds, some of them standing around a tartan travel rug spread on the carpet. Three gas burners and three steaming pots of food were being tended by two women on their knees.

George was shocked, quite apart from the fire risk and the possibility of ruinous stains to carpets. He knew he could only sleep six guests in total without a fire certificate and would have to ask the others to leave. Taking in the scene he had told them quietly 'You better bring your pots to the kitchen. My wife will help you cook there.'

Isa laid the table for the whole group and let them eat in the dining room. The rest of the family had no accommodation and had planned to sleep the children in their house with one mother, the rest of the family in the people carrier. One phone call to a friend and they'd got the rest of the family settled into a self-catering house close by.

How well they did, finding a solution to suit them all. George said he happened to remember a quote from Mahatma Gandhi, which he told them. 'Happiness is when what you think, what you say, and what you do are in harmony.' They'd smiled and folded their hands together, nodding agreement. Isa showed me an embroidered tray cloth which one of the women, Aya, had given her as a mark of their gratitude. 'Her name sounds like mine too.' she smiled.

Inertia

I had an hour's drive ahead through beautiful Argyllshire, as the sky cleared, and the gloaming was settling in. This overnight visit was to be a joint one with Mark, one of my more experienced colleagues. We had those visits from time to time to ensure parity of scoring across the team.

During such a day of unexpected events and stories, I'd driven through outbursts of torrential rain, with little respite while scudding clouds were blown along. Now the wind had dropped, there were blinks of the low sun and the forests were breathing out new clouds which climbed the mountains towering in the background.

Run-offs from fields and overflowing ditches had created streams of grit and mud, and small pond-sized puddles to drive around in the rucked and buckled farmland. The rain had smoothed the ridges of the ploughed furrows which now looked like fossilised waves and the almost-full moon threw a path like polished steel across them. On the surrounding grassland the sheep, comfortable under their oily wool, had already settled for the night.

I slowed down at a remote inn on the hilltop, my headlights searching for the car park entrance. The beam highlighted the puddles and the tractor-tyres recycled as planters with the sludgy-brown stalks of Bizzy Lizzies and the skeletons of white Allysum and Montbretia from last summer's planting. One dim light shone above the doorway and the lit windows in the bar showed no occupants. The overall effect of the building's exterior, empty inn and the neglected car park was gloomy.

My Scotsman in the footwell was sodden and unreadable, so I dumped it in a bin then stood and had a good stretch just as headlights climbed the road towards me. Mark arrived in good time and swept into the car park crunching to a stop alongside.

'Hi, Mark. I've just arrived too. Look at this amazing evening view.'

'Indeed. Looks like your cracking up under the strain.' He chuckled. 'Standing there looking at the moon with your hands in the air wearing one wellington. I feel two new awards are called for, Eccentric Behaviour and Worst Dressed GCO. Definitely Christmas party entertainment.' He chuckled. 'Payback time for me.'

I'd been in the office just before Christmas when one of the admin girls had asked 'Is it okay for Mark to say this in his report?' He is writing to a farmer's wife.

'Madam, your poached eggs resemble a sheep's scrotum.' It was definitely not okay: we had fun with it. Mark, a very popular and witty member of the team, was awarded Creative Report Writer of the Year and won a pocket thesaurus. He was a talented comic scriptwriter and had produced some very funny sketches for us on such occasions.

Seeing the dismal surroundings, Mark muttered under his breath as we entered the inn. 'Were you depressed when you booked this? Do we have to stay here? Shall we have a drink and move on?'

'No. We're staying, I paid a deposit.'

We checked through my room first, comparing our observations with Dave Thom's report from the previous summer. There looked to be no improvement. The bedrooms were the result of a very successful sales pitch in the 1960-70s: budget-priced blue, mauve and gold striped wallpaper below the dado rail and a patterned one above. The co-ordinated bedspreads now looked very faded

Then into Mark's room; far too small to meet our minimum size requirement. Dave was always very thorough and if he had seen this room, it would have been on his list and noted as not to be used. 'That one's occupied.' was one trick some owners would try when wanting to hide the worst room.

The bed was a child size single, a hook on the back of the door with a couple of hangers was his wardrobe provision and the floor space beside his single bed was only chair width. The heater in his room was Baltic to the touch. Mark stood; his shoulders slumped like Tony Hancock feigning depression. 'Tomorrow morning, I'll wonder if I've died and am lying in an undertaker's cold store.'

'You'll certainly be cold enough. You could sleep with your clothes on.' I teased.

The lady behind the bar pouring our G&Ts was buxom, with an orange curly perm and bow-shaped, pinched scarlet lips, looking as if she'd stepped out of a Beryl Cook painting. She apologised for Mark's cold heater. 'I can't give you another room sir, they are all stripped down. It's just an old heater.' She nodded at him. 'Just give it a kick, that usually does the trick.'

The gentleman behind the bar was detached from the conversation. He ignored us. He was busy pouring two pints of Coca-Cola, then he lifted two bags of crisps and tossed them on a table in front of the TV. He settled himself there, his dirty white trainers on a chair, scratched his unshaven jowls then folded his arms across his food stained vest. There is no way his purple and white shell suit would ever have been able to fasten over it. We learned later he was the husband of the curly perm, and also the chef.

Mark had gone off to kick his heater and returned to stand with his back to the fire watching those two. 'That's it, you settle down there, never mind us, hungry travellers.' He frowned. 'Is that Neighbours they're now watching?' He spoke rather too loudly for my liking, then strode off. I waited, listening to hear if he was going to say something, but heard a door bang behind me.

Returning, he placed his chair beside mine close to the fire, stretched out his legs and looked up, muttering. 'That smell. The Gents' toilets. That's it. I remember it now. Edinburgh Zoo. They used to have an elephant house.' He looked at me over the top of his glasses. 'Disgusting.'

Logs smouldered red on top of the pile of hot ash on the massive stone-slab hearth. It had gathered chips and cracks, but the hearth and carved stone mantel were intact, and it showed a century or more of smoke-stains. The stone walls, metal window frames, old flagstone floor and wooden ceiling beams all reminded me of a similar place.

'Do you know the Drover's Inn at Inverarnan, north of Loch Lomond? It looks dilapidated from the outside and you could imagine Rob Roy walking in the door. But it is quirky, the food is great and it's busy.'

He nodded.

'This is Clan Campbell country.' I continued. 'The Campbells fought at Bannockburn, Robert the Bruce supporters.' I thought for a moment: 'And Inveraray Castle, the Duke of Argyll's home is not far from here. The dining room there is reputed to be the finest painted room in Britain. Remember the huge scandal when the Duke divorced his wife Margaret accusing her of infidelity? If those two behind us were interested in history; pictures, artefacts, they could make more of this place.'

Mark kept nodding as I prattled on, then asked. 'Did the Inn at Inverarnan have a goldfish bowl of bingo balls on the bar, irritating flashing lights and electronic burping of a gaming machine like that one over there?'

'I can't remember.' Nudging Mark for his growing cynicism I added 'Must be a different type of clientele here. This elevated location. Tables outside in the summer. It does have some character and potential. A bit of enthusiasm and TLC would do for a start.'

I went on. 'I stayed at a place on the Isle of Skye where the owner had bags of enthusiasm, marched up and down the hall dressed in his ancient kilt, playing the bagpipes at the foot of the stairs to announce dinner. The Persian-type carpets were pretty worn, the high-quality dinner service and silver cutlery didn't match but the food was great, and they had happy guests. Our standards were too prescriptive for them and somehow a low award didn't reflect the great quality of stay I'd had.'

I sighed. 'I just wish we could somehow include those old characterful places with eccentricities and give them a special category. But on second thoughts, it would be at odds with our trying to raise standards. They are featured in travel magazines, they're popular.'

'They don't need us then, do they, if they are already popular?' He chuckled, delivering one of his off-the-wall ideas. 'You could start your own brochure. MacLennan's travel guide to The Quirky, Eccentric and Dilapidated Places to Stay?'

'Okay. Maybe you are right. Let's hope the food is good here though.'

We heard the theme tune ending Neighbours, then shuffling feet approaching; she was wearing slippers. With arms folded, she offered us ain't-it-awful sympathy for having to travel in such dreadful weather.

'And what brings youes to this wee place this time o' year anyhow?' she enquired. 'One guest yesterday, and you two the day, business is pickin' up.' She laughed showing a missing front tooth.

'Oh,' Mark shrugged. 'We are just looking at a few properties around the area.'

'Work for an estate agent's, do youes? Want to sell this place for us? Find somebody to buy it?'

I smiled 'No we can't do that. This is a nice location. You have good views from here.'

'Aye.' She nodded. 'Have you decided on what youes would like?'

There was a limited choice on the dog-eared menu. A dish of the day, scampi, chicken Kiev, burgers or battered fish, and like McDonald's, chips with everything.

'What is your soup-of-the-day please?' I asked.

'I'm not sure, it might be Tomato and Basil. It was yesterday. Do you want me to find out?'

I thanked her, and she drifted off, seeming to have a natural inclination to inertia, then returned. 'Yes. Tomato and Basil, it is.'

She had to return again to ask the shell-suit what the dish-of-the-day was; it was lamb chops.

Mark asked to have his served medium rare and also asked to see the wine list.

'I'll give my hubby your order first. Back in a jiffy.' She tore off the slip with the food order and we saw the shell-suit chef lumber out of his chair like a bear roused from hibernation and disappear, hopefully, to the kitchen.

She handed Mark the wine list with some advice. 'Ma hubby tells me that our local lamb should be served, well-done sir. The flavour is better that way sir. Okay?'

Not believing a word of it, Mark went along with it to see what would arrive.

The wine list was a simple one of vintner's popular wines for small pubs and restaurants. Mark chose a Merlot. She went to find it. No luck. Then a Pinot Noir. Off again to check. No luck, but she returned with a Rioja in one hand and a Sauvignon Blanc in the other.

'I'm wearing out this floor going back and fore. This is all that's left. If you don't fancy one of these, I could go to the SPAR shop in the village? It'll still be open. It's beers our customers usually drink.'

We chose the Rioja and with a coughing laugh, she said. 'Hallelujah.'

Mark turned the logs over, placed another couple on top then sat back. While her back-and-fore was going on, a group of four locals arrived and were greeted like friends. They took a table at the far end of the bar and as she had predicted, ordered pints.

We saw a strip-light flicker into life in the dining room, then heard the repeated metallic clicking of a switch trying to ignite a gas flame. She came to call us through, but it was too cold and uninviting to want to eat there. We told her we'd rather eat in the bar area where we were, beside the fire.

She smiled. 'Aye. Youes'll be comfier there.'

I left the glutinous lumps of undissolved powdered soup-mix, looking like dark blood clots on the bottom of my soup bowl. Even a high-hatted chef cannot turn already well-done, dried out lamb chops into medium-rare ones. I had two Chicken Kievs, the buttery garlic piping hot and the crumb crust crisp so offered one to Mark. It helped lift his peeved expression.

The cheese course was exceptional. From the Dunlop dairy a wedge of Bonnet, a hard goat's milk cheese named after 'The Bonnet Toun' Stewarton, where the bonnets were made for army regiments. A small round of Isle of Mull Cheddar and a Lanark Blue, a blue-veined sheep's milk from a dairy near Carnwath, all labelled. There was also a small dish of home-made chutney, green apple slices and rough oatcakes, enough for a hearty ploughman's lunch.

Next morning an older lady in a floral overall served us the B.E.S.T breakfast (Bacon, Egg, Sausage and Tomato). Both the plate and the food were piping hot. We finished and picked our way back across the floor outside the toilets where the same lady was now sloshing it with a wet mop.

At check-out, she took our payments, then our business cards. 'Oh God, they'll love this. I haven't heard them moving about upstairs yet. I'll bet they're still in their bed, but I'll go and see.'

'Would they be the couple who served us last night?' Mark asked. 'Mr and Mrs Brown?'

'Aye. That would've been them.'

'We would like to see the other rooms if we may. Could you please ask them if this is possible while we are waiting?' Mark added.

'I'm sure it'll be fine, just go ahead. But they're all stripped down. She went off and we heard 'Oh, deary, deary me. It's terrible so it is.' as the door marked *Private* swung shut behind her at the foot of their stairs.

A little later, the same lady brought a large cafetière of coffee and the Browns joined us at a table by the cold ashes in the fireplace. Mr Brown still unshaven, wiped the sleep from his eyes as he slumped into a chair.

After a very short preliminary, Mark got started; the lukewarm check-in, his tiny cold bedroom, the long wait for our meal while they watched TV. He did try to draw them into the conversation. I could tell by his sigh Mark's frustration was building but they knew there had been problems and kept quiet with a subdued look.

Behind him there had been more reaction in the increased vigour with which the cleaner was lifting chairs and upending them on the tables, working around the periphery of our discussion. Muttering under her breath as if she was saying the rosary, she'd add exaggerated shakes of her head as she listened.

At last, Mr Brown cleared his throat and spoke up. 'What about your meal then?'

'Yes. Well, you would see that I returned the lamb chops. You could not cook them medium-rare because they were yesterday's leftovers, reheated. Would I be right?'

I winced at Mark's directness, but Mr Brown nodded. Mark added 'They were inedible. Mrs MacLennan had to share her Chicken Kiev with me because I didn't want a further wait for a replacement. You have a dog. I heard it barking out the back. It might have enjoyed them.'

From the background came a shout from the cleaner. 'That's it, son, dinnae you miss him an' hit the wa'. He's givin' this place a bad name, so he is.'

Mr and Mrs Brown lifted their eyes and looking at Mark. Mr B said, 'That's my mother.'

I whispered. 'Would you like her to join us?'

He closed his eyelids and said quietly, 'No.'

Mrs B opened her eyes wide forming an inaudible 'No' as if staring into an inevitable car crash.

Mark turned to look over his shoulder at the mother. 'I'm sure they will discuss things with you later.'

'You can bet your bottom dollar they will. His wee faither will be turnin' in his grave, so he will.' She was taking her anger out on the mop, plunging it vigorously into the water and leaning on it with considerable strength to squeeze it out again on the draining bit at the side.

The Browns lifted their coffee mugs in unison, took sips then kept their hands around them, staring into them as if they might contain an escape route.

I was uncomfortable with Mark's direct approach and chipped in. 'I'll give you feedback on my meal now if I may?' I said the soup tasted good, although it was not truly home-made. I mentioned the lumps and suggested checking for those and adding a garnish; croutons, parsley, cream. I praised the Chicken Kievs.

Mark looked at his notes. 'Now. The wines.' Another whack coming. 'If you have only two bottles of wine left until your vintner's next delivery, why didn't you just bring us those two bottles the first time or go to the SPAR shop and stock up? Going back and fore unnecessarily was slightly irritating for us and tiring for you obviously.'

'We did enjoy the wine and it was comfortable to be able to sit by the fire and eat our meal.' I added quickly.

Mark gave me a puzzled look, then leaned forward, resting a forearm on his thigh. He smiled. I thought that's good, he's going to lighten up. 'Look. I know how hard it is to carry food and wine stores not knowing if you are going to have customers or not, but honestly, would you have chosen to eat here last night?'

'Ouch, Mark, stop!' I thought. 'Enough'.

They shook their heads, agreeing with him.

'I thought so.' He added in a commanding voice, looking over the top of his glasses. 'Now to the housekeeping. It is good, but training is needed. There's a grubby rubbed line along the wallpaper where they clean the dado rail and above the skirting boards, caused by using dirty clothes. The mother froze, mid-wipe as he continued. 'Did you know that more damage is done to the fabric of a place by staff, rather than guests?'

The mother who was still out of Mark's sightline, glared at us open-mouthed and flung her drying cloth to the floor. He powered on unaware. 'There is a rim of black gunk around WC and basin pedestals and behind the toilet doors. Needs scraped off or power washed. You also need to find a pleasant-smelling air freshener for that area.

She stood the mop against the wall and marched off.

A knowing glance passed between Mr and Mrs Brown. Mr B took a long breath in and blew out a slow heavy one.

Mark praised the breakfast but remarked on the stained carpet just as the mother was returning fastening her coat and sat down by the bar, but close enough to listen.

Knowing she'd returned, I spoke up. 'Our colleague Laura has put together a booklet of very comprehensive easy to follow guidelines for housekeeping. I have a copy in my car I can leave it with you if you like. It will be useful for staff training too.'

From her chair, the mother shouted 'Staff training? You have to be jokin'. He's a lazy big lump and she's no better, just lets him aff wae everything. Ye canny blame me, I do my best but they baith need a right good kick up the arse.' Pointing her finger at Mark she added. 'You gee it tae them, straight son.'

Mark sat back with an almost celebratory smile, spreading his arms, raising his voice so she would hear. 'It is not all bad news mother. The star of the meal was the excellent local cheeses. Promoting local produce is wonderful. The chutney and oatcakes were delicious.'

I nodded my appreciation, then turning back to the owners said, 'Were they homemade?'

'It's me that makes these.' came a shout from the mother. 'And sandwiches and scones and pancakes and the sponge cakes in the summer, for the high teas. But do I get thanks for that? Not a bit. She takes it all for granted and never bats an eye. They'll rue the day when I pop my clogs, so they will. Mark my word.'

They signed for our visit, took the list of things to attend to and accepted the news that they had too many poor areas to have their award confirmed on this visit. They would need to improve in so many areas before it could be reinstated. They accepted the news without fuss.

I suggested they could research some local history about the Campbells, add pictures, frame newspaper clippings etc. but soon saw the futility of it. I paused waiting for a reaction but might as well have been speaking a foreign language. It would be true to say; they were not overcome with enthusiasm. Mark stood to leave; our business finished.

We shook hands and they thanked Mark, saying it had been very helpful.

Mother came forward in battle mode, thrusting her hands into her pockets taking a stance, feet-apart, but did remove one to shake our hands too.

'You're a real asset Mother.' Mark said, fastening his jacket.

She announced with a voice full of intent. 'Just you leave them to me. They'll get a piece of my mind, you bet they will.'

Douglas's Phone call

It was a sun-filled morning, the air was crisp and fresh. Steam rose from the frosted backs of the sheep and Mark got his car engine going while he scraped his windscreen and mine. While I was fetching the Housekeeping Guidelines from my car, the mother came running out. There was a message for you Mrs MacLennan from your office. You are to phone this number. It was my home number.

We had two students, Federica and Nagina staying with us while our boys were away at university. Two out and two in; it helped us with financially supporting the boys. I couldn't imagine why they were calling me, instead of waiting until John got home. Must be an emergency.

'Hi, Mum. How are you?'

My heart leapt; it was lovely to hear from him. 'Hi Douglas, how nice to have a call from you. I'm fine, thank you but, how are you? Why are you calling from home?'

'Well, I'm okay but Dad isn't. He said not to tell you, but I thought you should know. He fell out of a tree and has damaged his shoulder. He thinks it is not broken so doesn't want to go for an x-ray. We don't want you to worry though.'

'Goodness, where is he now?'

'At work, but you don't need to shout I can hear you okay.'

'In the office!' I said surprised.

'In the office. Yes, Mother.'

'How did he drive?'

There was a pause. 'He got his keys, put them in the lock, sat in the driver seat. He's a big boy he can look after himself. If he couldn't drive, he'd have got someone to drive him or got a taxi.'

'Okay. I'll phone him myself.'

'But Mum. I'm in a hurry. I washed my clothes in the washing machine in the flat and they've come out stinking. Worse than when I put them in. That Persil is just crap. What should I do now?'

'He fell out of a tree. What was he doing up a tree?

He was sawing it, but he is okay I told you. Mum, I've brought my washing home, would you do it for me please?'

'Well, hang them out on the washing line in the fresh air and I'll deal with it when I get home. Okay?'

'Okay.'

'How long did you leave them in the washing machine?' I asked.

'A few days.'

'A few days!' I did shout this time.

'One of the guys needed the machine so took mine out this morning and left them in a pile on the chair. They're all crushed and a stinking mess.'

'But Mum, I've found a pair of Steven's jeans. I need to go now I've got a lecture. I'll bring them back at the weekend. He won't miss them. Okay. Bye.'

I called John at the office. He said he was perfectly okay, but sore. I knew he would say that anyway, not to worry me. He said it was just bruising. He'd got a lift to work so didn't need to drive. Lothian buses had written to ask him to take a branch off the tree in the front garden; it was brushing against the windows on the top deck of the number 44.

Counselling Training

I joined Mark in his car, told him about the drama at home, then we discussed that visit to the Browns.

'They won't do a thing. That place will trundle along going nowhere. The old lady's tried and is frustrated with them.' he said with his hands on the steering wheel.

I could feel the heat in my face, from my phone call and our feedback. 'That felt as if we were good-cop, bad-cop.'

'We are the voice of their customers and they are paying for honest feedback, even if it hurts. Your softly-softly approach; they would just have given a nod to. They will do nothing. They are switched off. Lazy.'

I rubbed my forehead. 'But I would still have downgraded them. Did you know I'm a qualified Relationship Counsellor and I've nearly completed a Post-grad. Diploma in Counselling at Napier Uni? Do you mind if I tell you what I think was going on with our feedback?'

'No, I don't mind. But what! You must be mad. Counselling. Whatever for?'

'I'm learning a lot about myself and others. Did you notice their body language? They were cowed, like naughty children getting a dressing down. You were a heavy father. The more confrontational you became, the more I wanted to compensate. We were polarising. I would have wanted to hear more about; how did it get to be like this? What would they want their business to be like? How could we help get them there?'

'That does sound very counsell-y if you don't mind my saying. I've heard you at staff meetings, you can be pretty forceful sometimes.' He raised an eyebrow and smiled.

'I know. I can overreact when I'm rattled, and I feel so embarrassed afterwards.'

'You're forgetting something, counsellor. You heard her say right at the start, they would sell up if they found a buyer. His mother was right, they're switched off and you would have been wasting time with them getting nowhere. They would have nodded and smiled agreeing with you then do nothing. You're making things hard for yourself. They are lazy.'

'Oh well. Perhaps you're right. Maybe one day someone will buy it, give it a bit of atmosphere, cook better food, have a bit of ambition and energy and the car park will fill up, like the one at the Drovers.'

I opened his door to leave. He was smiling. 'I'll bet John has trouble with you, analysing him. Poor man, it must be hell for him. Having to fall out of a tree to get some attention from you.' He laughed. 'Give him my regards and sympathies, won't you?'

'He says he has an off switch.' I smiled. 'Where are you driving to now?'

'Dumfries and Galloway.' He looked at his watch. 'Time I was off. I must see a day's worth of cottages on a shooting estate down there tomorrow. I'll be chauffeured around in a battered old Land Rover and will dine with the family. Last time, we had venison casserole I remember, braised with red wine brandy and rosemary. Rosemary with a small 'r' of course. They had a rather good claret to wash it down.' I've got one in the boot this time. 'Bye then, see you at the next meeting. Counselling! Indeed. Meddling more like it.' He chuckled. 'Drive safely.'

Troon Beach

Big bold daffodils tossed about at the roadside as I drove on the A794 which passes through the Royal Troon golf course.

I wanted a handy place to stop and reorganise my stationery and files in the boot of the car and have a brisk walk before sunset. The South Beach car park was the ideal place and I soon set off appreciating the lengthening day, the scent of the sea and the view of Lady Isle with its open stair lighthouse. It was visible through my binoculars with the Isle of Arran in the background. I'd grown attached to Arran, having worked there. I remembered being at the top of Goatfell with John on a clear day like this, looking over to the Ayrshire coast to where I was now standing.

No doubt hoping to keep its reputation as an award-winning beach, tractors and pick-up trucks were working the long sandy shoreline clearing up seaweed, orange and blue plastic ropes and plastic bottles; the detritus which we humans had tossed away, and the winter tides had thrown back at us.

A black Labrador had taken charge of a flattened plastic 7Up bottle and dropped it at my feet to throw for him. I missed our own two dogs who spent their lives hauling stones out of the Water of Leith, carrying the last ones home in the evening like trophies for us.

I walked towards the industrial area with its unattractive slate-grey sheds and could hear the rhythmic clinking of the rigging against the masts in the yacht marina beyond. From there we had sailed in the Clyde with our friend Alistair in his beautiful boat Samoon, a Vancouver 34. It is a popular marina because it is accessible at both low and high tide.

Pete and his Cat

I have reason to remember this next visit in the Spring of 1995, I had booked myself into a small hotel in Troon.

My hand was poised to ding the reception bell on the bar of this small Troon hotel for the second time when his face appeared at the small round window in the kitchen door. He strode past me, lifting his eyebrows in a suggestion of a smile, talking on his phone, laughing and running his fingers through his mane of shoulder-length, wavy hair: those silver-grey streaks placing him in his late 40s, early 50s. In scruffy trainers, well-fitting jeans with designer slashes, black shirt, collar up, St. Christopher glinting among the hairs on his chest, he reminded me of an ageing rock star.

With the phone still to his ear, he lifted the hinged bar counter then mouthed 'One minute.' requiring me to lip-read, so as not to interrupt his phone call. Then 'MacLennan?'

I nodded and smiled. He stood back to look below the counter, chose a room key and handed it to me. With the phone held between his shoulder and ear, he eased the counter-top back into place and took me to the foot of the stairs. Hearing his voice, I looked back. He was still on the phone but gave me a thumbs-up and winked.

In my room, waiting for the kettle to boil I read the paperwork. A final warning notice had been issued. The owner would lose his Three Crowns Commended award if certain simple items were not provided; a full-length mirror in each bedroom, 8 hangers and 2 pillows per guest, however, more important than those, he had to provide an evening meal for residents every night.

There was a complaint; he advertised an evening meal, but guests had been refused one only a month before. I would have been angry too if I'd to push my elderly father in his wheelchair, slithering along icy pavements looking for a place to eat.

In my room, I had a medium-sized mirror, a tangle of wire hangers in the wardrobe and not enough pillows. What were the chances of an evening meal?

After an hour, I heard laughter coming from downstairs, so slipped my shoes back on, grabbed my book and went down to see if other guests might be having a more efficient welcome than mine.

The living-flame gas fire had been lit and there were tea-lights on each of the occasional tables in the foyer/lounge area. He was behind the bar enjoying a drink along with two gentlemen seated on bar stools. As I passed, he asked 'Can I get you something to drink? G&T, sherry, a pint, bag of crisps, a soft drink perhaps?'

'A gin and tonic would be nice. Thank you.' I got a thumbs-up again, while he continued listening to their conversation.

Shortly afterwards, as their drained glasses were pushed across the bar and they rose to leave I heard. 'The lady wants a G&T, so catch you later guys.'

I was not offered a choice of gins or tonics, but he arrived with ice and lemon, poured half the tonic in for me, placed the bottle on a coaster, with a ramekin dish of potato crisps alongside. Good.

He was now dressed in tight-fitting black leather trousers, a white grandad-collar shirt with the cuffs turned back and hair fluffed up like John Travolta's Archangel Michael, his open shirt revealing a thick gold belcher chain. He stood leaning on the mantelpiece at first. 'Room okay for you?'

I took a sip from my drink. 'Yes, thank you, nice and quiet too.'

'Driven far?' he asked.

'From Edinburgh today.' I replied. 'It has been a lovely Spring day too.'

He said, 'I might as well join you now my pals have gone.' He had a whisky or brandy judging by the colour and relaxed back into the sofa opposite. With one arm along the back, he checked out my legs and continued 'I'm glad of some company. It's a long day when there is not much to do but stand around.'

'The hotel's not busy then?'

'Too early in the year yet. I have four Irish golfers staying and that is it I'm afraid.' As if suddenly remembering his manners, he stood up again, leaned across the coffee table, looking down at my cleavage this time, offering a handshake. 'I'm Pete by the way.'

A right Jack-the-lad. 'Nice to meet you, Pete, I'm Reta.'

'I like to eat early Pete. When does the dining room open?'

'Well, there'll only be you. The golfers like to eat out. There's a pub just along the road and good Scottish, Italian and Indian on the main street.'

I could have just gone out to eat too but that would mean he was automatically downgraded. He didn't offer that I could eat in. I hesitated and made a slight twist to the side of my mouth, 'It looks as if it might rain.'

He laughed. 'I can take a hint. You women know how to get your way. Let me think.' He rubbed his chin. 'Okay. I have homemade lentil soup; I could add a shot of vodka to posh it up.' He looked at the ceiling for inspiration. 'Yes. I also have an M&S

venison steak in the fridge. Their venison is always well hung and tender. Would that appeal to you?' He laughed as if he'd surprised himself with the double-entendre. 'Just joking, sorry, my wife is always telling me off for my sense of humour. Well, maybe, then some oatcakes and cheddar?'

'That sounds great but no vodka in the soup please.'

We chatted for a while about this and that, my keeping the conversation at level one; the weather, holidays, how nice Troon is, the beach being cleaned today.

I looked at my watch and drained my glass. 'I'll just catch the news at 6.00. Could I eat about 7.00 then please if that's okay with you?'

'Okay-dokay, anything the lady wants, the lady gets.' He stood also and collected our glasses. 'I'll put a glass of vodka on the side in case you change your mind. Try it.'

I could feel his eyes following me as he walked to the bar via the bottom of the stairs. I'd change into my high-necked blouse and trousers for dinner and hope that maybe the four golfers would dine in too. But I'd booked the one portion of venison! Maybe he'd more meals in the freezer.

I sat alone with a tea light and a single artificial Calla lily as company. Eating alone had never bothered me before, but here! I concentrated on reading my course textbook; *The Skilled Helper*.

After a while, the swing-door from the kitchen was pushed open and he brought my soup with a small warmed dinner roll. The soup was steaming hot and an appetising colour had hearty chunks of carrots and onions with mixed herbs and I could taste a good ham stock. He'd put a shot of vodka on the side, giving me another of his winks. I tried a sip, then a mouthful of soup, then tried them the other way around but they went together as naturally as a pavlova drizzled with paint stripper. Whisky might have been a better choice; I don't like whisky, but half-a-teaspoon drizzled onto hot porridge with cream and honey does give it a beautiful warmth and richness.

His face appeared later at the porthole in the kitchen door to check if I'd finished, then he returned carrying a tray to the sideboard. My plates were removed and with a mocking formal style, he placed my main course in front of me, swivelled the plate, positioning it as he murmured. 'I hope Madam likes this dish, prepared personally with my own fair hands, especially for you.'

I caught whisky breath. I lifted my fork and knife and smiled. 'It looks delicious. Thank you.' The meat was very tender, typical M&S reliable standard. The rich sauce of venison juices and red wine was glossy and indeed delicious. He'd cooked red cabbage braised with apples, crisp French beans and crunchy roast potatoes which were very good accompaniments.

As he returned to the kitchen, a grey Persian-type cat, in a very practised little burst of a run, entered before the door swung back. It then padded over and considering just the right spot, settled beside my chair tucking its tail around out of the way of passing shoes. It studied me with seeming disinterest. Every now and again it would lift its nose and with the slightest quivering inhalation, seem to savour the aroma.

The kitchen door swung open again as Pete reversed against it, a bottle of wine and an extra wine glass in one hand and a very large glass of whisky in the other. He smiled. 'I can't have you eating alone.'

I kept my eyes on my plate and he settled too, on the chair opposite. I was very sure I wanted to remain incognito and didn't feel at all comfortable being in his company for the evening.

'I said to myself, it's a cold evening, I'll join her and share my full-bodied-fruity Merlot. It might warm her up a little!' He laughed and held the bottle above my glass.

'I'd enjoy a glass of Merlot.' I took a sip. He was going to get a low score for wine service. 'Yes, it is very nice, and I get the fruitiness. A good choice.' *Shit. I shouldn't have said fruity*.

He wiggled his hands beside his chin, Chewing the Fat style 'Ooo, the lady knows her wines then!'

'The venison is delicious too.'

'Sorted then. Cheers.' He lifted his glass to clink with mine. 'Good old M&S, as I said earlier. I've got a chef for the summer, but I can't keep him all year round. He taught me a few things though. Changing the subject, that book you've got there. Can I have a look?'

'Sure.'

He opened it and could see from the style of the layout; targets, highlighted boxes, that it was not a novel.

'You studying or something?'

'Yes, I am. I'm studying counselling.' *Maybe shouldn't have said that either. Too much information. That proved to be the case.*

'Oh, ho, that can cause trouble, I can tell you.'

I just smiled. 'I think your cat is angling for some of my venison.'

He put the book down. 'Are you bothering the lady Hector?'

'No, he's fine. I like cats, but I have a friend who freaks out if one comes near her.' *I wondered if Hector was always around.*

'Well as she's not here, there's no problem then. If people don't like Hector, we just ask them to leave, don't we Hector?' He threw his head back laughing, finding this hilarious.

I smiled, changing the subject. 'You have another guest I see. I passed a lady on the stairs earlier.'

'That is no guest. That would have been my wife. She's off to Glasgow to stay with her mother and meet up with our daughter. She's doing Hospitality Studies at Glasgow College. The daughter that is. Tell me, was she carrying a large case or a small one?'

'She wasn't carrying any cases that I noticed.'

He downed a couple of slugs of his wine and told me he was not sure how long she'd be away, or if she was coming back at all. He gave a laugh which didn't contain any joy. 'Just a joke. Never mind, not your problem.'

He swirled his Merlot, took another slug. 'She ignores the guests. Nothing personal. She ignores me too, most of the time.' He moved the whisky glass aside so that he could lean his elbows on the table, getting closer.

I continued eating and he filled the silence. They'd lived in Glasgow, near her mother. He'd surprised her two years before with a weekend at the Marine Hotel on the outskirts of town and she'd said she wouldn't mind living here. She minded very much when he surprised her by buying this hotel without telling her.

He gazed into his whisky glass, took a large swallow then looked at his palm, picking at some skin. 'She tramples all over my dreams. Always has done.'

'Buying this was one of your dreams then Pete?'

He'd had redundancy money and made a snap decision. He was also thinking of their daughter, so she'd have a job to walk into when she finished her hospitality studies.

He smiled, but not with his eyes. 'The wife said she wasn't moving to Troon. So, when I told her I'd already put our house on the market, she went ballistic. So. She doesn't want to be anywhere near me. She really doesn't.' He emptied his wine glass. I put my hand over mine, then he refilled his own and continued. 'She feels too far away from her ageing mother. I'm not forgiven.'

'That was a life-changing risk Pete. It seems you meant well, but it has backfired.' *Careful, this might be engaging a bit too much. I shouldn't have mentioned counselling.*

He shrugged. His happy-go-lucky attitude might be what was keeping him going. 'I tell you; it was scary in the kitchen. All those knives around and shmargarete has one helluva hot temper. I think she decided it was slightly better living here with me than being locked up in Cornton Vale.' His laugh was hollow.

She'd had to leave her job and they'd reached an uneasy compromise. He'd run the hotel; she'd ignore the guests.

'I made a mistake. Our daughter doesn't come near the hotel, even in the summer.' He picked at his palm again.

'Give her time. She can make her mistakes in other people's hotels, get good training then join you.' I placed my cutlery together on the empty plate and returned to safer ground. 'That was delicious. Thank you. Could I just have a coffee now please?'

He looked at me. 'I'm lonely.'

'It is a pity you're not busier. Time would pass more quickly, and you maybe wouldn't have time to feel lonely then.'

He rubbed his hands together, gave a sigh and seemed to cheer up 'Pudding? I took a small sticky-toffee pudding out of the freezer earlier in case you fancied it. If you are not in a rush to go upstairs, I could warm it up for you. The pudding that is.' He laughed again.

'Okay. That's one of my favourites but just a small portion please.' Remembering, if it's offered, I have to try it at least,

He stood and removed my plate, leaving the drinks glasses and returned to the kitchen calling to Hector, to follow him, but Hector, surprisingly, was not moving. He turned his head a full 180 degrees only following him with a slit-eyed gaze.

Maybe it was the way I pushed my chair back a little for a moment, but Hector took this as an invitation and jumped onto my lap. He arched his back, stretched, then tucked his paws in, settling himself and started purring. I stroked his head and he closed his eyes pushing against my hand. Somehow, he felt like a good defence.

Returning with the pudding, Pete had brought one for himself too and a cafetière of coffee. 'Hector likes you; he doesn't climb onto everyone's lap you know.' He smiled. 'Wish I was him.'

Bloomin' heck. That was it. Enough. I gave a kind of involuntary giggle at the audacity of yet another overt remark. I drained my wine glass. And ate my pudding fast.

'How about a small nightcap? On the house.'

'No thank you, Pete, I'm happy with just this, then I'll take my coffee upstairs, there's a programme I want to watch.' I hoped he wouldn't ask the name of it; I didn't have one in mind. I should have put Hector down but didn't until I finished my pudding. 'Well Hector, you will have to move now.' I started to lift him gently, but he dug his claws into my thigh. Right through my trousers. 'Ouch.'

'Oops. He likes being there. Don't you Hector? Come on now behave, you're hurting the lady.' He took two enormous slugs of whisky, laughed and stood up.

I tried to ease out Hector's claws. but he sank his teeth into the soft part between my thumb and first finger. I yelled again. I didn't want help from Pete so held up my one free hand to stop him. When Hector released his teeth and claws, I gave him a very hard swipe. He landed a few feet away and actually growled, arching his back and turned to give me a stare, the tip of his tail flicking like a whip.

'That was very sore.' I said, using the napkin to wipe my bleeding hand. I could see dark beads of blood on my trousers too.

He addressed his blooming cat. 'Hey, Hector. Say sorry to the lady. That's not nice. You have to sort out your style pal, not every lady likes it rough.' finding his own quick wit very funny, he threw back his head, laughing again.

'That hurt. You should keep him out of the dining room.'

'No problem, as I said earlier if the guests don't like him, out they go.' He was laugh-out-loud amused now. 'Woosh. They're off. Hector rules. Isn't that right Hector?'

I stood. 'Well, I'm off now too.' I said, keeping my eyes averted feeling very uncomfortable and just wanting to go. 'I'll say Goodnight.'

'Let me get you something for that. You lead the way darling and I'll be right behind you in a few minutes. I'll bring you something for that hand.' He was more drunk than I'd thought. He was still laughing.

I frowned. 'No thanks. I can tend to it myself. I'll be fine. Goodnight.'

He stood watching me go. 'Awe, come on, don't go. Stay and enjoy yourself. I'll fix your hand. The night is young.'

I ran the tap on my bleeding hand and checked my thigh, it was fine. Then I heard a gentle knock on my bedroom door. I couldn't believe it. 'Who is it?'

'It's me, Pete. I think I was out of order. I'd like to apologise.' He coughed. 'Are you alright? I've got some Savlon and plasters and the rest of the wine. It's a shame to waste it?'

'Apology accepted Pete. Thank you, I'm fine. Goodnight.'

'Oh well. I'll see you in the morning then. Goodnight.'

What a bloody prick. I put the chain on the door hoping he'd hear it. He'd have a master key. I waited.

He said 'Okay, I get the message.' Then I heard his footsteps, heavy and slow thump down the stairs.

I slept better than expected and when I heard the golfers going down for breakfast, I followed them, glad of their company. There was no sign of Pete.

The golfers were from Co. Mayo.

'Have you been there?' One of them asked.

'No, I haven't. But my father came from there.'

'Ah well, if he came from Mayo, he would have been a fine man indeed.' They all agreed.

Later, when I stood at reception checking my bill, Pete arrived. He looked pretty rough, unshaven and back in trainers and jeans. 'Morning.' He took over from the waitress and I paid, noticing that there was no charge for my wine.

I had my business card in my hand ready to give to him when one of the golfers arrived. 'Hey Pete, we saw this lady having a meal last night before we went out. We didn't know you served evening meals. You've never offered us one.'

Pete sighed and shook his head as the other golfers arrived. He slapped his palm onto the bar then pointed to the door. 'Out you go, enjoy your game while the sun shines. The pub along the road has a disco tonight, you'll get fed there, pull a bird, have fun. I won't tell the wives. Bye guys.'

As they gathered themselves together to leave, I put my business card on the desk. 'You are not going to like this Pete, I'm from the Tourist Board.'

He looked at it and raised his voice to catch their attention. 'Cut. Retake. Gentlemen, dinner this evening? The dining room will be open from 7.00. I'll see you in the bar and take your orders. Any allergies? Preferences?'

The golfers turned around, amazed. One of them said 'We like everything.' Another said, 'Anything would be good.' Then smiles passed between them.

'Very good gentlemen, I will see you then, if not before. Have a good day now.'

He looked at me. 'You see this hair' he tugged his bedraggled locks. 'I can't even get out for a haircut. See that car.' He pointed outside 'It doesn't go. It can't move. It is kaput. I can't even get it to the garage to get it fixed. I am trapped here every day, just in case some guests, just even one guest should decide to stay. Preferably one who doesn't give me a blooming heart attack. But no. I can't get out. I can't go anywhere.'

Then wondering about the impression, he had just made, he continued. 'I enjoy it mind, I'm not complaining about the work, my wife, well, you know now. She's a real bitch. You have no idea. The night before last, she did everything but throw me out till I reminded her it's my place.' Then he sagged, leaning on his elbows on the bar counter, head in his hands. 'Don't do this to me. Not now. How's your hand anyway?'

'Okay thanks, just a bit swollen but it will be fine.' I pointed to where we'd had a drink the previous evening and said 'Could we start by sitting there. I'll go and put my suitcase in the car. I can't do haircuts, I can't fix cars, but let's see if I can help with your business problems.'

Pete brought a pot of coffee for us, followed by the girl who had served breakfast. She looked fierce now as she pulled on her coat; she'd tied her dyed-brown hair with grey roots up in the fashionable tumble-down pile, applied thick black eyeliner and scarlet lipstick. She stood with her hands on her hips, tight-lipped, giving him a hostile stare. Yet another waitress-cum-cleaner having a problem with her boss.

'Well?' she asked, in a challenging tone.

'Will you excuse me for a minute I just have to let Marilyn know what is needed today.'

They went to the kitchen, but I could hear her shouting. 'You're full of crap Pete. Promises, promises. You don't keep them. I am not touching even a dirty dish today until I get the wages you owe me. I've got my coat on. I'm going, and my husband will be here tonight to collect what you owe me.'

I heard him mumble something then they returned to the bar, he opened the locked till and counted out some money.'

'Thank you. Why do I always have to get angry to get paid.'

'Because I like to see that fire in your eyes, Marilyn.'

'Oh, piss off, flattery will get you nowhere.' Then she looked at me, shaking her head and tossing her eyes to the ceiling, returned to the kitchen.

He had stayed open all winter, but it brought big heating bills and very few guests. He kept Marilyn going on an ad hoc basis because he needed her in the summer.

We started the tour of the bedrooms which were like mine, very good all round. However, in the last one, I addressed the issue of missing full-length mirrors, coat hangers and pillows.

'Do you have your last report, Pete?'

'It's somewhere around, but I'm sure that's a copy you have there. Right?'

'Yes, I do, and it asks, for the last and final time, two pillows per guest. Some people need two pillows Pete.'

He looked at the bed with one pillow per person, looked at me. then let out a long breath with an animated wink. 'Inside that pillowcase, there are two pillows. Right?'

'Show me.' I replied holding his gaze, not able to resist a smile at his attempts at recovery.

He pulled his hands through his hair.

'And a full-length mirror?' I looked at our truncated reflection.

'What's full length anyway? A small person could jump up and down, a tall person could bend their knees. Don't you think?'

'Why should your guests have to? We gave you specific minimum measurements.' I held his gaze while I opened the wardrobe. 'You have enough clothes hangers Pete, but they are a tangle of dry-cleaners' ones. What about the quality?'

He turned to me, mouth open, eyes wide, feigning shock. 'Would you believe it, they've gone again. Those naughty guests. They walk out to the car with their clothes on my expensive wooden hangers and leave me those nasty wire ones.'

'You will know that you can buy secure ones. My colleague Ms Wearmouth mentioned it and my colleague before her, I added.

He folded his arms. 'You're not going to play ball, are you?'

'Let's go downstairs and I'll go through my visit.'

Pete groaned, drew his hands down over his face. 'I can imagine you'll have a lot to say. But remember deep down, I'm as sensitive and innocent as that chap born in a stable. I've just hit hard times. I need another coffee. Would you like one? Then you'll have my undivided attention.'

'Yes please.'

He talked about having no money, not able to attract enough business, wanting to hold out till the summer season believing he could afford those pillows, etc. Then asked. 'That book you were reading last night, any advice in that?'

'Yes, it's simple stuff. Identify the problems, decide on the goals then take realistic steps to achieve them. For example, lack of income. You didn't charge me for my wine. That is money walking out the door. And I have a complaint here. A lady with her father in a wheelchair. You sent them out to eat. Besides their inconvenience, you could have given them a meal, that would have been income. Or those friendly golfers, that would have brought in extra money!' I had heard enough of his patter.

I could see from his file what my colleagues had discussed on previous visits. None of Margaret's suggestions had been followed up and looking at why this was, got us nowhere. He had a problem gathering enthusiasm which I can imagine happens when you believe you have tried everything, and it hasn't worked.

I did find things he hadn't yet tried. Go to the ferry terminal and hand out leaflets to the drivers. Ask the bigger hotels if you can take their overflow when they have coach parties or events. Offer the locals suppers with quiz nights. Read the local paper for engagement announcements, they might want to hold a celebration. Look for funeral announcements and contact the family to offer to do their catering or contact the funeral directors for the same purpose; get known.

He was looking at me with a grin which said, 'No way'.

We'd given him plenty of time and two opportunities to put things right or accept a lower award, but he refused to display Two Crowns. Running his fingers through his hair again he said he might as well put up a plaque which said, 'I'm a loser.'

'A kind of Fawlty Towers approach! I hadn't thought of that one. Try it.' I added.

I closed my folder. Put it in my case then told him how uncomfortable I felt with his behaviour, there being no-one else around and even his aggressive cat being in on the assault. Coming to my bedroom door with a bottle of wine!

He groaned, 'I'm sorry. It is too easy to drink when I work in the bar and I get lonely. I'm not normally like that.'

'I'll take that as an apology then. I must go now, Pete. I wish you good luck and more guests.'

I lifted my briefcase and stood. He stood too, and we shook hands. I told him he would now receive a letter asking him to remove his Three Crowns plaque and we'd send him a Two Crown one. But a momentary smile flickered in the corners of his mouth. Did I think he would change the plaques?

Scottish Tourist Board News Bulletin 1995

'As part of the Highlands and Islands Enterprise Economic Growth and Development Plan, fifty Scottish Tourist Board jobs will be based at Thistle House, Inverness.'

Move to Inverness

Our department was on the move. There were now around 24 GCOs and as our homes were scattered throughout Scotland anyway, there would be an obvious saving in employee relocation costs.

Our new office was light-filled and spacious and a great open-plan environment in which to get to know each other better. Our new admin team were keen and efficient assistants, who became affectionately known as our mums and we had one dad, each supporting a small designated group of GCOs. This was a welcome new start and the atmosphere throughout the department was one of hard-working support and fun.

We were a happy team and after a few days of in-house training, celebrated the move by our very own pop-up chef, Malcolm taking charge of a pop-up barbecue in the car park. Volunteers donated savoury accompaniments and desserts and our wine expert Colin chose the wines. It was real bonding fun; some had more fun than others and had a problem with recall the next day.

Born in a Stable

A warm spell in the West had stirred life into slumbering bracken on the hills, short green rods with their tightly curled tops stood just above the faded-copper winter cover. In the high canopy, the burgeoning buds of skeletal ash and sycamore seemed nearly ready to burst and on the woodland floor, the tender leaves of wild garlic were well up, growing in bunches. Wild-garlic pesto and wild-garlic soup time.

Time for me to return to Ayrshire to visit a stud farm which had a very fine self-catering cottage. Behind tall fences, four sleek thoroughbreds were grazing. They reminded me of the racehorses I'd seen being galloped in the shallows on the sandy beach at Ayr.

I pressed the buzzer on the secure-entry keypad. It took three rings to get an answer.

'Hello. Linda? It's Reta from the Tourist Board.'

'Yes. Yes. Hello Reta, you're in good time. Drive towards the house and turn left into the stable yard. I'll meet you there.'

I drove up the long avenue of cherry trees, the first flush of pink blossom just appearing. There was the smell of newly mown grass from the clipped verges and the gravel was immaculately weed free.

Linda watched me arriving and waved me over with some urgency, indicating where to park.

'Hello, nice to meet you again.' She shook my hand, through the open car window and I picked up her excitement. 'Leave your things. Quick. Hurry. Come on, this way. You'll have to keep quiet though.'

A mare was on her side in a special pen with deep straw on the floor. She was in the process of foaling,

There were silent handshakes as I joined the observers standing off at a distance. I stood quietly beside Linda and her husband and learned later the others were the mare's two owners and the groom.

The vet, gowned up and wearing gloves right up to his armpits, stethoscope hanging around his neck, stood with his hands on his hips. His assistant held the bandaged mare's tail, which was for hygiene reasons I imagined. The birth sack, like a grey opaque elastic sheet, hung loose where the foal's forelegs had been released. The mare made low grunting sounds, strained her neck as her sides rippled then the attendant pulled hard on her foal's legs. It looked too rough to me and I held my breath.

After that, he inserted his hand and did a round sweeping movement which stressed me more than it seemed to stress the mare. After what seemed a long wait, the head emerged with the second very strong pull and the vet swept the birth-sack back from the new foal's face.

On the next contraction, I was again holding my breath and again with a huge pull, the full floppy length of the foal was born, lying on the straw. There was a warm body smell. I was in awe of the whole gentle yet strong process and found myself blinking back happy tears. The vet, cupping the foal's mouth, removed any mucus from its airways and slicked the rest of the birth-sack down over its body. It was a steaming, wet chestnut-brown colt with a long white flash on his forehead and two white socks on his forelegs.

The attendant rubbed him down with some straw while he shook his head. It wobbled on his neck. His eyes were open, he was blinking. Fluttering breaths soon became a steady movement. No-one spoke. The mare raised her head, trying to reach round to nuzzle her foal. The vet did his final routine checks and nodded, grinning.

The gathered spectators were smiling, showing some degree of relief, quietly shaking hands with a bit of gentle back slapping as we moved further off. A bottle of Dom Perignon appeared dripping from an ice box in one of the stalls beside a box of glasses.

We clinked glasses and returned after a few minutes, to watch again. The newly born foal was on his knees, then with a little support from the vet's assistant, supporting his underbelly, he managed to stand with a few wobbles, his legs splayed out towards each corner like the spindly screw-in legs on a 1960's coffee table.

The mare was now standing, sniffing and licking him, making maternal low snickering noises and the new colt was supported by the vet while he instinctively attached for his first suckle. I watched this gentle bonding between them, one of the most moving occasions I can ever remember in this job.

I made a quick check over their self-catering property, the reason why I was there, after all. I noted and recorded the upgrading Linda had done since last year and acknowledged her excellent efforts. She invited me to join them for lunch, however, I had to rush off. Linda carved me a slice of ham and made me a sandwich to take with me before I rushed off. What a happy day.

Who's Highly Strung?

This particular April day in 1996 was sunny and unseasonably hot. At the first hint of heat, the Scots discard coats, jackets and jumpers as if one big warm-weather massage is easing their winter-mindsets. While my engine idled at traffic lights, I saw people stopping to chat, in short-sleeved dresses, shorts and T-shirts, instead of rushing with buttoned-up coats and buttoned-up expressions. Workmen on the first-floor scaffolding had bared their sun-starved skin and tattooed backs because tomorrow it might rain.

I had returned to the Auld Toon o'Ayr and checked into a B&B owned by Mr and Mrs Burnett. They'd complained that Jennifer, the previous year's GCO had seemed too nervous and highly strung to be able to give them a fair assessment. This year they'd already had their annual visit but were still unhappy. We'd sent them a man: 'What could he know about running a B&B?' they'd said in their complaint. They wanted a woman's opinion, paid for another visit and I arrived.

Alan had been the man they'd complained about, just because he was a man. I told him I had the happy task of standing in line to be the third GCO they might reject. Alan remembered Mrs. B and warned me she was of a nervous disposition and to leave plenty of time for the feedback in the morning.

Sitting in their lounge with tea and cake, I mentioned as an opener. 'I was born in Ayr and wh...' That was only my preamble, the clue being that my mouth was forming the next word.

'So was I, what a coincidence ...' It was the opener for a potted history of her life.

From then on, the conversation was one-way; my opener and her lengthy response. That was okay, I just had to listen.

Poor Mrs Burnett. Such was her nervousness; that when she rose from her perch on the arm of the easy chair to reach for the teapot, she didn't give herself time to uncross her legs. She hit the coffee table with one hand first, then her shoulder, then her hefty body weight. She also lost control of her wind.

Everything went flying; the teapot, the sugar bowl, the milk jug. I had a firm grip on my own teacup, thank goodness.

Her pale-green carpet had a spreading puddle of tea, overloaded with milk and sugar.

I stood. 'Oh, goodness! Are you hurt?'

'No, no, I'm fine. I'm so sorry.' She said grunting, getting herself up from all fours.

'Oh dear. What am I going to do now?' She wailed, looking around her immaculate swags-and-tailed lounge with its large print of Culzean Castle above the fireplace, collection of Royal Doulton ladies and the velvet three-piece-suite to see if any of them had been sprayed. Meanwhile, the puddle was settling into the carpet.

'Quick.' I said we'll shovel up the sugar. Kitchen roll. Toilet paper. We'll soak it up.' I sounded quite commanding. 'Let's just do it now. Quickly.'

She scooped up the sugar while I trod kitchen paper onto the stains and created a plastic bag full of the sopping mess. Some generous squirts of foaming Vanish, a few pats and wipes and things were almost back to normal.

A Walk Through my History

Back in my room I wrote some notes, replayed the scene and had to smile to myself as I changed into my trainers, jeans and a T-shirt. I tied my denim jacket around my waist and strode out to the esplanade to be amongst the late afternoon sun-seekers and burn off some of that lovely afternoon tea.

I passed the harbour, onto Newton-on-Ayr and looked at the outside of 48 Waggon Road, where my father had lodged, I paused there, wishing I'd known him. Then on to 8 West Sanquar Road where I was born during the war while a convoy was passing. Continued up by Ayr Racecourse, the home of the Scottish Grand National, across the park and up the lane to 16 Craigie Lea where my Uncle John, once lived. He attended the races and followed the form of the racehorses and jockeys. I had stayed with him so many times. He had a beautiful singing voice.

I turned back along the River Ayr where I walked with my first boyfriend Jim and eventually reached the foot of the High Street. I'd walked through many memories, covered a good mileage and my legs were telling me I'd walked far enough. The heat of the day had cooled, so I put on my denim jacket, buttoning it up. I did not expect what happened next.

I squeezed between a bus queue and two rough looking lads standing outside a pub; scruffy trainers, tracksuit bottoms and T-shirts with scary-type slogans. I did keep an eye on their lit cigarettes burning at thigh level as I passed.

One of them was really fired up. 'An' Ah says tae him prove it ye fuckin' bastard, prove it then.' He took a long drag, his pal nodded. He continued. 'He couldnae. Ah, kent he couldnae.'

I got past them without a cigarette burn in my jeans then tried to move out of the way of a drunk propped against the pub wall while people beside me were moving onto the bus. He lurched forward. Grabbing my arm, he spun me around, putting his red puffy face close to mine. I froze with shock.

He pushed me hard against the wall. My head bounced off it. 'Bitch.' He pushed me again. 'Bitch. Ah'll learn ye.' He kept going as I tried to clutch his sleeves. 'Ye'll no pit me oot. Ye'll no dae that tae me again.'

The two rough guys reacted quickly. As he drew his fist back, they caught his arm, shouting, 'Wullie. Stop that.' They tugged him off me and he staggered away at a good pace, towards the harbour.

'You aw' right hen? Are ye hurt? That was terrible. He must'a thought ye were the lassie frae the pub. She jist pit him ootside a minute ago. He must'a saw yer jeans and yer jacket an' thought you were her.'

'I'm okay thanks.' I whimpered. But I wasn't. I walked quickly away, gulping air, trying to hold back tears. I decided if I saw a police car, I would stop it and give them a description of him in case he attacked someone else. All the way back to the Burnett's there was no sign of one, but it was just as well, I'd changed my mind anyway, imagining myself returning to the Burnett's in a police car.

Return to the Burnett's

I reached my bedroom, out of breath, a hankie with blood spots hidden in my hand. The bathroom mirror showed me an overheated face with smudged mascara and frightened eyes. I used my compact mirror to see the back of my head which confirmed the huge tender bump was just grazed. I could have used some ice for the swelling but there was no way I was going downstairs to ask for some.

Why are showers never hot enough when you need a bit of a sting? I stood there letting the hot water soothe me a little.

I didn't feel hungry or want to go out again for dinner, so had the Penguin biscuit and a chamomile tea from the tea tray and ate the apple which had lived in my handbag for a few days. I felt sorry for myself as I spread night-cream on my face and got into bed. I curled on my side and watched something or other on TV at an impossible angle, but it didn't matter. I wanted to be lost in sleep and it happened.

I woke very early the next morning to see thin slices of sunlight penetrate between the slats of the Venetian blind, casting strips of light and shadow on the wall. I raised the blind. The sun was adding a golden light to the tops of the trees and shrubs. A blackbird was on top of one, facing east enjoying its early warmth and singing to confirm that this was his territory. A new day. I was fine. I put the kettle on, made myself a cup of tea then climbed back into bed with it.

I'd slept well considering, but the bump on my head was tender. I had bruises on both arms. I watched the gauze-pale moon hanging there making its slow progress across one of the small windowpanes. Reaching the edge of the window frame, closing one eye, it was still there, closing the other eye it was gone. I could look at last night's attack one way or the other. Keep it in view or put it in the past.

I found the funny side of last night's attack. What if I'd met Mrs Burnett in the hallway, out of breath, my face in that stressed out mess, carrying a bloody hankie. She'd have been phoning my office. You've sent me another one. A neurotic, fighting GCO this time.

I hadn't heard of anything like this happening to any of my colleagues and it most likely wouldn't happen again. I put the TV on and listened to Breakfast Time and the forecast and eventually drifted back to sleep.

I am right-handed, so it was a habit, to hold my new zip-top briefcase in my left hand and close the zip with my right. When I pulled my briefcase out of the foot of the wardrobe it was turned around the wrong way. The room had been locked. Mr and Mrs Burnett would have a spare key. One or other of them had been prying. When I turned the briefcase around, their previous visit report was back to front. They'd have a copy of that anyway and fortunately, all other membership files were secure in the car. I had written nothing but complimentary notes of their lounge, for this visit yet, so the snooping must have been very disappointing.

I got dressed, wrote more notes and was thinking through my feedback when the vacuum cleaner was pushed back and fore on the landing, with a slight nudge against my door. This was one way of telling me it was getting late for breakfast. Checking my watch, I couldn't believe it was nearly 9.00 am.

On checking out, handing her my card, Mr Burnett hovered in the background. I smiled and addressed them both. 'I wonder if you might already know who I am and why I'm here?'

They looked at each other. 'Oh, No. What a surprise. Goodness.' She said, blushing. He looked away.

Two guests were on their way into the guest lounge, so I asked if we could sit somewhere else while we had a chat. There in the open-plan kitchen-lounge area a tray was already set with three cups and saucers and Mr B picked up the pen which was waiting by an A4 pad. They had been snooping indeed.

The dishwasher was sloshing away. There was not a sign of breakfast dishes, worktops were all clear and shining, except for two half-drunk glasses of orange juice and a concentrated juice carton.

My colleague Alan was right, the feedback took an hour longer than usual. A red rash on her throat climbed as she challenged every single score on her report. They were perhaps hoping that at least one of us would evaluate their place higher than the ones she'd met. When we got to scoring the breakfast menu, I commented on seeing the concentrated juice carton when her menu said fresh orange juice.

'It is just as good as fresh and cheaper' She said with some authority. 'We blitz the pulp of a fresh orange and add it and guests can't tell the difference.' But I did now.

Since last year they had completely refurbished one bedroom. They had bought flat-pack self-assembly oak-veneer furniture, which was good quality, but no higher quality than what they were replacing.

My colleagues had told them year after year, their showers were tiny and the very small ensuites were just too pinched for space to get them the Deluxe grade they coveted. There was nothing they could do about that except extend the house and build new ones. Was it really worth it?

Mrs Burnett seemed to have no control over her body temperature. Beads of perspiration gathered on her forehead.

The nub of the matter was fuelled by the fact that their neighbour two doors along had a Deluxe award and Mrs B having assessed it for herself was sure it was the same quality as their own. 'And!' She raised her voice. 'My neighbour even agrees with me and she should know.'

She had a good go at all of us then. 'Sending us a man last time too. What would a man know about running a B&B anyway?'

'That's right, what would a man know.' Mr B had been nodding agreement, stoically behind her all the time. His role in life was to be her echo.

'Everything has to be kept in good order, it takes dedication to ensure everything is ship-shape?' She added. *As if I didn't know.*

After being so challenged and doubted I couldn't resist using this opportunity, *ship-shape.*

'Alan, whom you saw last time, he was a, let me get this right, a CPOMEAH, Chief Petty Officer Marine Engineering Artificer in the Royal Navy. He had to keep everything ship-shape and the 'H' at the end means he also had to look out for holes in the hull and plug them. He certainly has an eye for detail. He and his wife have just bought their own B&B too.

'You're all in this together. It's a fix.' Was her response as she removed my teacup and stood? Time to go.

News Bulletin 1997

'1997 will see the introduction of the first of Scottish Tourist Board's Welcome Schemes. After consultation and discussion with relevant national bodies, Walkers Welcome and Cyclists Welcome awards will be offered to those hosts who recognise the varied needs of those guests.'

Welcome Schemes

Further Welcome Schemes were planned for Anglers, Bikers, Children, Golfers, and one for Ancestral Tourism.

Many establishments already made those guests very welcome and these new schemes would now formalise the requirements. This was sold as being a useful marketing tool. It could have been if there had been some way of finding them in an index of accommodation, but there wasn't. In order to find a Walker's or Children Welcome property for example, a potential guest would have to thumb through brochure pages searching for the symbol. This needed correcting.

An Unexpected Visitor

I noticed as I drove in the narrow lanes between the fields that spring, work was in progress; the shiny clods which frost had broken down had been raked to a fine tilth and the heavy machinery was making the drills and dropping in seed potatoes at regular intervals. They would be ready for harvesting in around three months' time. The light sandy soil and the salty air give the Ayrshire potatoes a mouth-watering flavour all their own. My grandma told me, 'If you can flick the skin off with your thumb it is a true fresh Ayrshire tattie.'

I was to be staying on a tenanted sheep farm and it was lambing time. Tenants were reluctant to make structural alterations to the house, such as creating ensuite facilities. Permission from the owner was needed and should the tenancy be terminated; they'd lose their investment. Therefore, the bathroom would often be the family one, with plastic ducks removed, or not. There might even be no wash-hand basin in the bedroom, however the hospitality usually more than compensated for the lack of facilities and such was the case staying with Jean and Will.

I was once again the only guest, it being still early in the season and was pleased to join the family for their evening meal at a well-scrubbed pine kitchen table. Grandad sat at the head of the table, their two young children, Will Jnr (known as Jnr) and Beth, a one-year-old who was restrained in a highchair, enjoyed dropping her spoon and having me pick it up.

I asked about their farm work and Jnr, who told me he was seven-and-a-quarter, was well informed on sheep farming. He'd listen to his father, wait for a gap, look at me and ask, 'Did you know …?' and finished with, '… Aye, that's what we do. That's what we do here anyway.'

'Daddy. Can we work the dogs after dinner, and I can show Reta my puppy? Say yes Daddy.'

I'd love that I added.

After dinner, Grandad, pipe in his mouth opened the front door for me, flipped on his cap, pulled his collar up, indicated I should go around the back then headed off, walking down the road to see his neighbour. Clad in my anorak and yellow wellies I joined the others ready to tramp along the muddy path to a small field.

Will had already let Floss and Jnr's young puppy Glen out of the kennel yard. Jnr climbed onto the field gate and stood with me, adopting an air of experience beyond his years; his commentary telling me that he'd work with Glen when they were both older and they would enter competitions.

Five black-faced ewes lifted their heads, still chewing, some had a quick nervous pee, wary of our presence. Floss kept a watchful eye on Will, so keen to be working. 'Away to me.' and she headed off to the right in a wide circle, Glen followed anticipating a game. The sheep stood in a huddle, turning to watch their movements. One sheep took a step to the front and faced Floss, stamping the ground.

Different whistles meant different commands and a voice command. 'Lie down' brought Floss to an instant crouch while the pup chased after a couple of hooded crows, barking until they took flight. Floss stayed down waiting for the next command. With 'Stand' and 'That'll do' the flock was worked around the field towards a pen. Floss, with Glen panting alongside her, crept forward keeping low, moving a little from side to side. Once the lead sheep walked into the pen in the middle of the field the others followed. When Will opened the gate again Floss instinctively ran around to the far side of the pen to chase the sheep out. Her job done, she returned at a slow trot with her master, the young dog pouncing at her mouth.

Jnr. jumped down off the gate and turned to me. 'I can't work Glen in the field yet because look ...' he showed me the gap along the front of his gums with two jagged edged incisors just coming through. '...I want to learn to use the whistle. Daddy says I should use my tongue, but I can't, so I'll wait until my big teeth come in.'

I slept a little then tossed and turned; I had a counselling exam the next day, Saturday so I put on the bedside light, made a cup of tea and sat up to read some notes. I noticed a movement on the edge of my vision. A field mouse, tiny as a wren, stopped. 'Have you lost your way?' I thought.

With those big transparent ears and appealing huge black eyes, it had probably seen me, but then seemed unperturbed. I watched it ripple across the room in little bursts, examining the carpet for crumbs. I used my old briefcase for my counselling work, and it was standing open on the floor beside my bed. It climbed the few centimetres to get in then ran around sniffing the corners, probably detecting the smell of a sandwich, long gone. Then it moved towards the lid, stretched to reach the lowest document compartment, pulling itself up. The hinges were slack, and its light weight was enough to topple the lid and slam the case shut.

I got out of bed and slowly lifted the lid. It sat hunched with its head in a corner, its tiny body trembling. Because I was used to handling pet mice when our boys were young, I was able to lift it. Its tiny heartbeat pounded in my hand, so I laid it on the carpet. It raced for cover under my bed.

I had enjoyed that little interlude, but if it could climb a stalk of corn, it could climb the valance and sheets of my bed. I clapped my hands and shook the bed and saw it make a dash for the skirting board below the window. It did a limbo-leg-stretch and disappeared. I marked the place with a yellow-sticky note so that Jean or Will would know the exit point at least.

I breakfasted with four other guests who had arrived very late after dinner the night before and once they had left in the morning, I told Jean the purpose of my visit. She was a bit flustered because I needed time to see around the house, discuss those two new Walking/Cycling marketing opportunities with her and she had orphaned lambs to feed. They were penned in the barn. I quickly saw the other guest bedrooms on my own, there were no changes,

I gave her feedback on the food and services and I had the documents signed off quickly.

Then I closed my folder. 'Something happened which I must very quickly tell you about, but this is not part of your official visit. I had a visitor during the night.'

She threw her hands up. 'He didn't? Did he? I have spoken to him about that before. He goes down that road to our neighbour and comes back rolling from side to side. They can get through a bottle of whisky between them sometimes. I'm so sorry, I don't know what to say. I can only apologise. You see he gets up to go to the toilet and forgets his way back to his own room.'

'Stop.' I laughed. 'It was a field mouse.'

Being an old farmhouse, it is difficult to keep the wee creatures out but keeping the old man out was very important too. Their tenancy agreement didn't allow them to put Yale locks on the bedroom doors, but the case of the night-wanderer gave credibility to my suggestion of a compromise; put a snib on the inside of the bedroom doors. We had an agreement.

'I have something to ask you if you don't mind. This is my last visit of the week and I'm heading home now. Would it be possible for me to help you feed the lambs?'

She stood. 'Of course. What are we waiting for then?'

I changed into my yellow wellies, jeans and a jumper and I had the best time amongst those strong frisky black and white bundles as they tugged at the teat. I introduced the possibility of them considering advertising; Come and Feed the Orphaned Lambs but this didn't go down well. They were too busy with farm work already.

A Lamb with a Strange Name

While with the lambs I told her about staying with two very welcoming ladies in Little Erradale in the north-west. I was the

97

only guest that night and invited them to join me for my evening meal.

We had just finished our main course of Haddock Mornay and I drew their attention to the field outside their window. 'Am I seeing a little black lamb on the ground beside that sheep?'

They looked at each other, then at me. They were obviously excited, 'Oh! That's our first lamb. Just born.'

'Do you know I'm from the Tourist Board?' I asked.

'Yes, but we didn't like to say.'

'Neither did I. I have my wellingtons in the car.'

The three of us left the table and tramped over to see the new arrival. The first new-born lamb any of us had witnessed. They called her Haddock; that's what we'd been eating at the time.

I could become a vegetarian.

Nervousness

Next day, Saturday was a Transactional Analysis counselling exam day. I also had an essay to hand in. I was very grateful to Andrew, who was now our resident student. He'd taught me some editing shortcuts on our home computer the previous weekend and wished me luck.

I was so nervous. Sometimes I can hide it from others but not from myself; there are signs. The exam was in the afternoon and we needed to do a grocery shop in the morning. Waitrose in Morningside has a rooftop carpark and the rain was bouncing off the tarmac there. John wheeled the trolley to the car, handing me the keys, saying 'You get in, I'll load up the boot and put the trolley away.'

My tail-lights had disappeared down the car park ramp before I realised I'd forgotten he was with me. At least I remembered him before I reached home. Poor John.

Scottish Freshwater River Pearls

The days rolled along the following week with uncomplicated visits. Just what I needed; passing on simple tips like numbering the corners of a mattress, turning and flipping it every month to spread the wear, or that in some grand hotels the staff keep to the left using the stairs to spread the wear on carpets. Instead of closing for a Spring Clean, they stay open and deep-clean one room at a time when it is free. Just pleasant visits to pleasant people and easy.

I parked in a layby on my way to the tiny village of Badachro in the North West Highlands and was surprised to see a scatter of mussel shells on the bank of a shallow, gravelly stream beside my car. Freshwater pearl mussels have been protected under the Wildlife and Countryside Act since 1981 and it is illegal to harvest them. They are extremely slow growing, the largest can be up to 100 years old so regeneration of those mussel beds can take many decades.

Skeldon Memory

The river pearls brought back a memory of when I was four years old. My grandma took me to visit family friends, the McVicars at 3 Plantation Cottages in the tiny village of Skeldon, by the River Doon in Ayrshire. I was happy. They spoke softly and were kind.

Jimmy, (who was my Uncle John's best man at his wedding), took me with him as he searched for river pearls. I sat on the bank being told not to get my new Clark's sandals wet. Jimmy put his hand down into the very cold river and brought up mussels which he dropped into my Mickey Mouse bucket and held my hand all the way home.

Back in their kitchen, I watched him open the shells and press the pale orange flesh gently with his thumb. In one of them, he squeezed out a pearl the colour of the moon.

That evening, I sat on his lap and cuddled into his warmth and stillness by the fireside as he puffed smoke from his pipe. I loved his big rough chin and gentle smile.

He asked my grandma to keep the pearl for me. She had it set into a crown mount in a gold ring and wore it herself, reminding me it was mine and I'd have it when I was old enough. In my teens, one day she gave it to me. Her knuckles were now too swollen, or we could have shared it.

This was the most valuable piece of jewellery she ever owned.

I left feeling bewildered

Badachro village is spread out along the shore of Badachro Bay, a natural haven for yachts on the south shore of Loch Gairloch in Wester Ross. I had arranged to meet a self-catering owner there. I called at her bungalow; wild unkempt garden, sea-sprayed windows and a badly scuffed door. It stood open but there was no answer. I went back to my car and a neighbour told me that was her, standing on the beach looking at us.

I waved. No response. I picked my way down to where she stood, watching me approach. The skin on her face was swarthy, her bare legs had reddish mottled-tartan shins from sitting too close to the fire. She wore a jumper over a white nylon blouse, the collar of which was none too clean. At her wrists, protruding from the jumper, one cuff matched the collar of the white-ish nylon blouse and the other didn't, it was pale-green and cotton. She was cleaning her filthy nails with a Kirby grip.

I introduced myself and she walked very slowly with me up to the back door of her self-catering cottage which I noticed on my form, was the same address as her own home. She remained silent as I praised the good weather and the view. I was not very optimistic about the impending tour of her house.

She had no conversation, filled the kettle, put it on the gas and sat at the kitchen table.

'Is it okay if I look around now?' I asked.

She nodded.

The rooms were furnished with old oak and mahogany pieces which were good enough, although had probably stood in the same place for decades. Her own clothes were in them. In one room, one of the beds was just a pile of single-bed mattresses; even if draped with a clean sheet, this did not constitute a bed.

In the lounge, a gentleman was stretched out on the sofa with a Guardian newspaper over his face. Thick socks paint splattered chinos and a well-worn jumper protruded from under it. No movement from the newspaper, just a gentle purring let me know he was alive.

She'd made a cup of tea, just for herself.

'There's a gentleman asleep through there.'

'Where?' She asked, this being the first word she'd said.

'In the lounge.'

'Possibly. Or perhaps just a friend.' she replied with an aristocratic accent and an expressionless look.

There was definitely a disconnection somewhere. We hadn't seen her cottage before and she only planned to let it for July and August each year, so he shouldn't have been a guest.

'I see your home address is here. Do you live elsewhere when you let the cottage?'

She shrugged.

'Have you had a chance to read the information booklets we sent you?'

After quite a long wait she answered. 'I prefer radio 4.'

'Do you have any help in running the place in the summer?'

She got up to look at the gentleman in the lounge and returned without saying a word.

There was no category in which to score the owner's mental state or character. I began to feel like an interrogator, so chickened out. 'I will send you my report on your cottage and some information on what self-catering owners are offering for their guests. Is there anything you'd like to ask me while I'm here?'

No reply.

You should get my report within a couple of weeks. Okay?'

She nodded, and I thanked her for her time.

Walking back to my car I was stopped by the same neighbour I'd met earlier. She'd been waiting for me, anxious to talk. 'I heard from the grapevine that you are from the Tourist Board. You should know, when she has guests and they leave for the day, she creeps back in for a sleep. Heaven knows where she goes at night then. She has been found sleeping on the beach in a blanket.

I did not want to gossip, but I was concerned. 'Does she have any relatives or friends locally. It seemed to me that she could do with a bit of help.'

She doesn't want help from anyone, keeps herself to herself. She inherited that place. Just appeared one day. No one knows where she came from. We have very good B&Bs and cottages here and she's giving the place a bad name. Speak to anyone they'll tell you. We try to keep an eye out for her, but it's not easy.'

I was not able to confirm an award for her and that was at the other end of the scale from a large country house just around the end of Badachro bay which I visited next. The same chatty neighbour told me she heard it was let to cabinet ministers and pop stars. I visited it later that day and she was right, it was just one of the best. It sat in its own grounds with hired staff if required.; bone-china dinnerware, Le Creuset pots and casseroles, wonderful paintings and a helicopter pad on the lawn.

I called John from a drafty phone box that evening and told him of my bizarre meeting. He asked me if I'd like him to open the envelope with my TA exam results. I'd passed.

Battling Bella's Bar

I love the month of May; the clocks now on summertime, the heat of the sun greening up the fields and hedgerows.

I was walking on a cliff path in Berwickshire, returning to my car after a cottage visit and caught the coconut scent of the luminous yellow gorse. The strong growing bramble shoots were attempting to arch across the path claiming more territory. There must have been a shoal of fish just offshore because keen-eyed gannets were wheeling above the sea, folding their wings in the last few seconds before plummeting below the surface for a direct hit.

I drove further south on the A1, then parked up to write my notes. Children's voices carried from the playground; pushchairs and bicycles parked at the side; the public grass had been given at least its first cut. The beer-garden tables were back in use. A tinkling-tuned ice-cream van arrived at the beach and in no time a queue of customers had formed, deciding on their choices.

Blackbirds had taken up their seasonal perch on high places, singing to announce their territorial presence and impress the females. A bit like the slick-haired youths, who perched on the back of the benches, catcalling at the girls. They were playing hard to get in their trowelled-on foundation and stiff lacquered hair, carrying big handbags, wearing big jewellery and wobbling along, arm in arm, with bent knees in ridiculously high stilettos.

I'd spent four interesting and enjoyable days visiting people who had refreshed the paintwork, planted their window boxes with red geraniums and purple petunias, paid fastidious attention to spring cleaning and were filling their freezers and cake tins with home-baking. It was the May bank holiday weekend and the tourists were returning.

The next day was Saturday and John was driving down to join me; a couple of nights off in a luxury hotel with no report to write, no feedback to give and some long walks if the good weather held. But not yet; one seaside pub with rooms to visit first.

I hoped the roadside-door would open onto a cosy bar and restaurant, but it didn't. It was not a funky style or an eclectic mix, it was just scruffy. The open-plan dining area had faux red-leather banquette seating around the walls, was tightly packed with tables and chairs and was obviously popular, despite the smoky atmosphere. The tables were all occupied by diners and those who just wanted a drink stood or sat at the bar end, puffing away, some of their floor area taken up by two large dosing Labradors. I stepped over the dogs to ding the bell on the bar beside the *Call for Reception* notice.

One of the locals told me. 'He won't be long love; he's just gone downstairs to see to a new barrel.'

'Okay, thank you.'

The cheery young barman appeared soon, apologised for keeping me waiting and seemed to enjoy the bustling business. He pulled the first few glasses of froth from the pipeline before serving a couple of pints then asked me to follow him along the corridor leading to the bedrooms and public toilets. I was asked to fill in my details in the huge registration book lying open on a counter; guest names and addresses, dates of arrival, room numbers displayed for all to see. I signed in with Edinburgh as my address and no room number. He didn't notice.

I passed a few bedrooms with the doors wedged open, I could smell the newness of the carpets and pine furnishings; there had been a refurbishment. However, it looked as if this business was a pack-them-in, stack-them-up one. In my room, there were three single beds, one bedside cabinet with a bedside light and a wardrobe. The lady owner had applied for a grant to achieve a Three Crowns Commended award, but it looked as if she'd fallen well short of the requirements.

A crackling-crisp waterproof mattress protector meant I could waken in a puddle of perspiration so removed it. I smiled to myself recalling my colleague Colin's experience. He'd stayed overnight and failed them. Above his bed was a sign: *Wet beds will be charged at £5 for a single and £10 for a double.*

Downstairs I had to squeeze sideways between my fellow diners' tables and my own to reach the last free space on the banquette seating. The gap was so tight it would have ripped the tassels off a sporran.

The busy waitress called across to me. 'You collect a menu and your drinks from the bar and place your order there too love. You'll have to be quick though, we stop serving food at eight o'clock. You have ten minutes.'

I squeezed back out. The barman said, 'That'll be £3.50 for the wine?'

'Could you add it to my room please?'

'It's cash only for bar sales love.' He told me it was cash only for food too, I was required to pay the waitress in advance, and she needed to cash-up before she left. He also told me. 'There's a hole-in-the-wall outside the bank. Just turn left then go along the main street, then on after the chemist. Sorry.' He grimaced in sympathy and I was reminded again. 'You'll have to hurry though, last orders at eight o'clock'.

Feeling disgruntled, I hurried to the cash-line thinking Service Standards! Guest Orientation, or Product Orientation? Guests did not come first here.

Breakfast was served from 7.00 am. There was no sign of staff at 7.15. The downstairs bar-restaurant windows were still shuttered, but in the other direction along a short corridor, I heard the Radio One music and light from under a door. This might indicate some activity in the kitchen. The only other light was from the green illuminated emergency system in the corridor. Feeling bold, I found the light switch, flicked it on and did the same in the breakfast room. The air was stale in there, the atmosphere gloomy, there being no ventilation. No staff, so no welcome, no newspapers to pass the time. Tables were partly set; the cups turned upside down on the saucers, canteen style and the cutlery placed. That was it.

I'd seen better breakfast buffets. A large opened packet of Kellogg's Corn Flakes and one of Rice Krispies, blister packs of marmalade and sugar in stick-packs. On a narrow shelf above stood ten pre-poured 120 ml. (almost medicine sized) glasses of orange juice, needing stirred to redistribute the juice evenly. Had they been there from the night before? There was no menu.

I sat for about ten minutes then heard coughing advancing from the kitchen. A wiry little middle-aged man carried a tray and set it down on one of the tables. 'Morning.' he said as he placed milk jugs on each table.

'Good morning. Nice day again.' I smiled.

He reached my table last. 'I don't know, I've not looked outside yet.'

I stood and walked towards the cereals. 'Could I have some milk for my cereal please?'

He looked into the small jug on my table and said 'If that's not enough, just take some from one of the other tables. I can top them up. Now. What can I get you? Full cooked?'

'And what is in the full cooked please?'

'Bacon, egg, sausage, tomato, mushrooms, beans and fried bread.' He coughed; a smoker's reaction to using his vocal cords first thing in the morning. 'Excuse me.'

'Any other options?'

He thought for a moment, scratching his stubble and grinned, showing his nicotine-stained teeth. 'You can have it half-cooked if you like.' His laughing gave momentum to his coughing and he thumped his chest with his fist adding 'Oh, excuse me. That's a laugh though, eh?'

I laughed too, with surprise. 'I think I'll go for a small portion of the full-cooked then please.'

I noticed hard-grey skin on his heels; he'd shoved his bare feet into slip-on slippers. The back of his hair was still bed-messed.

Breakfast arrived, on a hot plate. One skinny-pink-latex sausage and one rasher of microwaved bacon with a white gelatinous puddle on it, a pullet-sized egg, a tinned tomato, a couple of mushrooms and half a slice of fried bread, oozing oil. He got the small right and it was cooked.

Other guests arrived and went straight to collect their juice and cereal. They knew the system. I noticed too that the 'Full cooked?' was automatically brought to them.

My no-choice white toast, a blister pack of butter and one of low-fat spread arrived with my bill. He didn't clear my empty plate, so I pushed it to the side. The cheap bread collapsed under the stress of being buttered, so thin I could have fed it through a printer.

An hour later I carried my suitcase downstairs to put in the car boot before paying. I imagined I would be too early to meet the owner but would enjoy a brisk walk until she was ready.

The bar/restaurant area was still shuttered but there was enough light from the corridor to let me see my way to the entrance. When I reached the bar, one of the Labradors, bounded towards me stopping only about a metre away. Barking then growling with bared teeth, his hackles raised from his neck to his tail. The other one joined in.

I yelled with shock, then shouted, 'DOWN'. This was their territory, but it worked. I stood my ground and the alpha-male turned around, with tail wagging low and slow, his hackles calming and his lips quivering in an uncertain smile.

The breakfast waiter appeared. 'Okay, boys. It's okay boys, settle down.' They lay down again watching us.

'Trying to get away without paying, were you?' he chuckled, rubbing his hands together.

'I was going to put my case in the car and come back to pay.' The look in his eyes said Aye right!

I produced my business card. 'I'm here to meet Ms Higginbotham, the owner.'

'Aaaah, Yes?' He nodded.

'Is she here?'

'Awe Christ. There is just me here. Awe man, she'll be mad. Will you need to tell her I was late with breakfast? And the dogs, Christ, she'll go ballistic.'

I offered a bit of empathy. 'I imagine, it being a Saturday morning and a holiday weekend you didn't think anyone would be up so early.'

He brightened, hearing the escape route. 'That's it. You're right.'

'But what's with the dogs?' I added.

'I'm supposed to walk them then put them in the car. But I slept in.'

'Will she be arriving later?'

'No, she lives in Glasgow, she's got a business up there too and only comes here now and again. She'll be so mad. We don't call her Battling Bella for nothing. Not to her face though. I better get back to the kitchen eh! You alright?'

A week later, after Ms Higginbotham had received my report, one of our admin team took an irate call from her. She'd demanded the three Crown Commended award, after discovering that the one I'd given her would not allow her to receive this. She wanted to meet me at her pub. She'd wished it known that I had tried to leave without paying. As if!

I'd failed them on basic Code of Conduct: Proper Standards of Courtesy and Efficiency, and given low marks for Dining Room Atmosphere, Check-out and Breakfast Buffet. Also, for Three Crowns in bedrooms, there was the absence of enough bedside lights, mirrors, chairs and luggage stands. She'd also have to remove beds to meet the space requirements in the bedrooms for the number of occupants.

Three weeks later I returned to meet Battling Bella; her gathered heavy brows gave her a killer look. Rabbie Burns would have described her as 'nursing her wrath'.

She'd recruited support. I'd met the Chair of the local Accommodation Association before when I visited his property. He had been friendly enough then but not now. He was batting in her team. A local councillor with an apologetic smile, twiddled his pen nervously looked baffled as to why he was there. I arrived just before a representative from the Scottish Borders Tourist Board. The others had been there long enough to empty the cafetière and leave two biscuits. We were not offered refreshments.

I rolled out a walk-through potted version of my experience. To start with, those whom Battling Bella had briefed were vocal in support of her in the amount of work she'd undertaken. After hearing about the registration system, the poor payment system for residents to eat and drink, the very limited breakfast choice, the incident with the dogs, they lost eye contact with me and withdrew into silence. She had not achieved the necessary scoring to be able to meet the requirements for a grant: Three Crowns, Commended. I summed up with 'If you can implement all my recommendations, we will send you another GCO when you think you are ready for a second visit, incognito of course.'

Thank goodness looks can't kill, otherwise, my blood would have been dripping on the wall behind me. The next person to cross her that day would wish they hadn't.

Bernat Klein and AGA cookers

I was working back in the Scottish Borders in 1997 and in springtime there the fields were jumping with new life. What an office view and entertaining distraction from report writing.

The more socially mature lambs held sporting events. Competitions in running, the four-legged leap, the headbutt. Then a refreshment break. Young M-e-e-e-es, looking around in all directions listening for their own mother's deep B-a-a-a-a. They'd charge at their mothers and thump her udder so hard they'd lift her back legs off the ground. She'd hardly seem to notice as their tails wiggled with joy and she continued chewing.

They were curious, a group of them in a skittish gathering having the courage to see what my car was doing in their lay-by. I watched their antics as they ran off to play king of the castle with an old tree stump, the highest spot in the field.

I was on my way to an AGA cooking demonstration in the Scottish Borders. By chance, I happened to pull in at the old entrance to Bernat Klein's office to check the address of the Aga shop and was shocked and saddened to see the dilapidated state of his original iconic glass and concrete modernist building.

Reta MacLennan

We occasionally came across Aga cookers in self-catering houses. I wanted some tips for owners to pass on to their guests who might be daunted by the fact that this large cooker has no controls to instantly regulate the heat. It just needs a different approach to cooking and is very easy to use, once you understand the system.

During registration with coffee at the Aga demo, I got chatting to an elderly gentleman who just happened to have been the Head Design Technician in one of the local textile mills. He had worked with Klein. He was very knowledgeable about his life and work and was a very enthusiastic and active member of the Local History Society.

Klein was an honorary graduate of Heriot-Watt University, where I worked in a past life, as Secretary to Professor Joe Gloag, the Dean of Humanities. I had attended one of Klein's talks on Textiles and Design. He told us that he found inspiration in the Borders landscape, likening it to a patchwork quilt; the ribbons he wove through his cloth depicting the many paths and streams.

This gentleman added to that, telling me he also found inspiration in the colours and textures in the deciduous woodlands, dark conifer plantings, rough tilled land and the grand herbaceous borders at Floors Castle. He said Klein's enthusiasm was catching. His eyes came alive, he put his cup and saucer down and used his hands in an animated way and I could hear in his story how keen his own sense of engagement had been. It was very touching.

I told him I had two regrets: that I hadn't had the courage to approach Klein after his talk to tell him how much I'd enjoyed it and that I didn't keep the mini-skirt and waistcoat which I made from a yard and a half of bright-ribboned pink and green fabric, which might now be collectable.

Changing the subject, I told him 'I have another regret. I've just been listening on my car radio to a repeat of the Live Aid concert at Wembley two years ago. Hearing the crowd stomping and clapping to Queen's We Will Rock You.' I'd wanted to be there and should have tried to get tickets. He laughed. 'I was there with my son.' With that, he punched the air.

From the four-oven AGA, we enjoyed the light, warm buttered scones served with our coffee. When we were seated the demonstrator produced finished dishes which she had prepared previously. From porridge and meringues in the coolest oven to roast beef, roast potatoes and apple pie from the hotter ones.

Her voice was full of concern with scatters of warnings throughout; 'You mustn't … don't ever … you can't expect it to …' and 'it takes quite a while to get the hang of it', was actually correct, but as a sales pitch, it was a wonderfully successful deterrent. Some slunk off with a brochure and only the most stoic stayed to listen to more warnings.

She didn't mention other important things or there would only have been me left. There is no window to check how cakes and pastries are doing, they need turning half-way through cooking to ensure that they are not scorched on the hotter side. My sister-in-law Mary had a Rayburn, our friend Alistair had an Aga and they both had burn scars as far up as the elbows to prove it. AGA gauntlets, and they are expensive, are the only real protection against injury.

Nevertheless, those who like a challenge are rewarded, the sense of achievement when you have mastered the knack, the succulence of the roasted meat, the lightness of the sponges, with the added bonus of a warm kitchen and hot water had convinced us to install one when they were much less expensive. Our yachting friend Alistair got us one at wholesale price.

One major disadvantage is because cooking smells waft up the chimney, there is no warning when whatever is in this lovable oven, is burning.

When I had my outside catering business, I put a whole tray of leftover tomatoes into the lower warming oven one Friday, to soften, so that the skins would slip off easily. I could then puree them and keep a stock in the freezer. Returning on Saturday evening, the smell of something burning met us as soon as we opened the car door. The tomatoes had morphed into black briquettes and I threw the lot into the wild steep banking outside our garden boundary.

Our two dogs thought they were a treat. They sniffed them out. The first briquette was chewed in the kitchen and fractured into a thousand black particles. Thereafter I could tell by the way those dogs slunk in, tail down, glancing askance, lips hiding their trophy that they had found yet another one. They would not unlock their jaws to have it removed, so they were banished outside at some distance from the house and watched until they had enjoyed it. That was the only downside of AGA cooking that I could say had been a real problem.

Unconventional Welcome

Like my colleagues, I was a practised map reader with a good sense of orientation, but this country house B&B address gave little information on its location.

I phoned again on my way there. Sand martins were skimming and wheeling across the smooth-flowing river Tweed outside. A first sign of summer perhaps? As I waited for someone to answer, I noticed the spotlessly clean phone box, polished panes and mirror with taxi business cards neatly fixed along the window edges. Perhaps the people in the little adjacent cottage looked after it. *Unnecessary grading again Reta.*

I hung up and redialled: Maisie's directions were very unclear when I'd made the initial phone booking. It sounded as if she had been shuttling the phone from hand to hand, giving me invisible signals like my grandma used to. That insistent back-seat non-driver who never learned to know her left from her right would shout 'That way, I told you' signalling with a wave of her arm behind me in the back seat.

An out-of-breath Maisie answered the phone this time too and tried again to give me directions. 'When you see a beech tree on a corner, och, maybe it's an oak, turn that way. Stay on the road, (good advice), cross the cattle grid and follow the wall beside you till you see the gates. If the tractor is at the grid it will be getting cleaned out, so double back and come in the back way.'

Feeling no more reassured than I had the first time, I tried to get some bearings but knew as soon as I said, 'And which way would I be coming from to do that Maisie?', I had set myself up.

She paused. 'Well, you'll know that better than I! Won't you? Don't worry people always get here in the end.'

I made a note; improve written directions for guests and Maisie, and check signage.

Half an hour later I turned into a long driveway lined with rhododendrons, their purple buds bursting out of their constraining winter jackets. Dodging the potholes (make another note) I drew alongside the groundsman trimming the grass verge.

'Hello,' I shouted above the clattering of the rotor blades. He nodded, then reached forward to kill the engine. 'I'm looking for Mrs Bradinghurst-Smythe.'

The Mrs is not at home but himself is. Try around the back of the house or the stable block; you'll see the clock tower.' Then starting up again and giving a huge smile added 'If you find him, tell him Tom wants a word.'

My wheels crunched to a stop on the gravel in front of the grand house. I parked looking out over the ha-ha liking what I saw. The house had a distinct Scottish Baronial influence with a sweeping view towards the blue-hazed Eildon Hills. Five horses were grazing along with a few black-faced sheep in the foreground.

I stepped out of the car, making time to assess the exterior. I had a good stretch then heaved my suitcase from the boot. White-harled walls, crow-stepped stone gables climbing up to tall stone chimney stacks, steep-pitched roof lines, a pinnacled turret and corbelled window bays. The carved sandstone coat-of-arms and 1881 above the doorway were still in sharp profile and the building looked to be well maintained.

Ladders were propped against the front wall and an old sheet spread on the ground, another note, (window frames being repainted). The oak front door, weathered to a satins-silver stood wide open and the black and white checked tile floor of the vestibule appeared to be the glorious original, waxed and polished.

I pulled on the large polished brass bell and could hear it ringing deep inside the house, maybe in the original kitchen. No response. A well-used antique oak chest holding croquet mallets stood open against the vestibule wall. Walking sticks and golfing umbrellas were stored in the stump of an elephant's foot, complete with dark brown horny toenails. Feeling slight revulsion, I stepped into the hallway. 'Hello, anyone at home?' No reply.

Leaving my case there, I checked around the back of the house which was more modestly designed of course. On a bench beside an open door sat an elderly gentleman. He had bushy grey eyebrows, a ruddy outdoor complexion with a red kerchief tied at the open neck of his short-sleeved shirt. A Tilley hat, a pair of old khaki shorts, knee-length stockings and old paint-stained trainers tied with string made me think of a vintage boy scout doing bob-a-job. He was wiping the paint off his hands and a bottle of turpentine stood at his feet. I noticed he automatically cupped his hand behind one ear. That might be why I got no response to the bell.

'Hello. I'm looking for Mr Bradinghurst-Smythe.'

'Well. You have found him.'

'I've booked to stay in the B&B here tonight, I'm Mrs MacLennan.'

'Well pleased to meet you. I'm the eccentric old patriarch himself. Benedict by name. Ben will do.

'Well Hello. I'm Reta.'

'You must excuse me for not standing to shake your hand.' He had a public-school accent and resonant commanding voice. 'I suspect from your smart city suit that you've not arrived on a horse.' He chuckled.

I laughed and said I liked horses, but on the other side of a fence and I wished I was not afraid of them. I also told him I had driven down from Edinburgh.

'Ah, that city of financiers and frolickers. I must go there and talk to my banker very soon; however, reluctantly, I may say before I am summoned into his presence. No horse then, so might you be from the Tourist Board. Eh? Am I right my girl?'

I dropped the incognito, not wanting to play games with him and was invited to sit beside him in the sunshine for a moment until he finished cleaning up. I joined him; his genuine friendly style being an engaging welcome.

Then leaning towards me he spoke softly out of the side of his mouth; as if there was anyone there to hear him. 'Still in my working togs and not giving you a proper welcome. If the bride knows, she'll make a fuss. Maybe we won't tell her eh?'

His conspiratorial humour was persuasive, but I explained that I'd feel awkward. 'I'll just say I arrived earlier than expected, was delighted with my welcome and was made to feel very much at home.'

'Splendid.' He offered me a high-five, grasped my hand and I now had the turpentine smell on it.

His eyebrows rose when I gave him Tom's message. 'If you have any inspirational ideas about how to break the disappointing news to him that our almost-clapped out grass-cutter is repairable, that the spare part is arriving soon, and we'll be fitting it ourselves, I am willing to listen?'

We could hear the clatter of Tom's machine approaching so with hands on his thighs getting ready to stand up and squinting into the sunshine he gave me instructions. 'You see how the sun is just about to touch the top of that cedar over there?' Without waiting for an answer, he continued. 'That tells me it is Tanqueray-10-time. You'll find everything you need in the fridge. Off you go my girl, the kitchen is that way.' He nodded in the direction of the back door of the house. 'You will join us of course? The bride will be pleased to see that we are off to a good start. You'll want to freshen up first. Your room is upstairs second on the right.'

After freshening up and changing into jeans and trainers I went back down to prepare the drinks. As I approached the kitchen, I heard a flustered female voice and bantering laughter. I hesitated. Ben saw me and waved me on in.

I assumed it was his wife who was quickly stowing shopping into the fridge and cupboards with her back to me. Ben being caught still in his old clothes, minus the boots was being scolded while Tom, seated at the table looked on with a warm-hearted smile. This seemed to be a comfortably familiar scene.

Ben had beaten me to it and was already dispensing G&Ts. I stopped at the open doorway and knocked to let her know I was there while Ben slid a wedge of lemon around the rim of my glass, plopped it in and held the glass out towards me with an exaggerated wink.

She was still blethering on.

He moved behind her, placed a gentle hand on her shoulder and her drink in front of her. I learned later that she was 'the bride' and had been for 52 years. 'Penny my dear, this is Mrs MacLennan and we are to call her Reta. As you rightly predicted, she is indeed here to run her finger along the top of our doors, and look under the beds, but first, she is going to join us for an aperitif.'

Penny turned with surprise. 'What! You have arrived! Of course, I came in the back way so didn't see your car. I do apologise. You are hopeless Ben. Did he look after you, my dear? Ah well, that is just who he is I'm afraid. Untrainable, totally untrainable.' And with a laugh, shook my hand.

I assured her I'd had a very good welcome as I'd agreed with Ben I would, and he changed the subject. 'MacLennan, that clan originates from Kintail I believe and has a long history of producing fine pipers.

'Yes, I married a wonderful MacLennan, but he doesn't play the bagpipes.'

'I was a boarder at Strathallan School and used to play them very well. We had our own pipe band you may know.'

I nodded.

'I can still play a tune but haven't got the puff anymore. The reunions are wonderful fun. When we old boys get together and get the chanters out. Great times, great memories.'

We then heard a vehicle arrive with a repeated beeping of a horn. A door banged shut and a shout came along the passageway. 'Anybody home. Come and see this.' We all did.

In the back of a small pick-up truck was a girl in her twenties, with a peacock in her arms, no less. He looked around, the ends of his tall head-feathers bouncing as he turned his head. The young man let down the tailgate and the girl shuffled her tight jeans to the edge and was helped down. 'Where should I put him Ben?' she asked calmly as if this was just a normal delivery of goods.

'By Jove, my girl, you're a champion. Where did you find him? Welcome home boy. How did you trap him?'

She had a look of no-big-deal and explained that she and her boyfriend were sitting on their back doorstep enjoying the last of the sun when he just strode around the corner. She jumped on him before he realised what was happening. 'Ben my arms are aching, where do you want him?'

Penny was already beckoning at the open door of an old washhouse and the unanimous decision was he'd be fine there for the time being. There was a pulley and fixed rails that he could roost on, so he was to be confined there with the hens' feed and water till he had settled in, hopefully, to stay. His long-bedraggled tail feathers swept the floor as he shook the others into place and considered the grain.

The young couple Denise and Mark joined us for a drink in the kitchen to celebrate his homecoming. This hardy bird had survived in the wild for two winters, had been sighted many times on farm gates, pecking at the roadside on fallen grain but any attempts to catch him were thwarted by the fact that he could fly up some height into the trees. I was told it is unusual for peafowl to leave the place of their birth, so his arrival was indeed a reason to celebrate.

They accepted the invitation to stay for dinner, but Tom regrettably had to leave, knowing Maisie would have his supper ready. I felt very relaxed in their company watching Penny sip,

Keith Floyd-style, as she cooked. I set out the cutlery and mats on the kitchen table for dinner.

Penny's confidence and an ease with AGA cooking outdid that afternoon's demo and I learned more from watching her than I did then. She was busy moving pans around on the top plates and oven shelves and with the long-armed oven gauntlets reached right to the back of those deep ovens. The appetising aroma of creamy asparagus soup, AGA baked ham glazed with brown sugar and cloves, Cumberland sauce, roasted veg and steamed early potatoes from their polytunnel, sheened with butter and chives, made my tummy gurgle in anticipation.

My glass had been topped up and perhaps again as I watched Penny. When we all sat down to the main course, in went an Eve's Pudding, which came out later with a crisp crust over a fluffy light sponge.

A bit like my head after the quantity of gin then wine I think I'd consumed. I needed the solid support of the bannister to reach my room that evening and got ready for bed, mostly with my eyes closed.

I woke very early the next morning, drifting in and out of sleep, recalling the previous evening and drafting my report on the back of my eyelids, reluctant to let the day begin just yet. I realised once again why my job description required GCOs to have a strong constitution.

However, I was dressed, and the report was up-to-speed when Ben's commanding voice carried upstairs, 'Are you awake up there? Breakfast awaits. This is a working day for you and for us. Arise.'

I shouted back from my doorway. 'Coming. With you in two minutes.'

In the dining room, a large mahogany sideboard was set with an impressive buffet. Crystal bowls of cereal and jugs of fruit juices, sundae glasses of early forced rhubarb flavoured with fresh ginger and topped with thick creamy yoghurt, a small platter of the ham, cold this time, and the same of line-caught smoked salmon from the Tweed. Under the lid of a silver bain-marie, full cooked breakfast choices with scrambled eggs. I imagined they had shown me the full normal breakfast so that I would be able to score it, however, Maisie told me 'One guest or a house full, breakfast is the same, everyone likes a choice.'

A large portrait of a stern-faced distant relative, distinguished enough to have commissioned Sir Henry Raeburn to paint his portrait, graced the wall behind Ben's chair at the head of the table, and Penny and I sat either side of him.

They owned a beat on the Tweed and advertised salmon fishing with B&B and evening meal. There was even a cold room where the catch could be cleaned then frozen if wished or left with Ben for smoking over oak shavings.

With his forearm on the table, he leaned towards me and I got the message: pay attention. He told me that the Tweed runs for almost 100 miles through the borderlands of Scotland and England, with the estuary in England of course, and is managed seamlessly by organisations on both sides of the border. He claimed it is the most prolific salmon river in Europe and fishermen come from all over Europe and beyond to fish here.

'Salmon fishing on the Tweed contributes many millions to the local economy and supports hundreds of jobs. It's a thriving business' He leaned further towards me: 'As long as the fish keep coming, and the fishermen keep flying in and you bring the visitors here instead of letting them drive through and up to the highlands. That's up to you lot.'

I recalled an American guest I once met. He'd visited Pitlochry and his lady tour-guide told him that in Spring on the Tummel, the salmon can be seen running up the Fish Ladder. The American had said, 'She must have thought I was stoopid. I know salmon don't have legs.'

Ben threw back his head roaring with laughter and said, 'Well, he *was* stoopid.'

Maisie entered to clear our plates and offered around a basket of warm scones and croissants.

'I see you have given us some of your homemade lemon curd this morning Maisie. Would you have one of your small jars to give to Mrs MacLennan to take away?' Penny asked.

'Maisie makes them as a small parting gift to remember us by, jams too when the berries are ripe.'

She smiled and nodded, and it gave me an opportunity to compliment her on the great breakfast.

Ben wanted to tell me more. 'Did you know, the origin of the word Tweed comes from mistaken handwriting in a letter from a Borders gentleman to a London merchant, where Tweel, being the Scot's word for twill, was misinterpreted as Tweed. The name has stuck ever since'

I hadn't known that and told them that John's mother and father made Harris Tweed. They covered the whole process from shearing their own sheep, gathering *crotal,* (Gaelic for lichen growing on the rocks) boiling the wool with it to get a yellow mustard colour then hanging it on the fences to dry in the wind. When everyone was making Harris tweed, the *crotal* was in short supply: it meant walking for miles to find it and then taking risks to reach it.

His mother did the carding and spinning then his father spent many winter hours weaving on the loom they had in a shed at the end of their house. As a small boy, John remembered his father's hands throwing the shuttle back and fore and his feet rhythmically treading the battens to shift the warp. We still have one of those blankets he wove and treasure it.

Ben topped up my glass with fresh orange juice. 'I have had a Harris Tweed jacket since I was a young man.'

Penny raised her eyebrows and turned to me. The patches on the elbows are worn through but if he could get into it, he'd still be wearing it. Impossible man.'

Penny took her turn hosting the local hunt and this had given her an idea for another business. She was establishing a network of country house B&Bs willing to offer accommodation for riders, stabling for their horses and kennels for their dogs. She had invited the British Horse Society to look over the stabling and grazing for horses as a guarantee of standards.

One of the other stopovers was a member of our grading scheme already, but none of the others were. Penny thought, that publicising her enterprise with us would be a good marketing move: she was right. I was glad to have her list of B&Bs and we would contact those who were not already with us and offer membership.

After I had paid, seen around the other rooms, given further feedback and got a signature for my visit, Ben gave me their standard receipt. It was a folded card with a sepia watercolour print on the front. The painting was of the front of the house, with Ben standing holding the reins of a horse. He said. 'He won first place once in the Working Hunter class at the Royal Highland Show that one did. We had some celebration that year.'

The little watercolour was signed in the bottom left-hand corner, BB-S. That receipt was the best I'd seen or have seen since.

Broch Inspectors, What Next!

In the car, Radio Scotland was just a muttering in the background until I heard the words 'Broch Inspector'. I'd read about brochs in the airline brochure as I was flying to Sumburgh airport to do a presentation to a group of hoteliers. There are well over 100 brochs in the Shetlands alone and around 500 in Scotland, mainly close to the coastline.

Brochs dating from the Iron Age, are round towers, built of stone and have a double skin with a staircase between the walls. They might have been fortifications or small farming settlements, sometimes having a well inside.

However, I thought out loud, 'What? Why on earth are they being inspected. Another glamping experience?' Surely Historic Scotland would have something to say about that. It seemed plain daft to me.

I was the daft one. My colleague Sam had heard about this and explained that it wasn't broch inspector but *brocken spectre* (from the German Brockengespenst) and it is a phenomenon which can happen when standing on a high peak or mountainside with the low sun projecting a person's gigantic shadow onto the clouds or mist. Some have experienced a halo-like rainbow of colours around their shadow's head. Spooky and spectacular indeed.

SUMMER 1997 – 2001

Scottish Tourist Board News Bulletin 1997

The Scottish Tourist Board has announced that it will launch the world's first ever quality-led 'Star' accommodation grading scheme. For hotels, guest houses, B&Bs and self-catering units, stars will finally mean what customers have always thought they meant, quality.

'We are also working towards creating another first; a UK common standard. In-the-field tests have been well received in Wales and both tourist boards have forwarded their work to the English Tourist Board, the AA and RAC "in a spirit of open consultation".'

Our Head of Department, Tony was heavily involved in the process of this and it was not an easy task.

Star Scheme

We had a change of title from GCO's to Quality Advisors, which we thought better described the focus of our work: an approach which was more inclusive, working together in partnership with the membership.

We were currently awarding Crowns for facilities and four descriptions for quality, from Approved to Deluxe displayed together in all advertising. Now one symbol, stars, from one to five, would advertise both the facilities and the quality combined.

We were trained in the new star scheme in one week in July 1997. It felt grounded in common sense, comfortable to work with and the measuring of quality on a scale from one to ten left us more room for fine-tuning.

This change would have the same shake-up effect as happened in 1992 when we introduced the Deluxe grade. Amongst those establishments at the higher levels, some would convert to four stars, those who had further invested in top-class facilities and reached a world class standard in services, would now have five stars. These changes would put a burden on the industry to further invest in their time, money and training however, in pursuit of rising standards, change would be inevitable. Businesses which stood still, would by default move backwards.

I ran workshops, gave presentations to Area Tourist Board members, hotel, guest house, B&B and self-catering sector groups, focusing on improving quality and building a good working relationship together under the title 'It's the Difference which Makes the Difference.'

Green Tourism Business Scheme

It was also the year in which the Green Tourism Business Scheme was run out across Scotland, developed out of a partnership with Green Business UK. The focus was an environmental one, to encourage saving in energy costs, raise awareness of waste and how to avoid it. This approach held both ethical and financial business benefits and we were now encouraging uptake, assessing and advising on systems for awards at three levels, Bronze, Silver and Gold.

Career Choices

Life for me was now out of balance. I was far too busy. I'd temporarily reduced my tourist board contract to a three-day week to accommodate seeing my counselling clients and focus on my final year of a part-time post-graduate Diploma in Counselling Studies at Napier University.

I loved my work as a part-time trainer and supervisor for two agencies; Lothian Centre for Integrated Living for Meg McCallum and the Pastoral Foundation for Mary Lawson. Both ladies played an influential part in my personal and counselling development and career. I felt a loyalty to them for the opportunities they had given me, and I knew I'd soon have to make the hard decision to choose between the tourist board work and counselling work. Doing both was just too much.

Staying connected

Also, in 1997, we were issued with mobile phones, not fashionable Blackberries, but clunky-black-plastic bricks with a ringtone. We imagined an end to standing with one finger in an ear in drafty phone boxes, or in noisy bars and hotels. Not quite yet. Mobile signals were very patchy in the glens and the islands, especially in the less populated villages or townships.

Nevertheless, networks would extend in time. All but a few of us were delighted. One colleague felt it as an intrusion 'I don't want to be contacted on visits!' Another golfing colleague felt dismayed, 'No more fly rounds of golf then.' and our colleague who had to phone home every evening at 6.00, now had fewer reasons not to.

In a hilltop layby once, I spotted a parked car, door wide open with the driver standing holding something to one side of his head. At one time I might have thought he was ill, but now it could only mean he had a signal. A precious signal. I braked so hard I expected to smell burning rubber and reversed to the beginning of the layby. (We were taught to do that in an advanced driving day so that a car with braking problems couldn't drive into the back of us.)

I strolled towards him just as another car braked hard and slewed in between us. This would be a queue then. I was first. I did get a strange look as I stood close to him, not in touching distance of course, until I pointed to my phone. When he finished, he said 'Stand here, line up that telegraph pole with the tree the other side of that bog. If you can't see the tip of Skye, move to the right a bit. Pass it on. Good luck.'

Dragon Landlady

Her brochure entry read 'A warm welcome awaits'. An uninspiring and all too common fall-back description. We encouraged operators to highlight their own uniqueness instead. This description could have been read as a warning 'You might be welcome. I'll decide once I see you.'

My telephone booking was rather off-putting. She sighed. 'Just one! Only for yourself! I don't know if I can be bothered. It's not worth my while for one.'

She just couldn't be arsed. I wanted to get in there and deal with the complaints on her file. It was high summer so I led her to believe I'd tried several other places and they were all full. She had no single rooms and only when I coaxed her by offering to pay the full price for two people, pushing my luck in asking for a discount, (I would only be eating one breakfast), did she allow me to come.

I felt amused and intrigued but could never have imagined the extent to which this lady would go to displease her guests. I was looking forward to the challenge.

Arriving on the steep downhill approach to Oban from the Tyndrum junction, a lovely expansive view of part of the promenade, the harbour and ferry terminal opens up. But, having enjoyed this often I turned left to avoid the traffic, using the quiet shortcut on the back road to my B&B, past a small loch with swans,

I arrived at the same time as a young hiker lugging a backpack the size of herself. It was a humid sticky afternoon in June, and she'd had to climb up a long steep brae to get here. Perspiration was dripping from her chin. She looked ready to collapse as I helped her off with her backpack. She leaned on it, to get her breath back, drying her face as I rang the doorbell, telling me she'd trudged all the way up from the train station. I wondered what she'd had to pay for the pleasure of staying here.

Mrs Reluctance opened the door wide and glowered at us. She wore a floral overall and fluffy slippers, her grey hair looking as if she'd just pulled the rollers out and hadn't had time to comb it.

Tutting at the sight of the backpack, she frowned at the girl. 'You're not coming in here with that. It'll scart my wallpaper. You can leave it in the lounge and take out your nightie and toothbrush and whatever else you need for the night. But you'll leave that thing in the lounge.' Then she flung open the lounge door for her.

It was amazing that this dying breed of ageing dragon-landladies had managed to survive. As the other B&Bs on her terrace and the street downhill all displayed a tourist board plaque, it was likely that wanting to keep up with the competition, she had decided to join the club.

She *had Please refrain from* …. notices stuck to the back of bedroom doors, didn't issue guests with keys, locked the front door at 10.00pm, and charged £2 for a bath plug. Wasn't I lucky to find her? Maybe, a very optimistic maybe, I could make her aware of today's guest expectations and persuade her to move with the times.

During my feedback in the morning, she was prickly and complained about the staff in the local Tourist Office; they sent her no one. I suggested that perhaps because of the complaints she had received, they were reluctant to give her more business. Had she talked to them about it?

She unfolded her arms, clenched her fists and gave me a wry smile. 'No chance. I hate them down there. They are useless. I've told them time and time again.' She then counted off stipulations on her fingers 'I won't take people who have long hair, it's disgusting having to pull hairs out of the plug holes. I won't take obese couples; they will break my bed springs. I don't like foreigners; they have different ways from us and I won't have sticky-fingered children or babies that bawl in the night. Those people at the TIC know if they book one of those to stay with me, I'll just send them right back down the hill, quick as a flash.'

She wasn't finished. 'And I'll tell you something else, those people who are breaking God's law by sleeping together, I will not go into details, they can take a hike. That is not going on in my house either, I'm a Christian.'

I wanted to laugh, I found this so incredible. 'You didn't ask me if I had long hair when I booked on the phone?'

'No, because I would have turned you away at the door and sent you down the hill to that lot. It is their job to deal with folk like that, not mine. This is my home and I'll decide who stays in it.'

She still refused to give anyone a house key and went off on an attack again. 'Ten o'clock is late enough for any decent person to be out and about in the town here. And another thing, some of them have the cheek to ask for an early breakfast. They think I should get up and dance to their tune just because they booked the first ferry out in the morning.' Up came the pointed finger. 'I tell them straight, and they don't like it, they can get breakfast on the ferry as soon as it leaves the pier. They just think they can take a loan of me.'

'Do you charge those guests for breakfast?'

'Indeed, I do, I've bought the food, so they have to pay for it.'

With the danger of the list of dislikes and house-rules continuing I cut in at this point. I told her we would not be able to convert her 'Award Pending' to an actual award this year on account of failing to meet the basic Code of Conduct - to ensure Proper Standards of Courtesy: I got no further.

She showed me to the door with '... and don't you come back.' before she slammed it behind me.

This was one Teflon-coated mean-minded lady and I did not want unsuspecting guests to find themselves on her doorstep through reading our advertising. Driving off, I did wonder what in her life had nurtured such a cantankerous attitude and behaviour and felt slightly sorry for her: she'd never feel the joy and gratification in pleasing people.

However, if any two or more slim, bald, straight, God-fearing Christian Caucasians, with little luggage, who liked to be tucked up in bed by 10 o'clock and didn't need a bath, decided to stay with her, well the breakfast was okay.

Luxury with attitude

That afternoon I relaxed in a comfortable armchair enjoying tea and cake in the lounge of a guest house on the promenade in Oban, looking over to Kerrera. On arrival I was grateful for the jug of iced water which was delivered to my room on such a hot day and grateful too for having my case delivered to my room by one of the two gentlemen owners. A welcome contrast to my previous night's stay.

They had bought the place six months earlier and inherited the waitress who came with the purchase. She scurried around, fearlessly correcting both wayward and docile guests' behaviour almost standing over them in her unique way, keen to keep the breakfast service moving along.

She amused them with her chatty banter. 'Did your mother not tell you to clean your plate?' or to the Americans who helped themselves to huge portions of everything from the buffet then grazed, leaving most of it. 'It's obvious you didn't have to starve during the war.'

She was to be 85 in October, and they were retiring her then.

'Oh. You Sneak'

I crossed the Connel Bridge and drove north to a B&B, my last night on the mainland before crossing to the Isle of Mull. I was surprised to see a very old 'Listed, Commended' plaque mounted on the wall beside the front door. This lady had not been visited by us before. A further surprise; a dog might have been quite happy with my accommodation.

'You will be cosy here. It's just for one night.' This elderly landlady's departing words were more in hope than reassurance as she left me standing in her back porch. She departed to her cabbage-smelling kitchen avoiding eye contact.

My bedroom was the back porch. One step down to the back entrance to her bungalow with a tiny window and the back door locked and no key available. The single metal folding bed had two mattresses; at least the bed linen was clean and well ironed. A hook on the back of the door served as the wardrobe facility and a dining-chair, its seat covered by a tea cloth served as a bedside cabinet. A cemetery of dead insects, a screwed up sweet wrapper and a bristled hair-roller, hair included, lay under the chair in vintage dust.

There was more. The bathroom walls were covered in vinyl wallpaper; very suitable for bathroom walls, except those walls were papered with oblong pieces in a variety of shades and colours, curling up at the corners. They were sample pages from a wallpaper pattern book.

My towel would have been better recycled as a floor cloth. A well-worn bath towel cut up the middle, the old edges sewn together, the raw edges hemmed.

I had experienced enough to fail her already and wanted out, out, out. I phoned the Oban TIC to help me find an alternative bed for the night, but it was a busy summer, hot weather and to top that Runrig was playing at the Corran Halls. There was no room for me at any inn. I might even have considered a stable. I drove around looking for a vacancy sign but found none. So, unless I slept in my car, which was not on either, I had to return to her back porch.

She only advertised one room and at breakfast, I sat opposite the couple who'd been staying in that room. The one I'd booked. I imagine my landlady had moved me out for a more lucrative booking. He was a trucker in a white sleeveless vest, Gloria tattooed on one muscular bicep and *Remember Bannockburn* on the other. His wife, who *was* Gloria, with several chins, gelled-up bleached straw hair and dark-roots, smiled a lot; she was a happy soul. They tucked into their breakfasts as if it was a feast, mopping up the grease with their toast. I couldn't enjoy mine; the big-cooked-breakfast was greasy and there were blue spots on the sausage. The dominant taste in the coffee was chicory.

I had a look at what Gloria had written in the guest comments book as they left after their three-night-stay. She'd written '*Fabulous. A home from home. One of the best.*' This proved my point that guest-comment books can praise the worst, it just depends on an individual's expectations and their own standards.

Suitcase already in the car, I returned. The front door stood open. She stopped sweeping the linoleum in the long lobby to read my business card. I watched shock set in as a red flush burst onto her cheeks. 'Oh, you sneak! Coming in here and pretending you are a tourist.'

She was angry and needed persuading to even sit with me in the lounge for feedback, so it was not the best situation in which to approach the nitty-gritties. There was no way my attempts at building a relationship worked, so I arrived at the crossroad of our parting ways quicker than I would have liked.

'Do you have any help with the cleaning?' I asked as gently and sympathetically as I could.

'Are you suggesting there's a problem with my housekeeping?' was her retort

'Let me show you the problem where I slept.' She followed me to the back porch. I lifted the tea cloth, revealing the dead flies and debris. 'When I booked you told me it was a nice room with a double bed. I could imagine you didn't want to lose a better booking from that couple I met at breakfast. But you mustn't let this porch to a guest.'

I thought she was going to pass out, her rage was palpable 'You come into my house, insult me and expect me to stand here and listen to your complaints.' The floor brush was there where she'd left it, standing against the wall. She raised it as if to strike me, I backed away, turned and made for the door just as she gathered speed along the lobby towards me.

From the safety of the front path, I said 'We can discuss this. I'm here to help.' But my last words were to the second slammed door of the week.

I felt very uncomfortable and somehow responsible as I drove away. I could already see the next day's headlines in the Oban Times. 'Pensioner Drops Dead after a shocking visit from Tourist Board.' I called the Oban TIC immediately and asked them to phone her and check that she was okay and asked them to tell her I would be writing with a way forward. They did just that and called me back to say that she wanted to apologise; it was just the shock of it all.

A few months later my colleague Colin did her requested follow-up visit and I just happened to be in the office when he returned at the end of that week. He saw the approximately 150cm x 125cm porch and the narrow Z-bed with dead flies on the windowsill this time.

The outcome? He advised the lady that perhaps tourism was not for her and removed the plaque from outside her house. He dropped it on my desk saying, 'Mission Accomplished' Many years later when Colin was clearing out his archive, he found that plaque and sent it to me. A memento of my worst overnight stay ever.

R&R with G&T

I had an hour and a half to spare at the end of the day after my two day-visits before taking the ferry to the Isle of Mull so headed out to Ganavan Sands.

The tide was drawing away, passing Kerrera so gently it left barely even a ripple on the parchment sands. It was another hot day and I enjoyed strolling to the rocks at the far end, feeling the coolness of the wet sand on the soles of my bare feet, paddling in the trapped shallows on the Atlantic shore. It was refreshing and cleared the memory of that morning's experience from my mind.

I then walked back to the noise of the beach-side bar, throbbing with head-banging music and head-banging teenagers, throwing their heads back in unison, flinging their long hair over their faces into the middle of a circle.

The outside deck tables were all occupied. 'Come with me' the barman smiled. He lifted a chair, strode outside, and carried it down to the firm sand at the water's edge. I followed, my bag over my shoulder, shoes in one hand and the ice clinking in my glass of Hendrick's and full-fat tonic in the other.

'There you are Shirley Valentine.' he smiled again. 'Enjoy'.

'I'm loving this. Thank you.' I circled my shoulders, closed my eyes enjoying the late afternoon sun and felt the tonic fizz on my tongue, the music rising into the ether. I reminded myself that I meet so many more wonderful people in this job, than the inhospitable ones.

Meet the Americans

The Cal-Mac ferry turned away from Oban pier creating a churning-white-foam in its wake and I found a space at the rail beside two American ladies.

One of them said 'Excuse me, can I ask you a question?'

'Sure.'

That place we are leaving, Obaaan, are we leaving Scotland now?'

'No, you are still in Scotland. We are heading to the islands on the West Coast. The Inner Hebrides.'

'You'll have to excuse me. Of course. We couldn't see a passport check, but we just wanted to be sure. We get so confused. We have been touring now for almost three months. It sounds awful, but we've had enough, we just want to go back to our own beds at night now. Oh, but pardon me, you have a beautiful country, and everyone is so friendly and helpful.'

'I'm glad. That's nice to hear. And you are seeing it on a beautiful hot day too.'

'You think this is hot. You should come to Texas.' She laughed. 'We are travelling in Europe to escape a summer high of 95°F in Houston, Texas. Do you mind if I ask you another question?'

'No, not at all.'

'I am Charlene, by the way and this is my friend Rosie. Pleased to meet you. Are you Scottish?'

'Hi, I'm Reta and it is nice to meet you too. Yes. I'm Scottish.'

'Would you mind if my friend takes a video of us together? 'Only if you wouldn't mind? If you could just be talking to me about what we see here she could capture your lovely Scottish accent.'

'I'd be glad to.' *Wow, I didn't expect that.*

So, as her friend filmed the scenery I found myself sounding a bit Hebridean, it must have been my attempt at good diction. I told her Oban had a local distillery and the little I knew about McCaig's Folly, on Battery Hill. After a short while I ran out of things to say and the camera was still filming.

I thought, then continued. 'I was there once with a boyfriend in my teens; we had plastic tumblers, drank Mateus Rose, bought it because of the shape of the bottle really and we thought it so romantic. We cuddled together watching the sunset change from a glorious red to orange then darken to a deep violet as it sank behind those islands there.' I turned to see them. 'Kerrera and Lismore just there.'

Rosie with one eye still looking through the lens panned back to us and I made a playful frown. 'But. He was a heavy smoker and vain; couldn't pass a shop window without checking his reflection, taking out his comb and stopping to comb his perfect blond wavy hairstyle. So, I dumped him. I saw him later when he would have been 30-ish and he had a wig, so obviously a nylon one too. Maybe he wore out his hair, combing it.'

She switched the camera off. I gave a mischievous giggle, asked if that was okay, then the three of us burst out laughing.

Still laughing Rosie said. 'My first husband had one of those awful hair pieces. I told him it looked like a fireside rug.'

They'd bought a Colin Baxter coffee-table book of Scotland so would be able to read more about Oban in there.

I joined the now thinning queue snaking its way past the hot-buffet food, sliding their trays to the till. I was addicted to the high-calorie Cal-Mac steak pie with crisp topped puff pastry, soft on the underside, loads of thick brown gravy, a shovel of chips and a shaken-strainer of tinned peas, washed down by a mug of strong black tea. Basic comfort food. I always finished my meal in time to watch from the forward deck as we passed Duart Castle on the port side and the tail of Lismore to starboard.

This would be my third season working in the Inner Hebrides. where pegged-out washing whips horizontally in the sun-filled Atlantic wind, and if not fastened on securely, could finish up on mainland Scotland.

This time, approaching the Isle of Mull I felt a glow of anticipation almost akin to returning home. I had so many memories; having been welcomed into so many homes, the *Balamory* brightly-painted houses, the tapping of feet to the fiddlers' music in the Mishnish, Elvis the otter visiting Tobermory harbour for a fish supper, hens scratching the grass by the roadside. A world of passing places where a raised hand acknowledges the courtesy of pulling over.

Picking up Problems at the TIC

Slick and fast docking at Craignure saw trucks, tour buses, caravans and cars soon tailing each other, off snaking left towards Iona, or right for Tobermory. I was driving to Tobermory but stopped at the TIC in Craignure to let that traffic get well ahead of me. The locals would anticipate the straight runs and shoot past at every opportunity, red brake lights warning of the occasional sheep enjoying the retained heat of the day by bedding down on the tarmac.

Once all the people looking for information at the TIC had been attended to, Alfonso the manager had time to bring me up to date with the latest news. Glances passed between the staff when I said I was staying with the MacVicars that night.

Alfonso was Spanish and had made his home here some 30 years ago. In perfect English, even with a hint of a local accent he told me 'We've persuaded them to join your grading scheme and are hoping you can sor …. help them out. They used to have a guest house in Inverness. But. Well. You'll see for yourself I'm sure.' He'd even adopted the Hebridean sure, which can actually mean perhaps, or I hope, or possibly.

Anonymity

I sang along with Yvonne Lyon's honeyed voice on my CD player 'So many places, so many faces, so many places to call ho-o-o-me.' That so fitted my mood as I parked at Tobermory harbour to check the location of the MacVicars' guesthouse.

A battered old Land Rover sped in and braked hard alongside. A tall tanned young man climbed out, sleeves rolled up, folded his arms, crossed his ankles and relaxed back against it, the engine still running.

His eyes were creased to slits by the breadth of his smile. 'Fine evening. How is it going then?'

'Fine thanks, yes a beautiful evening. Have we met before?' I was sure I would have remembered this Isle-of-Mull Adonis; Action-Man jawline, eyes the colour of bluebells with a seductive gentle-timbre in his voice.

'No, but I know who you are. You can't drive around this island in a white Opel Manta an' no' be spotted. My mother said if I saw you, to tell you that she'll have lunch ready for you. You better stay for lunch or she'll be offended.'

I got out of the car. 'And your mother is?' I asked thinking of who I might know well enough to offer me lunch.

'Jessie Wilson?'

'Oh yes, over at Dervaig? I remember your mother now. How kind. I'd love to join her for lunch. Could you thank her for me, please? I'm looking forward to seeing her again. Sorry, I don't know your name.'

'Robbie.'

We shook hands then. He had a knuckle cracking grip and let go just before I thought I was going to buckle at the knees and have to thump him. 'Tomorrow it is then. Will you be there too?'

'No, Unfortunately not. We're working with the sheep tomorrow. I'll likely be out at the fank with just a sandwich and a flask. She said she wants you to see the neighbour's cottage across the way first because our guests are not leaving until the 12.20 pm ferry. She wants time to clean our own place first.'

He grinned again, slid back into the driving seat and was off with a wave out of the open window leaving me wondering if his gleeful smile was because he'd heard about my antics last time I'd visited.

Mother of Adonis

It happened last summer. I'd read the notice on the self-catering cottage door, *Be with you as soon as I can*. There was no car by the cottage which probably meant that the guests were out, however, our policy was, I was not to enter unescorted in case I nicked their jewellery.

One of the constant problems we had was this: accepting coffees and teas on day visits meant looking endlessly for loos. There are very few on the islands when you need one and needs must. I was desperate for a pee and couldn't move for a minute, my last coffee catching up with me. The cottage had no garden as such; the sheep had kept the grass short and when the urgency passed I hurried around the back and quickly squatted, imagining I was hidden by the bracken. When I stood up I noticed a bungalow half a mile away and a woman waving as she got into her car.

This had been Jessie's first sight of me. I was embarrassed and apologised of course but she laughed. 'Ocht, it makes a change from watching the sheep.'

Jessie was a source of local news, embellishing it with what was not printable, and she had a dry wit too. Her homemade roughly painted table at the gate by the roadside held a range of goodies. On this visit, there was a box of free-range eggs, jars of deep-red glossy hedgerow jelly and a plastic bag with crocheted tea-cosies.

There was a small biscuit tin with a label on the fence saying *Donations* and a notice in another plastic bag held down against the wind by a stone. It read *Help yourself and please leave your money in the box. All proceeds go to our local branch of Help the Aged, and I'm one of them.* It was signed, *Jessie*.

The Know-it-all

At the MacVicar's, I pressed the doorbell. After a short wait, the door opened just a crack: a lady's eye appeared first, hollowed and tired looking.

I heard a tutting and an irritating whisper from behind her. 'Come on Janet, open the door properly.'

I hesitated, imagining they would speak first, but they just stood there, two middle-aged folk, summing me up; and me them. I had an instant impression of unworldliness. She had an indoor pallor, very pale face-powder and a faded-patterned apron. Small and slim in a tweed box-pleated skirt and twin set and a Women's Guild pebble brooch pinned at the neck, she seemed a timid, beige person.

In contrast, he had a ruddy complexion and a kind of chin-up proud, chilling smile. He was cube-shaped, a mesomorph, short in the legs with highly polished shoes. He had a cravat tucked in at the neck of his lovat-green shirt and a sleeveless Fair Isle pullover. Both shirt and pullover were tucked into his trousers, the belt just held up by his hips, the buckle at an angle below the circumference of his belly. He seemed a tucked-in person.

I broke the silence, smiling. 'Am I at the right house? Mr and Mrs MacVicar's?'

He elbowed past her, shook my hand and lifted my suitcase. 'Yes, yes.' He announced with authority. 'We know who you are. You are visiting Janet's cousin here this week too. I'm Jack, pleased to meet you and this', he looked behind him and lifted his eyebrows. 'Oh, she's off, *was* my wife Janet.

I saw her back disappear through a doorway as she tugged at the knotted ties of her apron.

Jack followed, opened the kitchen door, muttered something to her and she returned, minus the apron.

I smiled 'Hello I'm Reta. Pleased to meet you.'

I felt an awkwardness in her limp handshake. I asked who her cousin was as an intro to a chat, but Jack interrupted pulling himself upstairs by the bannister, carrying my suitcase. He turned and commanded from the landing, still a hint of irritation in his voice. 'Offer Mrs MacLennan some tea Janet'.

She nodded agreement and went through an introductory routine, her hand shaking as she patted her immaculate greying-brown hair, checking the bun at the nape of her neck. She showed me the lounge and dining room; offering me some tea. 'Please make yourself at home. Jack will light the fire in the lounge for you. I know it is summer, but he still likes to light it. It makes the room cheerier.'

'I'll just freshen up and come down in about ten minutes then.'

Her fingers hovered at her mouth. Her delivery was stilted. 'Oh, sorry I forgot to ask you to register, didn't I? Jack will be annoyed, sorry, would you mind doing it now. Would that be okay?'

Of course, that was okay.

A smell of lavender furniture polish didn't quite mask the mustiness which hung in the wardrobe and drawers. I flopped back onto the red-and-purple candlewick bedspread on the squeaky trampoline of a bed; I could have been bouncing in a 1960s LSD induced hallucination, looking at the sun-faded orange carpet, fuchsia pink emulsion on the ceiling and walls and gaudy pink and red roses climbing the curtains. This was a psychedelic time-warp of a room.

I soon sat by the crackling sticks on the newly lit fire when Jack arrived with the teapot. Janet carried the tea tray followed by a miniature white poodle, prancing like a Lipizzaner stallion. Janet brought over a small table, placing a plate of biscuits and slices of sultana-cake beside me. He poured my tea, then one for each of themselves and I imagined we would sit together, but they pulled out two dining chairs from a small table about 6 feet away and sat; just watching me.

'I offered the plate. Would you like to share this with me?'

'Oh, no, no, you enjoy them.' Jack smiled.

I tried light conversation several times. Jack responded then, silence. They watched their dog who watched the cake travel from my plate to my mouth. When gazing didn't work, she stood on her hind legs pawing the air with a panting whine, her tongue lolling out of her mouth.

Jack smiled, like an adoring daddy. 'This is our Trixie. You can break up some small pieces for her if you like. She has no teeth, but she'll manage.'

With the proximity of panting-halitosis and the awkwardness of feeling like an exhibit, ten minutes of listening to my own voice felt like ten minutes too long, I folded my napkin and thanked them, glad to be out of there.

Jack asked me when I would like dinner served which took me by surprise. Some guesthouses did provide evening meals, especially in remote areas but I hadn't been offered one when I booked. I told him I'd had a Cal-Mac's steak pie on the ferry and could only manage something very light, perhaps in an hour.

I sat alone in the dining room feeling wary: the cutlery was set for three courses. I was just not hungry but was duty bound to at least see and taste what they served. Food kept coming. Starter: a light one-egg cheese and tomato omelette with tiny salad. Main: flippin' haddock with chips and mushy peas. Dessert: bloody hell, apple and raisin crumble with custard.

I made a huge effort; Jack frowned at the increasing amount of food left on the series of plates. What was it *about I have already eaten a steak pie dinner* they didn't get? Nevertheless, patting my stomach, I apologised for leaving so much very good home-cooked food.

He raised his eyebrows in a way which indicated a rhetorical question. 'But you'll have space for a coffee in the lounge, I hope? We have a surprise for you, it is something we do every night we have guests. You will enjoy it. It's unique.'

I nodded, smiling, but it was not a genuine smile. I waited until Jack had left the room to lean over the table and slowly ease myself to a standing position. I managed it without bending in the middle and waddled to the lounge as if carrying a full-term baby bump.

The lounge layout had changed since I'd had tea and cake there earlier. The alcove entranceway now had the upright piano and a stool positioned there, ready for a performance. An archway separated it from the lounge proper. Six upright chairs had now been placed in a curve facing the pop-up stage. A small occasional table with a cafetière of coffee, home-made tablet, a slice of lemon drizzle cake and two After-Eights was placed in front of my chair, in the middle. At that moment it all seemed as attractive as having

141

to eat sheep's eyeballs: With my hands on the seat of the chair I lowered myself down very slowly.

Jack appeared in his kilt. His sporran sat at a sharply inwards-tilting angle below his belly. He leaned over and stoked the fire, settled the coals with the poker then pointing it at me, told me with certain belief, not expecting a response. 'Just-let-me-turn-round and-say, you are going to be pleasantly surprised. Oh yes. You are indeed.'

He closed the window all the curtains dropping the tied-back ones in the archway behind him as he left. He then popped his head back in, smiling. 'Five minutes.'

If I'd known how cringingly embarrassing this unique experience was about to be, I would have feigned illness. The minutes passed. I heard thunder rumbling and booming in my intestines. The room lights went out. I heard Jack whisper 'One, two, three and ...' then two loud introductory chords, held there by the sustain pedal, announced the start of a Scottish Strathspey tune, giving Jack time to make a bit of a ceremony about tying back each curtain again.

My exit was now firmly blocked. But perched there, suffering there actually, I would have been missed. I was an audience of one. The room was lit only by the glow from the fire and a small spot lamp which stood on top of the piano. It wobbled in time with the thumped-out chords, casting a quivering beam of light onto the sheet music, Janet's nose, her breasts, hands and the piano keys. He stood to her right: the page-turner.

She wore a white blouse with a lace jabot, and I wondered if her long pleated skirt was the MacVicar tartan: it matched Jack's bow tie and kilt.

It was not just the lamp which shook, her voice did too and when she struck a wrong note she faltered, corrected it and lost the rhythm. The song was cheesily Scottish; dark lochs and windswept glens, a golden eagle in a sunset, a young girl broken-hearted as her true love tramped off in full battledress across the heather hills heading for Afghanistan.

I felt sure there would have been a road and maybe even a bus out of whatever village they lived in, or surely there would have been a send-off and a local could have given him a lift.

I felt a giggle rising; I imagined Ronnie Corbett in drag at the piano and Ronnie Barker in the kilt turning the pages. I coughed to hide my distress and volatile nausea threatened to make an appearance.

I smiled, applauded and rose stiffly from my chair. 'You'll have to excuse me.'

I was truly underwhelmed and wanted out before laughter and vomit burst out of me, landing on their carpet.

'But we haven't finished.' Jack frowned.

'I'm truly sorry but I've had a very long day and need to retire now. Thank you for that little performance.'

He presented me with a home-knitted tape of her music. 'Well before you go, just-let-me-turn-round-and-say there are more tunes on this tape. Janet writes her own lyrics and composes the music herself. We sell it to our guests but please accept it as a gift. You can play it in your room, I've put a tape recorder there for you.'

'Thank you, that is very kind. I'll do that. I will say goodnight now, thank you for the meal and entertainment.' I turned at the lounge door thanking him once again. Janet had already left ahead of me.

He smiled. 'Sleep well.'

Next morning, still feeling full I decided to be firm regarding quantities of food. The sideboard was already laden with cereals, fruit juices, fruit salad and yoghurts and a menu was at my place setting. Eggs cooked as you like, plus standard other options. My choice of a boiled egg with toast soldiers was swept aside.

'That is for children you should have our Hearty Scottish Breakfast, you'll find it is excellent, very impressive.'

'First, let me say I played the tape last night. I love Scottish music.'

'You enjoyed it then?'

I was put on the spot. 'It was very entertaining. I managed to say. 'Now I'm sorry I just can't manage a full breakfast this morning after last night's huge meal, so just a very small portion please? And I must insist, a small one please.'

'Have a little of that smoked salmon while you are waiting. He smiled, pointing to the sideboard. 'Don't stint.'

I resisted. A steak platter arrived with one of every item a Full Scottish could include. I wanted to tease him with 'What no kipper?' but didn't risk it.

'That'll set you up for the day.' He rubbed his hands together as if he was about to sit down and eat it.

'Could I have a small plate please and I'll help myself?'

With a tut-tut and some reluctance, he brought me a dinner plate. 'I'm sure you'll manage, just tuck in.' But Trixie was there already. Licking her lips. My alter-ego whispered just scoop the lot under the table for her. As if I'd dare!

One of our young slim trainees used to drop what she couldn't eat into a plastic bag, then tuck it inside her sock, hidden by her trouser leg. She stopped that after an owner's salivating Labrador, followed her to her room once.

I came downstairs to check-out and heard Jack's booming voice coming from the other side of the kitchen door with an exaggerated articulation and slow delivery as if speaking to someone he considered to be an idiot. It reminded me of a carer who spoke to my mother that way once. Mum asked her if she was on drugs.

I waited a minute, then knocked. Jack came to the door smiling, 'Come in. Take a seat.' He pulled out a chair at the kitchen table for me. I paid my bill and took out my paperwork for their visit.

Jack took command at the table with me and turned to Janet with a stern tone. 'You can turn that noise off now.' She reached to the CD player and silenced the sound of gentle surf and whale songs, looking out of the window as if she'd rather be with them, than with us.

Before joining us, she finished tipping coriander seeds from a packet onto the surface of a small pot. It joined the other pots labelled parsley and cress standing on the windowsill. The food-mixer arm was up, the recipe lying open in a ring binder and there were ingredients all ready to mix. Vegetables were washed and lined up beside the chopping board ready to chop.

The three of us sat together at the kitchen table. Janet looked worried and I sensed her fragility as she studied her bitten nails. A pen and writing pad lay on the table beside a copy of our booklet, Criteria for Guest House Classification, the pages fringed with yellow Post-Its.

Jack kicked-off with a complaint. 'Just-let-me-turn-round-and-say, we get very little business from that TIC. But I know something. That place over the road belongs to the Manager's wife's auntie and we see the cars arriving there alright, but not here'.

'Have you spoken to Alfonso about needing more business from them?'

'Just-let-me-turn-round-and-say; *He could be dizzy if he kept this up*. it is a waste of time. He is not local. He doesn't understand how to run his TIC. The business should be shared out equally amongst us. The auntie over there has the new Five Stars grade, I have worked out that we will be Four or maybe even Five too.

Ignoring his misplaced optimism, I said. 'Speak to him about it.'

'No, no. Once we have our award, the guests will come piling in then, and we won't need them, him or his staff. By-the-way, there is something else you won't know. If I gave him a few drams we'd get the business alright. But his tongue will be at his ankles before he'll get a drink out of me.'

Judging from my room, and what I'd seen of the public areas, he was in fantasy land. I asked, 'Have you stayed at any Four or Five-Star guest houses?'

He waved that aside. 'We are caravaners, but I've done my homework and I am confident we have covered everything in your booklet. Mind you, we don't agree with all of it do we Janet?' He picked up our new guidance booklet on facilities, fluttering it and patted Janet's thigh. 'Janet missed one or two things, but we can always fix those. Yes Janet? Won't we?'

She turned the back of a porridge oat packet towards herself, studying it like an embarrassed teenager.

'You have the other booklet too Jack? The one which we issued when we moved over to our new Stars grading system?'

'No. What other booklet? I know nothing about that.'

'The one which explains how we measure quality?'

'This is all we were sent, I am sure?' But Jack's sure had that same ring of the Hebridean sure. Janet got up and went to their small filing cabinet beside a desk to check.

'It has a lilac cover Janet. In the meantime, could we start by looking at the outside of the house, the parking and the garden? Do you mind if we go out the back way, I'd like you to show me around and I will explain how we grade properties as we go along?

He stood, puffed-up with confidence. Told Janet to put the kettle on, we wouldn't be long then announced. 'I'll lead the way then.'

I made complimentary noises about the location and the fine stonework then explained how we start with assuming a value of 10/10. 'We take a point off for each item or area which is not excellent. So, I can see the paintwork is peeling on the rear window frames. Do you see where that length of guttering has slipped down?'

He nodded.

'You can see where the algae have penetrated the red sandstone, it has been dripping for quite a while there. It is likely the mortar needs checked around that chimney stack too, just where the buddleia is growing out of it That all brings your score down to 6/10 which means *just good*.'

He frowned and said, 'These are mere details, it is a fine stone-built house.'

'Indeed, it is, but we measure the condition as well as the quality. You'll find it all explained in the other booklet Jack; the one Janet is looking for?'

He frowned, and I continued with the Grounds and Gardens scoring; there were bespoke-designed wrought-iron gates but rusted with long grass preventing them from closing. The lawn had been mown, but the edges not trimmed, the driveway was rutted, the red chips long ago flattened into the soil.

Upstairs, the first bedroom had an ensuite shower, WC and wash basin arrangement behind a partition wall. No door, no window or extractor there for the WC facility.

'Did you get Building Control approval for this ensuite Jack?'

'Not yet, but I will.' He said very confidently.

'The ensuite in my room was fully enclosed with its own door within the bedroom and it has an extractor. In this one, the guests' privacy is affected, and ....'

He turned away before I had finished, walking into the hallway.

I followed him. 'I was going to say, a shower and washbasin within the bedroom is okay, but a WC must be enclosed behind a door, that ensuite needs a ceiling with either an extractor fan or opening window.'

He again waked on and waited outside the next bedroom door. I listened carefully to the impressive list of improvements he had made, making notes as he spoke. 'I'll deal with the Building Control people and Planners. I'm sure there won't be a problem.'

Janet appeared and stood patiently beside us with an arm full of clean linen and towels to prepare my room for the next guests.

Irritated by her presence he eventually said, 'What is it now Janet?'

All she wanted, she was able to say in five simple words. 'Could I please get past?'

We reached the last bedroom. It was a joke. There was a bank of louvre-doored cupboards covering the wall opposite a standard-size double bed and twin beds. He opened all the louvre-doors one after the other. The first two formed a double wardrobe. Behind the next door along was a washbasin with a mirror. The next two along had a sideways-on WC; the toilet paper holder screwed onto the louvre door. This WC looked impossible to use, without the door remaining open. When he opened the last set of double doors the white shower curtain escaped, billowing out like an escaping ghost. This was his idea of a shower room. It contained a narrow shower tray with a Mira shower.

He then returned to the bedroom door and flicked a switch. A fanfare might not have been inappropriate as the whole lot blinked into strip-light life. If one guest needed to get up during the night, the rest of the guests would think it was morning.

I was speechless for a minute. How to discuss these terrible facilities, knowing he would disagree with me.

'What do you have to say about this then?' He beamed with pleasure, crossing his arms proudly. 'You have no idea how difficult it was to fit all this in here. This was originally a useless long wall of wardrobes. I converted them myself.'

'Jack, I can imagine that this was a lot of work for you, however, I'm afraid you have the same problem here. This arrangement offers no privacy and no approved ventilation.'

He leant towards me, raised his voice a little and spoke slowly pointing to the beds. 'This room can sleep a mother, a father and two children. The other bedroom you saw has only one double bed. All those guests will know each other very intimately. They are family.' This was followed with a mild threat. 'We are not going to be difficult now, are we?'

'What does Janet think about those rooms?' I asked as we left that bedroom and headed towards the stairs. 'Shall we sit with her in the kitchen now?'

He followed me, muttering. 'Huh. Janet doesn't have anything to say. She had nothing to do with the alterations.'

In the kitchen, Janet had prepared coffee and biscuits. She brought the cafetière over and filled our three mugs. Jack pulled out the chair at the head of the table and settled himself down, with a chairman-like air of authority

'Now Reta, what award are you going to give us?' He turned to Janet, 'It doesn't look like Five Stars though. Out with it then.'

I'd prefer to give you the feedback on my visit first and we can discuss.'

'No, no, no. Just get to the point. What award are you giving us?'

I felt a fluttering in my stomach, like when my neighbour was felling his tree and I saw it dropping towards his greenhouse. Something bad was going to happen right then, but I kept going.

'You have high standards Janet. I loved the quality of the food you produced and your baking. The housekeeping is excellent. Some of the furnishings have been of excellent quality originally but are of course well used, so that their condition is now what I would assess as *just good*, not *very good* or *excellent*. The soft furnishings, carpets and bedspreads, being well worn are in just acceptable condition.'

Janet didn't look up but said. 'All this furniture was here when we bought the guest house.'

He drummed his fingers on the table. 'We know all that, not everything is perfect, but I agree with you, Janet's cooking is outstanding. The award please if you don't mind.'

I addressed both of them now. 'These words, acceptable, good, excellent, we use to measure quality and some areas are holding back the scoring. The rough grass edges, the driveway and parking could all be improved. So, to sum up … I know you are going to be disappointed, but I have a way forward for you to consider and a solution. The scoring would bring you out at two stars. Regardless of that, I'm sorry Jack but because of the ensuite facilities not meeting the regulation standards, I cannot offer you an award on this visit.'

Jack seemed paralysed by shock and Janet covering her mouth, looked at Jack.

I continued, 'It is unlikely that you are going to be able to get planning consent and building warrant for alterations in the next few weeks when we are at the end of the current scheme year, so I propose that you have an Award Pending entry in our publications until you have upgraded the areas I will outline in my report. That will give you time to perhaps achieve the award you would like.'

He looked to be ripening up for a full-blown tantrum. With narrowed eyes, he pointed his finger heavenwards as if to call the wrath of God on me; thankfully the ceiling was in the way. 'NO. I won't accept that. No award. Now? On this visit? After everything, we did for you? Everyone knows we are having your visit and you will leave us with, he shouted *NO AWARD*. Indeed. No. That is not going to happen.'

Spluttering foam was gathering in the corners of his mouth. He lifted his coffee mug, took a drink and slammed it down so hard on the pine table that his coffee splashed around.

Janet jumped in her chair and Trixie stood, stretched, circled in her basket and lay down again, her eyes on us.

He raised a finger again, towards me this time, very slowly. I noticed his knee was bouncing under the table. Things were about to go off-piste. 'Just-let-me-turn-round-and-say, you're not half as good as your male colleagues who visited our guest house in Inverness. They knew what they were doing.' Then he called up the cavalry. 'You have a reputation around here. Oh yes, you are known as a difficult one to please. I will not accept this ... Award Pending'. It is an insult. I'm telling you now if you ... .'

He ranted for some minutes stripping me of any professional credibility, thumping the table with his fist, finishing with '... I have contacts, and you will have no job by the time you get back home my lady.'

For him, this seemed to be some sort of Armageddon. I kept a stony-faced response but felt the tension might snap my last fraying nerve. I gathered my papers together.

Janet, who had mopped up the coffee suddenly turned. 'Please, Jack. Please. Shoosht. Could we maybe just talk about this quietly? Listen for a minute.'

She turned to address me, but he shouted again. 'Janet. Silence.'

But, Janet with her eyes down continued. 'Maybe you'll remember I thought we should have new furniture? I wanted to redecorate right from the start. Remember? Put in proper ensuites?'

'Quiet Janet, keep out of this.' he barked, not turning his head to look at her.

'I'd like to hear what Janet had plans for.' I added.

She burst into tears. 'All I ever hear is "I know best Janet, leave it to me." She took a hankie from her apron pocket, then took off her apron and threw it down on the table. 'You're just a blind, stubborn, mean and arrogant, she searched for the right word, *prick*, and seemed to shock herself but did the Magnus Magnusson thing; she'd started so she was going to finish. She continued stacking up her disappointments and embarrassments.

He was dumbstruck, open-mouthed, feeling betrayed; her expressing her own opinion in front of me. I was now the only one seated keeping my eyes on my briefcase, while I was putting my notes away. I was thinking counselling: *Drama Triangle, Persecutor, Victim and Rescuer. I'd been seen as all three.*

His rage propelled him out of his chair, (*in Victim mode*) he charged across to the kitchen door; a flight response at full throttle and vented his anger on the door, swinging it to slam behind him. Trixie had been hard on his heels imagining it was time for walkies, but just managed to jump back before being chopped in two.

For him the issue was not now about ensuites or quality assessment, it was about the loss of face, making a mistake, not having control of the two women in his kitchen. Bloody misogynist.

'I'm sorry you are both so upset Janet.'

She dabbed her eyes and poured more coffee. 'I'm sorry you had to witness this. He's a good man really, he means well, but he's mean. We have the money, but he won't spend it to make the place nice for the guests. And playing and singing in the lounge; I felt so embarrassed. I hate it. I'm really and truly embarrassed, I think the guests are embarrassed too. I write a little and sing for my own enjoyment, not for others. I just don't want to do it.'

'Well don't Janet. I think you are right, even if you had been Maria Calla it is just too intimate an experience for a small guest house audience.' I closed my case. 'I should go now. I'll write my report and send it to you.'

I so wanted to leave but Janet asked me to stay, so she could show me the mood-board of carpet, curtains and wallpaper samples she'd had made two years before by an interior designer. She'd had it ready to show me all the time. She knew high quality alright.

'You are very attentive to your guests, your cooking, baking and housekeeping are superb. What you have there is of a high standard. If you were to go ahead with this, you will get much more enjoyment out of running it too.'

She knew that. Together we made a quick note covering all areas which needed improvement.

She seemed keen to go ahead with the planning, although feeling a bit apprehensive. 'Our children will back me. At least I hope they will. They have been telling me for years I should stand up to him. Maybe now is the time.'

Just as we were finishing, Jack returned. 'You still here?' was his opening. He then went to Trixie's basket and picked her up. He adjusted his chair at the table and sat down. Trixie responded by licking his hand as he stroked her, his security blanket, on his lap. Purple faced and looking at Trixie he said, 'If you could get that idle manager down the road to send us some business, we would have some income to spend on upgrading, but not until then'.

I heard a chink of hope there that things might shift. Janet held up our booklet, Notes on Grading. 'I found the other booklet Reta was talking about.'

'Oh, you'd lost it then?' He struck out again.

'It was in our Tourist Board file. There all the time. You didn't look either.'

I stood to go, ignoring the bickering. 'I will tell the TIC manager you would like more business and you are considering improvements. You could pop in yourself too Jack, with Janet. Do that. They'd love to hear about the plans Janet, and I have been discussing. There are other properties which are Award Pending, holding off on their award till they complete upgrading. It is not unusual. Where proprietors are intending to improve. We'll support that by giving you time and any further advice you think you need.

Janet interjected. 'Our own son told us, speculate to accumulate, he said.'

I already felt I'd stayed too long. I told them I'd send a detailed report and Janet saw me to the door, we shook hands and she patted mine firmly. Jack remained in the kitchen.

I drove off a bit disturbed by that domestic incident thankful for my own good fortune in being married to a gentle and kind man.

The next time I called in at the Craignure TIC to update them on my visits, I told them that the MacVicars had accepted an Award Pending. I was able to report that Janet was keen to undertake extensive upgrading. Alfonso, the manager asked. 'And Jack?'

'He is not a happy man, but I think he might come around to Janet's ideas. Jack will need to redesign his ensuites first though.

His assistant laughed. 'I win girls. She turned to me. 'We had a bet on. They said Jack would throw you out.'

My Matriarchal Family

I was not used to such a dominant male. In my childhood, Grandma was a strong matriarch, kind-hearted, but a true virago. Dear Grandpa's wishes were swept aside. In fact, the men who married their daughters eventually gave up having opinions of their own too. I can remember her reducing the value of the whole of the male species at the end of one rant with 'Ach, their semmits make guid dusters.'

I find it hard to believe now; my grandpa was called Bobby; my mum's husband was called Bobby. We all lived together. What name should Grandma not have chosen to give to my budgie: a gift for my birthday? Well, she did. No-one complained.

On one occasion, during the Edinburgh Festival, there was a Fringe event of alternative therapies. I volunteered to have my eyes read by an Iridologist. She was excited about finding such an example of something-or-other and asked if I'd mind her student having a look.

She peered into my eyes, referred to her chart and they nodded agreement. 'You have a castrating effect on men. I recommend you join a male voice choir.'

Well, was I shocked? Totally taken aback. The male-voice choir bit was silly, but I got the message loud and clear. With a husband and two sons, I was truly concerned: was I really like my grandma?

I told them the iridologists' opinion and asked if they thought I was too heavy on them.

'Yes.' was my sons' answer in unison, but with a hint of a smile not wishing to miss the chance of a wind-up too.

I'd subconsciously carried some of my grandma's behaviour into the next generation. Something to explore at my next personal growth and development group.

A Castle Stay

The rest of my visits that week since meeting the McVicars had been so very busy, cramming in as many visits as I could while on the island. They were good productive ones though, including my lunch with Adonis's mother, Jessie in Dervaig. When I commented on how handsome he was. She said. 'I weaned him on porridge when he was a bairn. That's what did it'.

Friday arrived, and John was to leave his car in Oban and join me on the Isle of Mull for a week's holiday. We'd planned a visit to the Treshnish Isles to see the sea birds' nesting colony there, the puffins in particular. I had one more official visit to do that night first and chose the accommodation because it was in the direction of Ulva Ferry, from where we would take the boat. I'd had a message from the office in the afternoon to say that we couldn't for some reason arrive before 10.30pm.

After enjoying an evening meal in Salen, we headed off to look for our B&B in a castle. There were no streetlights of course and its dark square bulk was outlined on a rise of land, in the moonlight. A restored fortified tower house, took shape before we approached the field gate entrance with the sign. I manned the gate and John drove through across the 400 metres of sheep-cropped grass. Our headlights picked out a parked car by the castle wall and a lady stepped out.

'Hello, I'm Jean. Pleased to meet you. You'll have to excuse me for rushing off, but the lady of the house sends her apologies, she can't be here. Now don't worry, I'll look after you.'

Jean explained that the father of the lady who owned it had had a heart attack, so she and her husband had rushed off to be with him. He lived in Oban on the mainland and they'd be away for a few days. This cheerful lady couldn't have met us any earlier because her daughter had MS and she had to look after her grandchildren until 10.00 when her son-in-law got home. I didn't mention why I was there; they had enough to deal with.

She handed us a huge iron key and a slip of paper with her phone number. 'Now be sure to call me if you have any problems and take this key, lock yourselves in. But I'll have to ask you what time you'd like breakfast so that you can pop down and open up for me in the morning. We're full tomorrow night but you are the only ones in tonight.'

We looked at each other. 'Say eight o'clock for breakfast then, would that suit you?' I asked.

'Never mind me. You're the guests. I'll arrive at about 7.30 if you wouldn't mind just unlocking the door for me. I work here every day, but I preferred to sit in my car just now; that place is far too spooky for me at night. I've left the lights on for you and a fire in your room, it can be a bit chilly with these thick stone walls.'

She left saying 'Don't lose that key now, it's the only one', then turning away, was into her car and off with a wave. 'You'll be fine.'

Once she had gone the only sound was the ticking of the cooling car engine and two sheep munching, chewing the cud as they lay against the castle wall.

We had the place to ourselves and I was very glad I was not alone, doing this visit. I looked up at the clear dome of silver stars.

'I cannot remember ever seeing the Milky Way so clearly before.' I said.

'On Harris, this is just the usual clear night sky.' John replied, getting our case out of the car.

'I have never seen the Aurora Borealis either. I'm going to start a bucket list.'

'It is not visible in summer. We don't need to pay for an expensive cruise on the off chance of seeing it. We'll go to Harris. You could see them every winter from Northton.'

A light shone out from a ground floor window and another high up on the tall stone wall: that would probably be our bedroom.

John had the huge iron key which if not the original 17th century one, was a convincing aged replica. The heavy door screeched resisting movement, needing a strong push. We headed across the vaulted hall towards the narrow stair which rose within the turret in the far corner. The wheels on my suitcase clunked over the flagstone floor as if it was a pavement, catching on the edge of the ancient rugs. It did indeed feel spooky, passing a suit

156

of armour standing to attention with its metal hand resting on the hilt of the sword.

We climbed the worn steps of the clockwise spiral staircase. John would have the advantage with the sword in his right hand if the man in armour should want to come to life during the night and attack us.

One full turn, then another, we saw the reassuring glow from under our door. There was no landing, just a worn-down doorstep off the staircase. I lifted the latch and yelled, nearly knocking John down the stairs with my fright.

There was a lady in a long silk-like dress, a lace cap on her head, sitting at the fire with a book in her lap. It took a minute for me to realise my mistake. She was a model in period dress and the fire was a couple of light bulbs and some red-net fabric waving in their heat in the fireplace. This place was one of our Visitor Attractions during the day and a B&B in the evening.

One more turn of the stairs to reach our cosy, velvet-curtained room, where a fire had been lit in the grate. It felt like stepping back in time as we climbed into a four-poster, wondering how they got it up the stairs. With the gentle glow from the flames and the total silence; we were soon asleep.

Next morning the mist was so thick I mistook it for a steamed-up window. I heard the gentle purring of a car engine, so took my time going carefully down the stairs. The key gave a reassuring loud clunk and the massive door swung open just as Jean turned off her car engine.

She stepped out and turned, giving me a view of her backside as she spoke, she reached across to the passenger seat for her shopping bag. 'What weather! Oh well, that was a challenge, as they say.' She laughed and stood up. 'Just as well I know when to turn the steering wheel crossing that field. Instinct I suppose. Did you sleep well enough? Yes, I'm sure you did.' And with another laugh she passed me and scurried off.

I closed the massive door, yawning. 'Good morning. Yes, we both slept well, thank you'.

She disappeared behind a low door shouting back, 'Nice pyjamas.'

At breakfast, although there was background heating from the night-storage heaters, a log fire did add welcome warmth and atmosphere in the inglenook fireplace. A castle-sized oak table was set in front of it. We felt like the laird and his wife and joked that medieval dress-code would not have felt out of place.

The home-made yoghurt swirled with zingy home-made lemon curd and topped with crunchy granola was a great start. Scrambled eggs with cheddar cheese melted through them, crispy bacon on the side and warm toast with fresh-farm butter followed. We felt pampered.

As we left, I asked her to tell the owners the purpose of our stay, that we'd had a very good experience and would phone them when they had returned. Jean waved us off, but her big smile was soon veiled by the mist.

Turus Mara Trip

Not a hint of movement. Fine moisture hung in the air; every blade and seed head of grass, every leaf holding tiny light-filled beads. None were dripping. The mist was so thick that finding the route from the castle across the field to the gate was difficult; our trip to the Treshnish Isles could be postponed.

Once we were on the road, curtains of mist lifted here and there and by the time we arrived at Ulva Ferry, it was thinning above the silent sea. As the passengers gathered, the skipper, Iain Morrison was confident it would clear. We set off and as the Hoy Lass left the pier we could see on the western horizon, just as he had forecast, the edge of a clear blue sky expanding towards us.

The tide was just right for us to tie up at the pier on Staffa and we enjoyed a short walk on the grassy island with its vast sea views. Then returning to the boat, Iain managed to steer us into Fingal's Cave. We stepped out onto a basalt rock pathway and walked further in. He played a CD of Mendelssohn's Fingal's

Cave Overture. The acoustics were perfect and as the echoing music rose and crashed, rippled and whispered on the Atlantic waves, it was a goose-bump experience.

To get ashore at Lunga, Iain picked up a pontoon anchored just offshore. He fastened it alongside the Hoy Lass and took us as close as he could onto the shingled shore. We stepped onto the beach then climbed past the nesting kittiwakes, guillemots and dark green shags within touching distance. They were quite unperturbed by our presence and camera snapping. Having been encouraged not to stop there but continue further on and upwards to the grassland above the cliffs, we passed fulmars nesting and saw gannets diving just offshore before reaching the puffin colony.

We would love to have seen Manx Shearwaters, however Iain told us that they are nocturnal and only come ashore at night when the parents change shifts on the nest. We couldn't see the nests anyway because they are in burrows on the higher slopes of the island. He also told us that their second largest breeding ground is on the Isle of Rum, where they are there in tens of thousands.

Puffins took-off in a blur of wingbeats using the uplift of the air on a seaward slope. Their return to land was astounding to witness. With a beak full of sand eels, stiff-winged, splaying their webbed feet, rocking about, they tumbled to crash land on their bellies near their burrows. With a quick shake to realign their feathers, and without losing one sand eel, they disappeared underground.

We were told that those hardy, comic little creatures fly thousands of miles in migration, can dive to some 60 metres to collect the sand eels and are known to live for over 30 years. One ringed bird was found a few years before our visit and was reckoned to be over 60 years old. That wee soul deserved a pension.

It was not advisable to walk among the burrows because our weight might collapse them, so a kind of commando crawl is what worked best. After some time, I rolled onto my back to give my arms a rest. Then dosing in the warm sunshine, I sensed movement close to me. Keeping my eyelids almost closed against the sunlight I saw a puffin right beside my head, having a good close-up look at me, turning one eye then the other to study my face. He made a deep throaty sound, like a slowly opening hinge that needed oiling, which although I am not a baby puffin, I found soothing.

We'd made a memory to treasure on that sail to the Treshnish Isles.

Kylehrea Ferry

It was now the following summer, a year further on and I was travelling to the Isle of Skye. I'd booked my visits starting from the south of the island and turned off the A87 just after Shiel Bridge. I passed through Glenelg, heading for the short ferry crossing on the Kyle Rhea straits. This stretch of sea which is only 600 metres wide had a tidal flow looking more like a river in spate on that day.

The small MV Glenachulish, which carries only up to six vehicles at a time, claims to be the last one in the world to operate a manual turntable for vehicles. I watched from the queue as it sped across towards us going with the strong tidal flow, swinging into a manoeuvre to approach the slipway. It would be a different story on the return journey, battling against that current, although it was an experience I didn't want to miss.

The cheerful crew pushed the turntable around, waved the cars off, while their dog avoiding the cars, had a sniff around the slipway. We were loaded on and as we churned across, I wondered if this was the same skipper as was in our friend Wendy's story.

The ping-pong sound which announced the safety instructions was followed by a male voice on the loudspeaker. 'Could we have your attention, please? There are three lifejackets on this boat, one for me and the other two for the crew. If you hear a loud whistle followed by a splash (wheezing laughter) that will be us abandoning ship.'

Apparently, the laughter was continued until the click of the off switch.

Neist Point and Tranquility

It was nearly midsummer, and daylight stretched until after 10 o'clock in the evening, I decided after dinner to stride out to the Point and back. Two people were returning to their car, but there was not another soul to be seen. It looked like about a mile, but I knew I would enjoy the effort of a brisk walk there and I'd burn off some calories.

I started down the long steep path, then up and down again to the lighthouse. Beyond it, to the left, I stepped sideways in case I slipped on the grassy access to the basalt rocks. I clambered out onto them and settled on one with another as a footstool. I was on the edge of the Atlantic Ocean.

The breadth of my vision was now filled with the water, the sky and the lowering sun back lighting the Uists and South Harris. I could clearly see the rocks in the water at my feet and yet as the vast expanse of it reached the horizon, except for the steady path of sunlight, the surface was as dark as the gloss on treacle.

I sat very still as the black-headed gulls, skimmed and tilted around me. One came so close I felt the shift of air from its wings as if for that bird, I'd merged into the landscape. Its head was more chocolate than black.

Their throaty, crackling *aaah* had no urgency, as they wheeled around, then suddenly they'd settled. Just gone. All was quiet. The sun drew in its shining path and melted away like a butterball spreading on and into a warm-treacle ocean. Just the sky, the scent of grasses, the ocean and me. I don't know how long I sat there in the sound of silence as the light was fading.

I was reflecting on my busy lifestyle. It had really become too much. Something had to change. Which job should I choose to stay with and maybe progress in? I liked the people I worked with in both counselling and tourism. Whichever one I decided on, I'd miss the other, the people and the work. In the beauty and silence of those surroundings, I let thoughts on those decisions go, trusting that the answer would come in time.

Walking back, while I could still find my way, I carried John in my thoughts. He was to join me again at the end of the week for this year's annual staycation holiday. Last year we were on Mull this time, while I was on the Isle of Skye. He had some engineering site visits to do, to distilleries and we would combine that with walking in the Quiraing and as many other guide-book walks as we could manage.

Who Would Believe it?

A tourist board visit only gives us a snapshot of a business and unless we hear otherwise, we trust that our stay is a typical one. I had such an outstanding experience staying with Charmaine and Peter on the Isle of Skye, I had been happy to confirm their Five Stars the previous year. With a clear vision and their own hard labour, they had beautifully restored an old farm steading, creating a unique experience for guests. The impeccable attention to service standards, top quality in everything from the doormat to the polished solid silver cutlery had all contributed to this well-earned award.

Now I was returning with John for two nights during our holiday. I wanted him to experience the luxury I'd enjoyed on my official visit. But it was not going to happen.

We felt relaxed and comfortable against the feather-filled cushions of their sofa in front of the open log fire, sipping our complimentary sherries and reading our books before the other two lady guests arrived. They'd booked in for a week and as they had no car, Peter had kindly collected them from the bus in Portree.

Fi was a quietly spoken watercolour artist. Miriam, her sister, was a disgruntled motor-mouth. 'I told Fi straight If I'd known this place was in the middle of nowhere when she booked, I wouldn't have come.' Turning to Fi she imagined the worst. 'It will probably rain all week and we will be stuck here in this damp bog.'

Fi's smile was one of embarrassment and defeat. I'll try to hire a car Miriam and the forecast is not for rain, so far anyway.'

Turning to us again she had a further complaint. 'Do you have a dog?'

'No. We used to though.' I replied, wondering why she wanted to know.

'Fi forgot to ask if they had dogs, there was one lying outside our bedroom door.' Looking around the room she hadn't finished yet. 'She knows I don't like them. I'm surprised that people who have dogs themselves would take guests' dogs as well. They give dog's beds in the bedroom too. That's disgusting. So unhygienic. Inconsiderate.' She shuddered. 'The folder in the bedroom says they even have a menu for them. Ridiculous. How they got a Five Star award I'll never know.'

She was right; she would never know. I wasn't going to enlighten her, but I might have blinked a few times as I looked at John. He got the message.

The two sisters dined first, and we ate with the owners afterwards. However, it turned out to be a meal we wouldn't forget. Long, stormy island-winters can drive some to knit beautiful jumpers, paint beautiful pictures and others to excessive alcohol consumption.

The meal was delicious. Fresh scallops harvested that morning. Succulent Duck-a-L'orange, then a deliciously citrus lemon cheesecake and finally a cheeseboard with port. With the exception of the scallops, the meal had come from their freezer, having travelled in their trailer from the Inverness branch of Marks and Spencer. Nothing wrong with that, when island supplies can be unpredictable. They were ensuring high quality.

We declined Peter's insistence in replenishing our wine glasses too frequently, but he was unstinted in attending to their own wine then whisky glasses.

As the evening wore on Charmaine became incoherent. There were only so many times we could say 'Excuse me' or 'Sorry I didn't catch that'. Her voice became an unintelligible background garble as Peter and John chatted on about design and engineering. When she laid her cheek gently on her table mat, started snoring with throaty gusto and passing wind, which Peter didn't seem to mind. We decided it was time to exit.

We excused ourselves hoping to save Peter embarrassment, but further embarrassment awaited downstairs. Their dog which had been waiting too long to go outside had deposited his dump right outside our bedroom door. There was no way we could not draw his attention to it. Shovel in hand, he attended to the problem with the same matter-of-fact detachment.

Next morning motor-mouth appeared for breakfast. 'Fi has a migraine. Apparently!' Miriam announced with open disgust and a nip of disbelief at the inconvenience. We wondered if Fi was allergic to Miriam.

We headed out on a walk, but soon a chilling sea haar rolled in, so we returned to the B&B for the car to try another inland part of the Island. Peter insisted we warm up in the kitchen first. The coffee pot was going the rounds along with the whisky bottle which stood beside the sugar and milk. There was a smiling gentleman in thick socks and a chunky sweater, standing with his back to the sink. It must have been his wellingtons at the door. We recognised each other, acknowledged the coincidence and he was first to laugh.

The last time we'd met he'd stood in his doorway, looking past me at my low-slung Opel Manta. 'Bloody hell, how did you get here in that?'

'Well, my directions say to meet at your house. I didn't know your driveway was along the beach and disappeared at high tide.' Turning back was not an option once I'd committed, so I just steered my way across the larger boulders which looked wheel-width apart and thought I'd worry about the return journey later.

'You've got balls lass; I'll give you that.' he laughed.

He must also have remembered I'd failed two of his three cottages because both had well-used furniture; one had been let to a shepherd and still stank of sheep and wet lanolin-wool, and the other, with damp walls and equally old furniture, stank of chip-pan frying, it being the only cooking pot apart from the frying pan.

Relaxing around the kitchen table with them, worse was to come. Out of the drenching mist appeared another neighbour with his Irish Wolfhound. He lifted the table leg to secure the loop of the dog's lead around it. Miriam looked very uncomfortable, but she had a coffee to finish.

The huge animal lay on its side under the table, closed its eyes for some time until it wanted to stand. Its long scrabbling legs caused quite a bit of disturbance but 'Lie down boy' seemed to quieten it. Then I noticed a huge heap of recycled-dog-pellets at its rear-end, like straw-coloured porridge; no smell though.

'We should move John if we are to make anything of the day.' I instantly decided.

Miriam moved her chair back a little to let me out and looked to see why her feet were sliding. 'Oh, God. Look. Your friggin' monster has shat all over the floor and it is on my shoes now. *Aaahhhh*. Get it out of here.'

Next morning, we managed to leave without witnessing any further embarrassing incidents, reassuring them that we'd enjoyed our time with them; which was the truth. As we shook hands I said. 'What happens on tour, stays on tour. Okay?'

Peter held my hand and patted me on the shoulder, smiling knowingly.

Enthusiasm and confidence

John left at the end of our holiday, as usual, I missed him during that following week.

Driving towards Portree, I was looking out for my next destination on a quiet lane off the main road when I saw his hand waving. He was waiting at the gate for my arrival, unclicked it and climbed on as it swung wide to allow me into the driveway.

'Hello, I'm James.' He greeted me with an open smile and eyes sparkling. 'Are you Mrs MacLennan?'

'Hello James, yes I am.' He offered a handshake.

'You said 2 o'clock,' he checked his watch, 'and it is'. How did you do that? Daddy can't. He's always late.'

He offered to carry my briefcase, I let him, and he ran ahead to tell his mother that I had arrived. Mrs Jackson came to the door drying her hands on her apron. She was also a smiley person. We moved to first name terms and James asked his mother if we could have a chat now with coffee.

'I'd prefer to see your cottage first and have coffee and a chat afterwards if that's okay. Would that suit?'

He whispered to his mother 'Please, please, please ask her to have the coffee now. Please? I need to show her what I've done first.' He looked concerned, glanced at me, then to his mummy.

He was a bit young to be learning to delay gratification, so I said, 'Okay James, let's have a quick coffee first.'

His mother smiled, stroked his hair and headed off to the kitchen. James pulled away from her, as a company director might if his secretary had done that, in public.

He excused himself for a minute, ran off, returning at top speed with a pocket folder under his arm, making a jumping turn to seat himself on the sofa next to me in one practised movement. He showed me the title on the folder Rose Cottage then handed it to me. There were neat paper-clipped batches of photos of furnishings and household items removed from catalogues or magazines, some handwritten notes and printed ones.

Swinging his legs with excitement, this 10-year-old then picked out the A4 sheets. 'This is the preparation I did for your visit.'

He glanced between looking at his work and watching my face for a reaction as I scanned the pages to get an overview. The first typed sheet read:

Rose Cottage
First visit from
Scottish Tourist Board
by
James Jackson

'I found your Guidance Notes helpful, so did Mummy. I've allocated a guesstimated value; do you understand guesstimate? Partly estimate and partly a calculation of what each quality score might be?'

I nodded and told him I was very impressed. I was actually amazed at his interest in taking this on as a project.

'Everything in the cottage is brand new, therefore I imagined, wrongly actually...' Turning the page for me, pointing to his tabulated scoring sheet, holding up both palms, he continued. '...that we'd get top marks. But here was my big problem. Mummy said the furniture in Buckingham Palace would be quintessentially ten out of ten. We had to consider practicality; our furniture and carpets had to be durable and easy to clean but I think my scoring reflects that.'

He looked at me and shouted towards the kitchen. 'Mummy she's smiling. That's a good sign.'

I nodded again aware that he was eager for my response. 'This looks very thorough James.'

'I know. It is accurate, that is the important thing. I think we should be in the middle of the Four-Star range and Daddy does too. Mummy and I included him because he is paying for everything after all, but he trusted us to be circumspect and budget accordingly anyway.'

He dropped his voice to a whisper and told me they had spent just over £6,000. 'Can you believe it? And that's not including the new bathroom and kitchen. That's a substantial amount, don't you think?'

'Just think how many bicycles, computers and toys you could buy for that James.'

He moved to the carpet, lay on his tummy leaning on his elbows, both palms holding his cheeks. 'Toys don't interest me, a professional computer with a colour printer would be amazing. But a computerised robot to teach! That would be something indeed.' He laughed 'That's just a joke, you understand we wouldn't get one even for what we spent.'

He had set out a spreadsheet with appropriate headings, leaving a column for my scoring beside his own so that he could check his accuracy. It was now obvious why he wanted the discussion first.

'You are a good help for your mother James, having done all this work.'

'I know. She said she was glad of my help.' He then got up off the carpet and looked out a grocery sheet from the pack. 'We send this to guests before their arrival. We are some way from a supermarket here as you now know. The booklet recommended we offer to shop for them. It makes sense, so we do that. As we don't know the people, obviously our list may not suit them, so I have left space at the bottom of the page for their own preferences. This is proving to be popular and they just pay us when they arrive.'

He turned to the next page for me. 'The second sheet is our welcome letter.' He watched my face while I read it. 'Mummy said I could set a tray with cups and saucers with some of her home baking and go with her to welcome them. The guests certainly appreciate this. When I offered them the cakes, they cleaned the plate.' He laughed again. 'I offered to put the groceries away for them, but they said they'd manage so I just told them the milk was in the fridge for them before I left.'

I kept smiling and nodding, listening to this wee chap in amazement.

Swinging his legs with enthusiasm, he was keen to tell me more about buying the new furniture 'We bought everything, right down to the doormat and a huge van arrived with three men to unload it; one of them was so tall himself too and we wondered if he would bump his head on the door lintel. He did once. Mummy said it was as if all her Christmases and birthdays had arrived together. We had a mountain of cardboard boxes and had an amazing bonfire in the back garden. Not very protective of our planet, climate change and all that, but it was fun and won't be repeated.'

He was unstoppable and hardly took time to draw breath.

'We decided to shop in the Edinburgh John Lewis store for the essential items, rather than the Glasgow one because I wanted to also visit the statue of Greyfriars Bobby.'

His mother returned with the coffee. 'Enough James. Mrs MacLennan maybe hasn't time to listen to your story, she has to get on with her work.'

He either pretended he hadn't heard, or maybe he was so enthused, he didn't hear. 'Of course. I'm writing a story about him, giving him a secret life after his master dies. I wanted to take a photo of his statue for the front cover of my story. The statue's nose is rubbed to a polish by people touching it for luck I imagine, but I can put up with that.' He pondered 'It might make it authentic leaving the shiny nose in. Would you like to hear about it?'

'Yes, indeed I would.'

She tried to stop him again. 'Mrs MacLennan has work to do.'

He lifted his eyes to the ceiling. 'We are to call her by her first name Mummy and she did just say 'Yes indeed I would.' and she is our guest. It would be rude if I didn't tell her.'

His mother shook her head looking at me. 'I tried.'

'Everyone thinks that Bobby after his master dies of course ...' He had a thought and stopped to check. '... You do know the story?' I nodded yet again. 'Well, in the story Bobby apparently spent years lying on his master's grave and only left it to get fed. I don't believe a dog would do that; they would be too disturbed by their olfactory sensors picking up tantalising scents not to want to follow them up.' He checked again. 'You'll know about that?'

Another nod from me.

'Bobby can talk by the way, so I gave him a secret life, working with the police, helping them find criminals. He bribes another street dog which also happens to be a Skye terrier, to lie on the grave during the day, promising him bones from the butcher's shop, that is why everyone thinks he lies there all day long, and so, then he can get on with his work.'

We sipped our coffee and listened.

He continued. 'I can't say all this is original, but it does have an unexpected twist. You look old enough to remember the film Lassie; Mummy does. Bobby has a friend, I thought about calling him Laddie, but Daddy, thought that was a bit of a naff name, *'laddie* being Scottish for a *boy* you know.' He laughed again, in agreement.

'However, Bobby is Scottish and what is special about him is that he can actually pick up the scent of guilt on a person. The palms of our hands get sweaty when we are nervous, and Bobby knows this, but he can detect guilt, that is the difference. Amazing yes? So, all the police have to do is find out what he or she is guilty of. They don't know a crime has even been committed until Bobby tells them he has found a guilty person. I will give you a copy if you like?'

I smiled.

'I know, it's exciting, isn't it?' He clapped his hands. 'She wants to laugh Mummy. She looks as if she is enjoying it. Did you really enjoy it? Really, you are not just saying that to please me because I'm a child?'

'No, I like your story. I think you should let others read it too. Does your school have a magazine? Would they be interested in including it in one of their issues?'

'Yes, we have a magazine. I am the editor and publisher. I format the magazine in newspaper style, in columns. Love it. But I

170

go to High School next year. They are sending me a year sooner than my age group because I get bored with what I'm learning in Primary 6. I'm useless at drawing, but I took photos in Edinburgh. One man had a large rucksack and a red woollen ski hat. I made him the suspect. It would have been excellent if a Skye terrier had been just behind him, that would have been serendipitous indeed.'

His correct use of vocabulary; 'Oh, my goodness'. I giggled, amazed at his endless enthusiasm and ability to be so up to speed with technology too.

'My birthday is next month, and I've asked Mummy and Daddy, for a Skye Terrier so that I can take photos of him. I could train him. People do train dogs to act in films of course, and I could make my own films because this could be a whole series of adventures. Wouldn't that be exciting to do?'

'Very exciting indeed James. But ...' His mother attempted again to introduce an ending.

He sighed. 'I'll just have a biscuit then. Mummy made them. Daddy, and I think she's just the best baker. I think that is why Daddy's waistline is expanding, he can't resist your baking can he Mummy.' He offered me the plate of biscuits too.

'Let's go and see the cottage now please.' I said wanting to give his mother some backup. 'I'll need you there too James to go through your list with me. I think it is very helpful. Would that be okay Mummy?' I added.

'She's not your mummy. You can call her Jean.' he piped up. He's Not What You Think, is the title of my first story.'

'James, enough, please. I said enough now. I mean it.' She said as she removed the tea things.

Their cottage was a short walk away and it was already 5 o'clock when James led us there, pinpointing views, naming wildflowers then taking the key from his mother to open the door for us.

They got the award they wanted, and James whooped and jumped with joy. Never before, and I imagine, never again will I meet such a mature and wise old soul in such a bright and enthusiastic young boy. It must be both amazing and exhausting to be his parents.

Graduation

In the summer of 1998, I had cause for celebration. I had completed my counselling post-grad course and it was my class's graduation day. My five fellow students and I held hands along the row of seats in Edinburgh's Festival Theatre, feeling the mounting excitement just before our course was called. When I walked across the stage to receive my scroll, I felt like dancing there. John, Douglas, Steven, my mum and her husband Bobby sat in the balcony: John told me they roared and clapped their support. Coincidentally, John had been the Engineering Director on the total redesign of the Festival Theatre and had been introduced on stage on the opening night. We never thought I'd be walking across it too.

I'd fulfilled a wish I'd held since age 15: I had enjoyed my studies and had an academic qualification, something I'd coveted since then. The photographer asked me not to smile so much, he couldn't see my eyes. Afterwards, John's sister Mary and her husband Roddy joined us all for a celebration lunch at the Sheraton Hotel. I was so happy to have them all there to celebrate with me.

I'd become very close to my fellow students on the course; we'd worked well together, learning from each other as well as coursework, laughed and cried together, exorcised ghosts. I had new insights and perspectives on my life and gained more understanding of what makes me who I am.

I lived with my grandparents as a child and remembered Grandma's directive. 'You will be a shorthand typist or a comptometer operator. We don't come from a family where we go to university. Don't you get above yourself.' I'd had to leave school after only two years and one term of senior school education and had carried some resentment; I'd wanted to be a vet. I attended night school for Shorthand, Typing and English. That was the best Grandma could think of, given her own limited education and hardships. Lying in bed that evening, having finally taken off my graduation robe, I drifted off feeling contented. *Grandma, I think I would have surprised you.*

Laptop Aptitude

In 1999, we were issued with laptops and Morven, our IT girl ran workshops. I whispered to the girl beside me. 'That's the hinges your pushing. Turn the laptop around, the logo on the lid should be facing away from you. Try lifting the lid then.' How we laughed.

Downloading onto a floppy disc to send into the office? Not a problem. This felt so cool.

We had continuous coaching from Marie and Rhonda in our department. Those girls were so patient with us, supporting us via our mobile phones and one-to-one in the office.

One gentle-natured girl, who was a very good QA needed extra support. She felt very challenged. Her mastering of laptop skills was up there alongside captaining the Starship Enterprise; it was never going to happen. Months later she'd still send an email then phone to see if it had arrived. I remember her frustration exploding into slamming the laptop shut, then when asked, 'Did you save it?' threw her head back and let out a howl; like one I remember coming from a delivery room in the Simpsons Memorial Maternity Hospital.

The Homecoming

I didn't recognise the car in our driveway. I came in through the garage to leave my cases in the utility room and as I bent down a familiar voice behind me said 'Hello'.

With the joy of surprise and relief, I hugged him. Our Steven, whom I thought was still basking on a beach in Bali at the end of his year as a world traveller was safely home. I checked him over with a mother's eye. He looked very well; fit and tanned. I couldn't quite believe he was with us, kept looking and listening to him over the dinner table to see if he had changed. He was still the son we remembered, gentle, with a dry wit.

That weekend, we looked through what seemed like thousands of his photos and two videos, one of him bungee jumping and another of him jumping out of a plane and I was glad I hadn't known about this until afterwards.

He then told us. 'If I don't get a job within three months, I'm going back to Australia.'

John and I hid our sense of impending loss with smiles, but inside, although we would want to support and encourage both our sons in their chosen careers, Australia is so far away.

He had a sponsor; the man who owned a tomato farm he'd been working on. He'd got on well with this farmer and being a mechanical engineer, he'd been able to repair his tractor.

He did get a job, which would be based in Scotland, on his first interview, but was off again for nine months to Guangdong Province in China this time, on a trainee manager programme with Foxconn.

Six Temps

By 1999 our Grading Scheme had grown year on year, the membership then standing at over 9,000 and still growing. We had to recruit six temporary QAs to help with visits during the summer months. They would visit self-catering properties only and where possible, only those which had already been assessed the previous year by an experienced QA.

When this was announced at an all QA meeting, I knew they would need training. I had to restrain myself from jumping up and down like the donkey in Shrek shouting 'Pick me. Pick me.' I got my Senior QA Neil on his own afterwards, he checked it out with Richard and asked if I could be allowed to take this on. By then I'd had experience in training and supervision of counsellors and was given the task.

I decided to use our own home as a training base for the first three days because it was partly refurbished to a high standard, the rest of it having to wait until we could afford to upgrade it. They would see a range of qualities to challenge and discuss and Edinburgh had a wide variety of properties to choose from for further practice.

They were mature, likeable people, easy to be with. They'd learned very quickly, worked well and like all of us, had brought previous business and life experiences to the job. After a fast-track, two weeks' training followed by a week of work shadowing they were flying solo.

Grading Newsletter:

It was important that they didn't feel that in working alone they were abandoned. They still needed to feel connected to the department. I started a weekly newsletter for them; sharing information, topping up training notes, giving input from admin on use of the systems and included some anecdotal information and this was run out across the whole team.

Richard, Neil, Tony, Lorraine, Colin and Marie informed us on membership issues, visits done, visits still to do, hotel acquisitions, Trade Overseeing Committee decisions, Scottish Enterprise Initiatives, Area Tourist Board activities, Marketing, everything in the larger picture which was relevant. There were also regular entertaining anecdotal contributions from QA team members.

We needed a Knowledge Manager and Kim won the job against tough competition. She filtered the blizzard of information for us so that we were always up to speed and informed.

Such was the continuing surge of growth in our membership within the tourism industry that Colin reported in our internal Newsletter on 7th February 2000, a grand total of 10,596 across all sectors: Accommodation, Hostels, Visitor Attractions, Green Tourism and Holiday Parks/Caravans. This was a staggering number of properties to visit in the 1999-2000 scheme year. Those temps who were covering all the self-catering properties made the difference between completion and failure.

Fablon Fixed It

Now driving in the North West near Ullapool the windscreen wipers were in top speed, dealing with the deluge of rain as I approached my next visit.

A lady appeared at the door of the farmhouse in her cross-over apron and wellingtons as my car arrived. She was a ruddy-cheeked farmer's wife who looked like a character from a second world-war film, her flat metal curlers, not quite covered by a land-girl style headscarf. She tented a raincoat over her head against the belting rain and waved me on around to the yard at the back of the farmhouse to the letting cottage.

The overflow of cow slurry from the byre had made its own stream to the lowest point on the hard standing, forming a very large greenish-brown puddle. The only space to park out of the way of farm vehicles was close to this. I opened my umbrella and stepped out. Closed my car door I didn't hear him coming before the backs of my knees buckled.

I'd just had an exuberant punch of a welcome from their collie-cross pup. Too late. Looking at him, I just knew there would now be greenish-brown stinking skid marks down the back of my skirt and ripped tights. I turned and tried a rugby stiff-arm challenge, but this was interpreted as an invitation to wrap his paws around my sleeve. What a good game.

The lady of the farm shouted, 'Down, you stupid mutt.' and he dropped his head, wagged his tail slowly in a submissive stance and rolled over in the muck.

I asked her if I could please use her loo to change my clothes and could she keep the pup away until I left. It was still deluging, so I wore both yellow wellies.

It was a quick visit, to a very basic property. I used her 1970s long-john coffee table, covered in badly-creased sticky-backed Fablon, as an example of how to make some small improvements. 'If you were to remove the Fablon and have this table sanded down and brought back to life with teak oil, I'm sure it would look great.'

She looked at me, disbelief in her eyes. 'I put that Fablon on especially for you coming; you cheeky besom.'

Her cottage was very clean and well stocked. She was far too busy to spend time on improvements, so was happy with one star. I told her there was a market at every level provided the price was right and she was happy with that.

A Storm in Stornoway

I was returning to the Isle of Lewis on the MV Hebrides. She cut smoothly through the calm surface of the Minch like sharp scissors through silk as it rose and fell like slumbering breaths in a giant rib cage. The sunlight rolled on the surface.

A sea haar was beginning to gather, hiding the rocky landscape before we docked at Stornoway and my tyres touched the tarmac for the third summer of visits. I was returning to yet another friendly and welcoming community. Interestingly, it is the uncanny visits, the awkward and difficult visits which stand out in my memory over the years. The impressive and better ones, though I remember them too, don't seem to be as entertaining in the telling.

I spent time in the TIC collecting brochures for the places I was going to visit, giving the rush of cars pouring out from the ferry time to get away. The staff were keen and engaging as the queue at the desk steadily ebbed and tourists holding their leaflets returned to their caravans, cars and bicycles and walkers hoisted their backpacks, some to thumb a lift.

Andy, who managed the TIC had one of those expressions which is only resting from smiling. He came over to greet me. 'Well a' well, it's yourself Reta, nice to see you again. You would have had a better crossing today. I remember a greenish tinge to your face last time.' His shoulders shook with gentle laughter and I was prepared this time for the strength of his handshake.

'Hello Andy, I'm glad to be back. Ten days this time.'

He called for one of the staff to put the kettle on and gave me the news of two local businesses. One guest house owner was struggling to cope with guests after the birth of their fifth child; the second was a farm B&B where the wife had gone off to live with her husband's second cousin and had opened a B&B there now. 'Himself's not that bothered, he's got a lovely young Polish girlie in to look after the guests. They are getting on very well together, she's a gleam in her eye and he has a huge smile on his face all the time.

We both laughed.

'Oh, but we're all very well here, thankfully, and busy, busy, busy.' He continued. 'Come away into the office now, we can get some privacy. That Castaways programme on Taransay last year fairly boosted the occupancy rates; the hotels are full and getting their rack-rate, no bother. Accommodation is in demand right throughout the year now. Aye, it's been grand.'

We chatted and listening to his soft Hebridean lilt and clear diction, I was aware of tidying up my own articulation again. When our tea arrived, he sent a document to the printer and asked the girl to bring it to him.

He handed the page to me. I'd be grateful if you could manage to call in and see some of those folks on the list; they have questions I can't answer. Only if you can spare the time mind. I didn't make any promises.'

'Sure. I will if I can.'

He'd more to say. 'You'll see there's a manny on that list. You just missed him, he and his wife were here not half-an-hour ago. They have an old black house; inherited from the wife's granny. Well, it was originally a black house, but he has patched the old stonework with breezeblocks. The original stones were lying there, half-buried too, he could have lifted them and done the job properly. It still has the thatched roof right enough. The furniture has had its day though. It's the old lady's furniture they are still using. It's all looking a bit shabby now.'

I was looking down his small list and recognised the name. 'Blantside? I remember his place; I did their visit last time.'

He continued. 'Well it'll be you he's gunning for, he's not a happy man, with his two-star award. He is up from London just now, they live there, but you'll know that already and was asking if any of you folks were on the island while he's here. He wants to see someone about his grading: and here you are, holding the short straw.' He beamed.

Andy continued as I was recalling their property. 'Right cheeky he was. He was standing at that very counter with a Blue Reef brochure for that lovely new self-catering in his hand, wanting to know how they managed to get Five Stars when they have just opened. It was itching him like the midge bites. I tell you! Do you think you could squeeze in a visit to them while you are here?'

'Did you know Rhoda, Blue Reef, called into the Inverness office to show us their plans. I was very impressed by them then and more so when I visited to assess them. I'll call the Blantsides first, if I may use your office for a few minutes?'

I requested a fax of all their reports from Inverness and had them in front of me when I called Mrs Blantside, I told her I was on the island, calling her from the TIC and when she realised it was I who visited their property last, she took a quick intake of breath.

She became quite fired up. Her voice was high with anxiety. 'So, it was you who gave us this plaque with Two Stars on it?'

'Well, it would have been sent out from the Inverness office.'

'You took away our Three Stars! Why did you do that? We have changed nothing.' There was a tone of derision in her voice.

'As I explained in my report, there has been inevitable wear and therefore deterioration. I see from my colleagues' reports and my own that the areas we drew to your attention had still not been upgraded when I visited, so that is why we had to change your award.

Did I hear her sniffling? Was it a cold or was she crying? This seemed way over-the-top to be the result of my phone call or my visit which had been six months previously. Then I heard 'Give me the phone Clemmie'.

She handed it to her husband. In an angry voice, he said. 'Now listen here! My wife. She doesn't keep good health at the moment, and I won't have her upset.' *So, she was crying.* 'I was listening to your call. I will deal with you regarding our award.'

'I'm sorry to hear your wife is not well. I hope she is better soon. She mentioned your award. The one you received last February. Yes?'

'Yes. No. The report was sent to our London address but there was a Two Star plaque in an envelope to this address. We didn't see it till we got here, and your paperwork is back in London. Why have you given us only Two Stars?'

'It seems as if our admin staff sent the plaque to where it was to be displayed ....'

He interrupted me. 'Answer my question, please? We had Three Star. Why now only Two? This is nonsense. An insult.'

'I made recommendations in my report to help you have your Three Stars reinstated.'

'Yes. I gather that, and we were happy with the Three Stars. I could accept that. We have kept this house as it was when my wife's grandmother lived here. There has been no change. It - is - original. It - is - an - authentic black house. We don't think you have taken account of its authenticity. Wear and tear is to be expected.'

'I can tell you briefly what is in my report. There is a significant deterioration in the following areas: worn soft seating, cigarette burns on the kitchen worktops, a broken drawer front, a leaking shower fitting and some evidence of rot in areas on the thatch. Most of the things could be fixed fairly easily, but the thatch, that could be expensive to restore. I took account of all of that, made recommendations for you to regain the Three Stars. I think Two Stars was a fair representation of its current standard. I got your award right Mr Blantside.'

He took a moment. 'Now listen to me. I'm looking at the brochure for that Blue Reef place and we cannot see why they have Five Stars; it is too new. Ours is a piece of living history. It is unique. It is authentic, and you must accept that things get worn. Our guests don't mind. In my opinion, TVs and the internet are not what today's guests are looking for in the Western Isles. Our guests come here to get away from all that.'

'I won't discuss another member's property Mr Blantside, but. I know that many guests appreciate being able to keep in touch with their businesses, family and friends and with their TV programmes while they are away from home, I will post a copy of my report to you so that you can read it while you are here. You will see the written suggestions for upgrading.'

'You must have something against black-houses.'

'There is already a black-house, with Four Stars.' *Oh heck. I knew as soon as I said it that fanning the embers of a smouldering fire was not the thing to do.*

'Where?'

'On Skye. However, to get back to your property ...'

'That's it then. It is personal. It is probably because we are English.'

He demanded I visit them that day and he put a condition on it. 'You will reinstate our Three Stars right now. I'll come around to the office and get your signature on that, then you can jolly well visit again. Only then will I consider spending a little money here and there on improvements my lady.'

I was close to my tipping-point now but recognised it. *Stay cool. Keep Calm.* 'I can't do that. I am sorry. We do support those who are upgrading by giving them time, but you have had three years and none of our suggestions has been acted upon. Can I ask you, is your property *Listed* with Historic Scotland Mr Blantside?'

'I don't believe so. But anyway, what has that got to do with anything?'

'They may consider your cottage to be unique and authentic too. It might just be of architectural or historic interest. It would be good for you to enquire because it will affect whatever improvements you can make, externally anyway, to the thatch. There may even be a grant available.'

There was silence on the other end of the line, and I imagined he was summing up the pros and cons. I continued. 'But can I also ask you, do you have enough bookings? Yes, we certainly do. We also have friends who stay and what on earth are they going to think when Four- and Five-Star properties are sprouting up all over the place like mushrooms, and we have this insulting award?'

'Do you have repeat business?'

'Certainly, we do, we are full most of the time. We have loyal customers and no complaints.' He continued in a lofty derisive tone. 'But I can guess what's gone on, there is something behind all those high awards. And you! Well, enough said. Our friends and guests agree with us, our property is perfect as it is. They like it.'

'Well there you are, you like it as it is, you tell me your guests are happy, they agree with you. There is a valuable market at every level. If your guests like your place enough to return, consider your business a successful one. I think you should celebrate that fact and consider if you need us at all.'

'What? What are you suggesting? You are telling us to leave?'

I had to hold the phone away from my ear again.

'You'll hear more about this. He spluttered'

'You have been visited by two of my colleagues before me, you don't agree with any of our assessments. There is always an option for you to leave.'

'I will report you for insolence.'

I continued. 'Feel free to make a formal complaint. I'll make a note of your comments and mine on your file, I will quote you on saying "there is something behind all those high awards" and you think I am prejudiced against you because you are English and because I don't seem to like black-houses. I will state that I won't respond to your demand to reinstate your previous award before I visit you again. We can send you another QA next year if you like, but if you are still dissatisfied you are free to leave our scheme. I don't think I can help you further. I'm sorry to say this but I'm going to put the phone down now. I'll say goodbye Mr Blantside.'

'But.........'

Click. *Blast. I lost it. I thought I was over the menopause.*

Andy had heard the raised voice and stood open-mouthed. 'Well, that's shocking. Indeed, it is. I'm a witness if you need one. Told you he was cheeky. But I'd love your job; such power.'

I finished my luke-warm tea and let that awful phone call go.

'Oh dear, Andy. This is not the start of my time here I would have wished for.'

'Oh, I know, I know.' He folded his arms and smiled. 'It is unfortunate really, but it can only get better. After you've done that visit to Mr MacInnes anyway. I see you are going to visit him. I hope that will be the last of the difficult ones'

'Yes, I'm starting off now. To Hushinish.'

'Oh, he needs sorting out, or a bit of help, I'll tell you. Tourists are coming in here furious. He's a rascal, a right rogue. Do you know his nickname?'

I shook my head.

'Scrook.'

Scrook

I'd lost my cool with Mr Blantside. *Something's going on.* Was he thinking I'd been bribed? I felt a rising heat. In all the years I'd been working for the Tourist Board, no-one had ever hinted at a bribe: until Scrook tried, with one of my colleagues. I read the long letter she wrote after her visit last year, giving lots of advice. It finished 'Finally, I am returning the £20 I found under my briefcase in the front seat of my car.'

I had the unenviable responsibility of visiting this member. There were ten complaints in as many weeks about him, his mother and his property. We needed to visit him urgently.

His name; Scrook. John told me everyone had a meaningful nickname in Harris and when he was a boy, were better known by that name than their first names. Among his school friends there was Cocky, Crimisc, Nico, Lal and Fagan; John's was Mocan meaning little socks (his knee-high school socks always slipped down). Among the men he mentioned were Sheriff, Cooky and worst of all, Crippon, not to be mistaken with *Crippen.* The girls were not given nicknames.

I passed two cyclists straining their muscle-power with the effort of climbing the Clisham to get through the North Harris hills. I was glad I had horsepower. After that test of leg-power they would be able to free-wheel down the mile or so on the south side taking in the extensive views.

At the foot, I turned West on the single-track B887 at the start of a 16-mile single-track road with passing places. In that treeless landscape, I soon passed the tall square chimney stack of the now-derelict Bunabhainneadar whaling station, then a little later, possibly the remotest tennis court in the UK.

The Opel Manta climbed in second gear on this very narrow road, sometimes with a sheer drop on the passenger side, at other times so steep my car bonnet was pointing at the sky and I'd no idea which way the road was going to go, stretching my neck to get the first hint of a bend to the right or left or straight ahead.

The road almost passes over the doormat of Amhuinnsuidhe Castle and two Land Rovers were parked there, a large party of gentlemen in shooting gear standing around them, champagne flutes in their hands. I felt like saying 'Yes, thank you, I'd love a glass.' as my car cut in on their party.

A grocery van had pulled up at a cottage and the sheep had come running, gathering at the open door, the tiny lambs staying close to their mother. As I waited for them to disperse, I was amused by them; their trotters, like black ballet-shoes tap, tap tapping on the tarmac as they danced around on their points.

No champagne, I had to make do with a snicker bar and a bottle of water and had no idea about the cost of either item. The van man had no price displays, he just massaged his forehead, muttering and placing his hand on the chocolate and the bottle, then out popped the total. 'That will be £1.50 thank you.'

I passed a cottage with a caravan beside it, roped down against the wind and the start of breezeblock walls being built around it.

Soon after, when out of the wind, I pulled over to eat my snack and out climbed my wing-mirror spider to repair his web. I'm one of the millions of car owners who have that variety of travelling spider. I watched it rebuild its web, as it had done for several years now, though I couldn't say if it was even the same spider. I never saw any insects caught in the web, just rips which were repaired when I stopped.

I refreshed my memory of the record-breaking ten complaints in Scrook's file; grouping them into categories. I formulated an approach with this man, whom the reports indicated was a hard-drinking owner. I wanted to try and achieve a good outcome for both of us.

Driving on, my car wound its way around rocky outcrops, past lochans of dark-brown peaty water, some no bigger than a domestic swimming pool and peat bogs with peats air-drying on the moors ready for stacking. The expansive views across to Taransay changed as my car rose to cliff tops and dropped to empty stretches of white sand with the blinding light on the

Atlantic stretching to the horizon. Scrook lived in Huishinish at the end of this single-track road.

I arrived. Scrook was sitting on his doorstep in the sunshine. I parked on his worn patch of grass to check that I was at the right place. 'Mr MacInnes?'

'Aye, it is.' Pulling the last possible draw from the cigarette stub cupped in his palm he then tossed it away and walked over to my car in his slippers, dungarees splattered with what looked like tomato soup, and a long-sleeved flannel semmit, brown under the armpits.

He took my hand in his calloused grip and clasped it with the other, holding on just too long. I introduced myself as Mrs MacLennan, wishing to keep a more formal approach.

'Well, a-well, it is good to meet you. I'm glad you've come. We are way out on the edge of the world here and I need you to bring me the tourists. I hope you are going to do that for me now. Are you?'

'I will try my best Mr MacInnes.' I smiled but felt wary. He had whisky breath. This confirmed one of the complaints.

'Come away over then and we'll see what's what.'

He turned, and I followed his carefully measured stride. His chalet was a timber flat-pack single garage, likely bought from a catalogue, the would-be car-access doors permanently closed by a strong batten. He led me around to the side door which had no lock.

'Before you say anything, we don't need locks out here.'

The rectangular interior was divided by one thin timber wall to my left. Two doors on this wall led to two bedrooms side by side. The first bedroom was so small the double bed duvet touched the walls. The second had bunk beds but space was so tight, sidestepping would be the only way to negotiate the ladder to the top bunk.

On my right, on the other side of the main area in the far corner was a shower room, leaving an L-shaped floor space forming the living, dining and kitchen area. Comfortable seating was only for two people, on a small sofa which faced the wall of the shower-room and the cooker sat beside it. No worktop, just the cooker.

I spent time listening to him. He found his life difficult and listed his ailments. We chatted about the wonderful location with the view of the white sandy beach just outside the window. I complimented him on the quality of furnishings, bed linen, carpets, ensuite facilities and the cleanliness. They were all very good. But we both knew what was coming next.

'You will know that when my colleague visited you in the Spring, she gave you a list of things to do.'

'Yes, yes indeed I do.'

'I need to talk to you about them and the many complaints we have received since then Mr MacInnes.'

He nodded 'Yes, yes indeed. I know all about them and I will explain. You see people don't understand what it is like to live here, there are no jobs and we have to do what we can to attract the tourists and they look for a lot for the money I charge. Aye, they do that.'

He advertised his accommodation as being suitable for four people, but it wasn't. 'Some of these complaints claim it's too small and they also complain about the lack of facilities for four people. I have to agree with them. There are only two chairs for the small dining table and this two-seater sofa. Four people need ….'

He interrupted, shaking his head and sucking in a long breath. 'Aye, that would be right. But common sense should tell them there is no room for more seats. That is just common sense, and they should understand that. I would have put more in if I could.' He emphasised this by pointing here and there. 'It's fine. Just fine. They should be out and about anyway.'

'I have a suggestion for you. But it is a big one. If you were to remove those bedroom partitions, do away with the bunk beds and ….'

'Bugger that, I put these walls up last year, they are not coming down for you, or the likes of you. No, No, I won't do that now. Not for nobody.

'All right, it is just a suggestion. But hear me out, if you did away with the bunkbeds, kept the double bed and had an open-plan arrangement, that would free up space. You could advertise it for two ...'

He interrupted again 'For two. Just two. But I'd get less money then. That's just plain daft. I need more money lass, not less. You bring me the tourists first and I might think about it.' He thumbed his cap back a bit, vigorously scratching his head, making low moaning sounds in Gaelic, then slapped his thigh with his cap: I recognised the Gaelic 'gu sealladh ort' meaning for goodness sake, which I'd heard my mother-in-law use when she didn't like my way of doing things.'

'I can understand that you don't want to undo what you have just built and that you need the income. But I've heard in the TIC there is a boom in tourism since the Castaways programme on Taransay and there are not many places just for two people. The quality of what you have is very good. They would enjoy the increased space. We need to find a solution which does not generate complaints. Think it over and see if you can come up with any ideas yourself.'

He paced up and down. After waiting a few moments, I continued. 'I notice the TV is on the draining board at the sink, that's not very safe. It is not possible to see it from the sofa anyway because it is tucked around the corner.'

He nodded in agreement, looking at the floor, muttering 'It is only there because you folks ask for one. It is not plugged in. We don't get a signal out here.'

'You could remove it then. A radio would be good instead. You also advertise an open fire.'

He shook his head as if to clear his thoughts. 'I know. I know there is no open fire, that's as plain as the nose on your face. But you see, if I say there is, it attracts them to come, everyone likes an open fire.'

He continued. 'But I know what the real problem is. You see, everyone is different, some people are not bothered about what is here, they just enjoy the shore, the walking.' Then his hands balanced like scales. He was weighing the weather. 'If it is sunny and warm, they are out and about and there are no complaints. Everything is grand. If it is raining, they come to my door with long faces asking for a refund. Aye. They're terrible that way. That is how it is. If I had a direct line to Himself up there, I would get them edge-to-edge sunshine, so I would.'

I was really struggling with his defensive logic. While I checked my notes, he strode to the window, looking out to sea, then turned and strode out through the door. I heard him outside shouting, either at the imaginary guests or at my list, raising his voice, speaking in Gaelic.

Coming back in, he folded his arms across the soup stains with an angry drawing-in of his brow. He looked down on me, sitting on the sofa. 'But a refund! The cheek of them. Refund! I tell them, no I'll not give you that.' He was indignant and agitated. This, of course, concerned parting with money he'd already been paid. 'So, I tell them straight ...', emphasising his annoyance with a nicotine-stained finger '... like I'm telling you now, it's the weather that upsets them. That is just how it is.' Then added 'Now.' as if closing the issue.

I stood, to be on his level and walked past the whisky fumes to the view from the window again. I quietened my voice hoping it would calm his mood. 'I'd like to help you with your advertising, filling in the tourist board form: TV, open fire, we will remove those items, washing machine and dryer, I'll come to those in a minute *What was I thinking about, I was dodging the bigger issue. It just wasn't the right moment yet though.*

'Well, again, as I said, they can't have everything at the price I charge. I'm depending on you lass, that's just how it is, and the view is lovely.'

His voice faded into a worried and disappointed tone. I felt quite sorry for him; he needed the income. He had built the chalet, was hoping for a good business, seemed to struggle with an alcohol problem and was perhaps slow-witted or wily, or both? But I had a job to do to ensure his guests were treated well.

'Let me read you this letter. "We booked the chalet but were put into a damp caravan beside his house because he had others in the chalet. It was covered in mildew and had only a chemical toilet." Would that be the same caravan I see there?'

'Yes indeed.'

'So, you are taking double bookings for the chalet,'

'Well, I wouldn't call it that, not exactly, some are quite happy in the caravan, and it is only for a few days anyway till the others move out. They don't stay the whole week some of them and I give them it a bit cheaper for those days.' He had a nervous tick, screwing up both eyes now. He thrust his hands deep into the pockets of his dungarees and clinked his change, swaying back and fore, then gave a little stagger backwards. 'What am I supposed to do then if people leave before the end of the week is up, let it stand empty? It works fine most of the time.'

I was making no headway. 'But it doesn't work fine.' I took slow breaths to compose myself. 'Mr MacInnes. They are writing to us to complain.'

'Ah, well they would. They think writing to you will get them their money back, but I know it can't. Isn't that right now?'

'But two lots of guests pay you for the same week and that.' I chose my word carefully 'is dishonest.'

He stood looking out the door, rocking on his heels and only said 'Ocht'.

I addressed another complaint, trying a different tack. 'I will read you this letter from a lady who was frightened. "There was supposed to be a washing machine and we wondered if it was in his house. I went to the door and got no answer. I opened the door and called to Mr MacInnes. He chased me away with an empty whisky bottle in his hand." Mr MacInnes, if you were me with a complaint like that, what would you do?'

'I wouldn't believe them, not one word of it. You give me their name and address and I'll write to them myself. I'll save you the trouble of telling them that they are black-hearted down-and-out liars. My old mother is at their beck and call every daylight hour God sends and they had no right chasing after me in my own home.'

'But is that where the washing machine is?'

'Aye, it is.'

'Does your mother have English as well as Gaelic Mr MacInnes?'

'Yes, we all do nowadays.'

I flicked to the last complaint; 'One lot of guests say here that she spoke only Gaelic so couldn't understand us.'

'A well, she maybe didn't have her hearing aids in, so she wouldn't know if they were speaking Gaelic, English or Russian.'

I felt appalled. I'd not moved his perspective one tiny bit. While he was under the influence of his favourite tipple, he was not going to listen to my reasoning. So, I summarised concisely, knowing full well that he was not going to like the kind of help I was going to offer.

'Okay here is where we are: if you are in our membership and people book the chalet you cannot put them in the caravan, you cannot take more than one booking for any one period of letting and you cannot advertise facilities which you do not have.'

'Oh, no? Indeed, I will. It suits me fine. You're just too swanky to see it from where I'm standing. And I'll tell you, for most of them it's hunky-dory. As I said it's the weather.'

I ignored this. 'We have a ruling Mr MacInnes, three complaints in any one year and you are automatically removed from the scheme. You have ten and because of this, I have to withdraw your award now. We are happy to come back and regrade you next year, but you would have to adhere to the rules. I need you to sign this form for my visit and I will write to you confirming what we discussed.'

'Are you standing there, having driven all this way to tell me that. What use are you then? I'd have been as well throwing the money I paid you in my fire. You are going to do nothing for me then is that right?'

'I am going to write to you covering all the things we have discussed. The TIC staff in Stornoway need to know this outcome so I will tell them when I am next up there. You have the whole of the coming winter to think about it all and make those changes. They will benefit you in the long run. You'll see.'

His rage peaked. 'Well, you can just get back in your posh car and get out of my sight. I knew right away when I saw you in that sporty car and your tight city skirt that you were not going to understand what life is like here. You have no idea. Have you?'

'But I do. My husband is a Herach, like yourself, born and grew up in Northton.' I passed him my pad with crosses marking where to sign, and a pen. 'Would you sign here please for my visit?'

'I'll sign nothing. And married to a Herach are you, well he made a poor choice of a wife, so he did.'

'I'm off now Mr MacInnes, I came to help you but, well, I tried.' The way to the door was clear so I stepped outside, my heart thumping in my chest, my cheeks flushed, a bit afraid of him. He followed me, bellowing in Gaelic, with the words, *telephone* and *boss* leaving me in no doubt about what he was saying.

A rush of hot air escaped from my car as I dropped myself onto the sun-heated driver's seat. He thumped the boot then worked his way along to grab my door as I tried to close it, vocalising his anger in English. 'I could bash you, so I could.'

I was afraid now and pulled my door handle hard. His hand slipped off; he staggered away a few steps before his knees buckled and he disappeared below the window. I fumbled with the ignition key, started the engine and moved slowly forward. My spider was bouncing on its web on the wing-mirror as I checked where he was. He was clear of the car, getting to his feet, so I took off before he had a chance to come for me again.

My exit was hampered by two sheep which had been watching, chewing the cud. I had to brake. They trotted out of my way but onto the road, running in front of me, so I had to drive slowly behind them until they chose to turn aside. *Stupid bloody animals.*

He was up, his mouth moving in a silent shout and arms flailing. It must have been his old mother I saw running towards him, waving a dish towel.

I couldn't shake off a gut-churning feeling of a horrible experience for some time after that visit. It followed me like a shadow. I wondered if I could have handled it better. The major difference between my counselling work and this job was one of rules; you join the club you play by the rules. By the end of the week, I was able to tell John about it and see the funny side. Black humour indeed.

Several weeks after I sent my report, I opened a handwritten scrawl.

'Dear Mrs MacLennan,

I hope you are well, as this leaves me here. Next time you are on the island I will show you what I am doing DV. *(God willing)* You will be pleased to know that things will be better next time. I want the tourists to come back and will be good to them. I have seen the doctor too and my ailments are being cured as I write.

Respectfully yours,

Sheamus MacInnes.'

John and I returned to Harris on holiday the following May with our son Douglas and his partner Eva. We called in at the TIC. Andy and John chatted in Gaelic, then I saw Andy wink at him. 'Now Reta, I have a very big favour to ask you, but I know you are on holiday.' He held out an envelope of photos to be returned to Scrook. 'John tells me you are going down to Northton to stay at your cousin Donald John's old home, and it is a grand drive out to Huishinish from there.'

'Oh, ho, ho. Andy, I'd normally love to help but as you say, we are on holiday.'

I looked at John. His quiet smile told me this had fired his curiosity to meet the local rascal. 'If you just want me to drop off some photos. We'll go then, he said.'

What a surprise. Scrook had made vast improvements: the chalet was doubled in size now with a new entrance and a small landing facing the beach. There was no sign of the old caravan.

His mother, a diminutive old cailleach, her face lined and weathered by decades of salty wind and sun, answered my knock that afternoon. Standing on the doorstep, she clasped my hand and addressed me in Gaelic. She didn't change to English as I enquired after her son and asked if he was around, so I beckoned to John, to translate. She held onto his hand while attempting to place him, looking for a connection to family or friends.

Meanwhile, there was a croaky, coughing voice from inside the house. 'Is that you Mrs MacLennan, wait there I'll be with you in a minute.' He appeared wearing wide-legged old-fashioned white underpants, a checked shirt with dried blood all down the front and a pair of mismatched socks. He had a black eye, a badly bruised cheek and a swollen cut lip. 'Come in, come in and sit yourself down.' he beckoned from the hallway.

I was more than reluctant. 'I can't stay Mr MacInnes, I'm on holiday and am here with my husband and family. Andy at the TIC asked me to return these photos to you.' I handed them over. 'I've got you out of bed and I don't want to disturb you. I'll come back another time, but I can see you have been hard at work with improvements to the chalet. It is looking very good.'

His mother, her English having returned, said. 'Come away over with me and see the improvements now.' Then she linked John's arm leading him over to the chalet.

Just at that, the phone rang in his hallway. 'Stay there a minute please, please. Don't go, stay there, I won't be a minute.' He reached for the phone and I stayed while John was on his way with the mother.

'Hello, hello. Oh, it is yourself, doctor. He listened, Aha, aha, aha. I want you to give me more pills, you didn't give me enough last time.' He listened again. 'Aha, aha, aha, well I can't be going up to Stornoway so often, the petrol is so expensive.' A pause again. 'Aha aha, aha. Oh well, it is like this. I would have to give them petrol money, so I can't do that either. ... Aha aha aha, ... well, I can explain. You see, I was going over to Bernera and I was afraid I would lose them in my pocket, so that is the only reason I took them all at once. I won't do that again. I take them one at a time now, as usual. Yes. With water.'

'There is no need for the nurse to call, I'm fine'. ... Aha aha aha. ... Well yes, I did have a fall, but how did you hear of that?' Another pause while he listened again. 'Oh, they make up stories, so they do, I just tripped that was all. So, could you post them to me? ... Aha aha aha. Oh well just give them to Lachi, he'll bring them to me. Will that do? Well then, I am much obliged and thank you, doctor, thank you, thank you. Goodbye now.'

He replaced the receiver. 'Come away in now, come in.'

'You go back to bed Mr MacInnes. Your mother is over there showing my husband around, so I will just join them for a minute, then we'll be off. You stay where you are, and I will see myself across. I will call on you right enough when I'm next on the island, so I will.' *Goodness, I was mimicking again. How patronising.*

I could understand his keenness to let me see the improvements, so screwing his face up, he crossed the pebbles, his socks giving little protection, calling 'I'm coming, I'm coming.' John, Douglas and Eva turned and just stared. They made no comment. Neither did his mother. She seemed unfazed by his appearance.

There were two good sized bedrooms, a sofa bed with two armchairs. A much-improved layout and a dining area.

He stood wheezing and coughing beside us.

'I am so pleased to see the improvements, what a lot of work.' I enthused.

'I keep it spick and span.' His mother added. 'His chest and his legs are bad now, so he can't work at the moment. This will keep him going and the money from the Social and a bit from the tourists will let him pay up the furniture and leave him a bit for himself. Where are you from again?' She raised her eyebrows. 'You are not from the Social, are you?'

'No, the Tourist Board Mrs MacInnes.'

'Oh, the Tourist Board. We are hoping the people who come will write good reports to you folks. Those rascals who came before were just as low as that floor there, so they were.'

Like many crofts with a modern house, the original black house falls into disrepair or is recycled as a hen house or store. The MacInnes's one looked renovated. It stood well back from the new-look chalet, had a bright red corrugated roof, white painted walls with pretty curtains on the windows. As we drove off, John told me that he had asked her about the old black house at the back.

'Oh, that! Ocht! It is just for the sheep.'

Many years later, when I had retired, and our own B&B was well established, I was telling two of our guests about Scrook. They announced, 'That would have been him we saw, sleeping in the phone box when we were there."

Ladies Beware

Towards the end of the millennium, we were being trained in the use of the world wide web. One gentleman colleague had been looking for certain items of dress for his Edwardian evening-wear outfit and discovered that his Glasgow supplier had closed up shop. He tried an internet search and was quick to inform us of its dangers in our QA Newsletter. Typing *stiff* and *collar* and *studs* into the search box produced an amusingly shocking result and he warned 'lady colleagues of a delicate nature, beware of the dangers which lie in wait in using the internet'. The Tourist Board firewall was playing catch up obviously.

Scottish Tourist Board News Bulletin 2000

'On 16 February the BBC announced: "Enterprise Minister Henry McLeish pledged £11m to boost the industry in Scotland, £5m of which is to improve marketing and put tourism online. The internet is seen as key to the growth of the tourism industry and the jewel in the Scottish Tourist Board's crown, is project Ossian. A central database, which is scheduled for launch in June, will hold information on all the tourism products and services in Scotland."'

Project Ossian

When Google went live on 4th September 1998 people took a while to understand the power of the internet; potential for business growth, worldwide advertising was at their fingertips. Some B&B and small self-catering owners couldn't imagine it would bring them more customers. They couldn't yet grasp the fact that by investing in an attractive website and having it optimised, put them on the same playing field as the big boys. Furthermore, by standing still, they would, in effect be moving backwards.

Some enterprising local Area Tourist Boards enticed members to attend their workshops and those seemed to be well supported but QAs could reach those who didn't attend. On our one-to-one visits, we now had to encourage them to have a good profile on the Ossian site; it was their shop windows.

Foot and Mouth Disease

In February 2001 Foot and Mouth Disease was found to be present in pigs in Essex. By March there were cases in Northern Ireland and Scotland and on 30th September the BBC announced 'The epidemic reaches the six-month mark with 3,750,222 animals slaughtered. The tourist industry says businesses have lost trade estimated at £250m.'

International news channels repeatedly showed one dramatic picture of pyres of burning carcasses, the animals' legs silhouetted black against a flame-filled night sky, the rising smoke forming clouds. We could only imagine the smell. Those pictures could have given the impression that the whole of the UK was one massive animal bonfire.

Farmers who had bred their own healthy stock were deeply affected by the cull which was intended to prevent further spread. Its impact on UK agriculture and tourism was devastating and a few farmers, heartbroken, were driven to suicide.

From March onwards that year, through the whole summer we were unable to visit any properties which required crossing land where animals grazed. B&Bs, holiday cottages, caravanning facilities, bothies and hostels used by walkers in hill grazing areas were all out of bounds.

Even before this tragedy, some livestock farmers had been struggling to survive. With the diversification grants which were available, some opened farm shops selling their own meat and dairy products; ice-cream, yoghurts and cheeses. They would attend all day, in all weathers at stalls in Saturday farmers' markets offering their own produce for sale there too.

Some who already provided B&B in their homes and self-catering in their farm cottages had also opened their farms as visitor attractions. We saw playgrounds and picnic areas created, even the construction of a yew maze in progress. Now all those alternative means of income were hit by the ban on entry to farmlands. Farming communities despite having been innovative were hit financially in all their diversified industries. It was catastrophic for them.

We phoned those businesses, read their previous year's reports offering to carry their awards forward to the next year. We noted those who had invested in improvements, promising an early confirmation-visit so that they would be advertised with their upgrade if that was the outcome. It was October before that happened, a whole seven to eight months before Scotland's countryside was open again for business.

Driving in the countryside now the views had changed; the grass grew long on the empty fields where livestock had grazed, hedged remained untrimmed and fences lay untended.

Just A Slip-Up

I was glad of city work that summer and in Inverness, I had to explain to one couple who owned a guest house that the Four Stars plaque I saw displayed beside the front door should not have been sent to them. They should have had a Three Stars one and I was not looking forward to telling them this. It had been a rare admin cock-up.

'Well, we just have to accept it. That is just life isn't it.' the husband said.

'The neighbours will think we have slipped in our standards.' the wife said.

'Never mind pet, we'll not make a fuss, we'll just do what we have to do to improve. It was just a mistake. We can all make mistakes.' the husband said.

'Okay love. You are right. We can all make mistakes.' the wife said.

I should have asked them to take the plaque down, but they were only a few points off the required score. Instead, I gave them ideas to consider. Power-wash the algae off the path to the front door, refresh the paint on the window frames, add more extras to your bedroom accessories, use fabric napkins instead of paper ones, and a few other things which did not require a major investment and they would creep into the Four-Star band. They were eager to do that, so I offered to return as soon as the work was done and have their new award processed. That felt like a win-win with that lovely couple.

A Free Presbyterian Welcome

The Western Isles escaped the Foot and Mouth disease and cars arriving off the ferries at the Stornoway terminal had to go through a disinfection process.

I arrived at my Stornoway B&B with my mother just after 8 o'clock on a Thursday evening. It was her birthday that weekend and I had collected her off the train at Ullapool, having invited her to join me as a birthday treat.

She would be happy sitting in the car while I worked on Friday, reading her book or taking a stroll and had been coached on avoiding making any comments on the quality of anything on tonight's overnight stay.

I had a moment's concern that her holiday was not getting off to a good start when I saw a message left hanging out of the letterbox at the B&B.

It read 'Dear Mrs MacLennan, A very warm welcome to you both. I've banked up the fire. There are some cakes and a few biscuits for you on a tray by the fireside. I've plugged the kettle in for you beside the TV and will be back as soon as I can.'

When she arrived, she was so apologetic. 'What a welcome to give you, I am so sorry I wasn't here. I was at a church prayer meeting. I might have asked the other guests to look after you had they been in, but that wouldn't have been right either.'

She sat with us for a while telling us what to see and do in the area and before leaving, made another apology. 'I have only one tomato left to go with your bacon and eggs in the morning. The other guests don't have any, so you can have a half each.

The delivery of fresh food flies off the shelf once the ferry has restocked the Co-op and I thought I had enough, but it has been very busy this week with tourists. So, you are on rations.' She laughed and had such an open and honest attitude, that having half of a large tomato was just fine. Her free-range hens' eggs had yolks the colour of an orange sun and the home-made preserves and her smiling service were a joy to experience.

Bird Watching

I had the week-end off and there were two places I had planned to take Mum. We had lunch at The Cross, the most northern pub on the Hebrides and asked the owner for directions of how to view the nesting colonies of seabirds. It was near the end of the nesting season, but there was still plenty of activity to see.

We crawled on the grass on our hands and knees to look over the top of the cliff. The cacophony of calls from common gulls, kittiwakes, fulmars and others I couldn't identify, was loud and constant. Well-feathered chicks still called from rocky ledges and a young common gull sat beside pink thrift almost within touching distance, quite unperturbed by our presence. Parent birds, wings flapping in reverse for landing, fed their hungry chicks and took off again in the uplift of air.

But the stench of the guano also drifting upwards on the air was potent, so we didn't stay long.

Callanish Standing Stones

John had given me his very comfortable Mercedes for that Hebridean visit as my car was in need of some small repairs before passing its MOT. Mum and I were both enjoying purring along in the comfort of this luxury car as we made our way to the West of Lewis looking out for the Callanish Standing Stones. There was no signage at that time, so I slowed to a stop at one point noticing two local gentlemen leaning on a field gate, just seeming to be passing the time.

Mum wound her window down a bit and asked, 'Could you tell us if we are on the right road for the Callanish Standing Stones please?'

One of them put his hand behind his ear to try and catch what she'd said.

I asked her to wind the window down further and pulled on what I thought was the handbrake. My seat shot backwards. The car kangarooed to a stop and Mum screamed. My feet had lost contact with the accelerator and clutch. In the panic, it took me a few seconds to understand that I'd pulled up the seat lever.

They heard us very well after the engine had stalled and just answered by pointing along the road. They were both shaking their shoulders with laughter and one of them took off his cap to wipe his eyes with it.

Those standing stones are thought to originate in the Neolithic era and while walking along the main avenue towards their centre. I marvelled at their size and structure. They stand on higher ground than the surrounding moorland and must have been transported there from some distance. The hewing, hauling and erection of those massive stones would have taken some strong manpower, knowledge and skill.

A creepy feeling came over me as I thought about the ritual ceremonies which were thought to have been performed there during the Bronze Age. The antidote to this feeling was remembering my colleague Kim's story which she heard when visiting a croft B&B close by.

A German lady returned to stay there every year around midsummer. She rose early each morning as dawn lightened the sky before sunrise; spent time among the stones, resting her cheek on them hugging them, running her fingers along their lines.

Curiosity led the crofter to ask her why she did this. The woman, with a serene, calm demeanour, talked about the spiritual atmosphere and the energy she felt from being near the stones and touching them. His typical islander response was 'I get the same feeling from a cup of tea and a Kit-Kat!'

South Harris Visit

Mum and I drove on south through the Harris hills feeling the tranquillity and seclusion when there were periods without another car on the road and the rocky landscape in late summer carried hues of pink to purple in heathers, and tufts of white bog cotton being shaken by the breeze.

Corncrakes rose from the boggy machair by the roadside as we approached Scarista House, our accommodation for the night. It sat almost on the edge of the ocean; the effects of the Atlantic gales evident in their garden where all vegetation was wind-trimmed to the height of the wall. From there, it was rowing distance to the Isle of Taransay where the BBC filmed the programme Castaways. Rumour had it that the TV celebrities came back and fore regularly to relieve their boredom.

We had a barefoot walk on the white sands that afternoon and a flock of lapwings rose from the shorter machair grasslands alongside Scarista Links Golf Course. There were four golfers playing that day; a rare one with no high wind, just blue sky and hot sun.

Unlike other links courses, this one was not designed by man. This nine-hole course is natural, being sculpted by the effects of the sea and windblown sand. There is an honesty box into which anyone wishing to play deposits £10. Nick Faldo played there once in the early 1990s when the green fee was £5. He signed his £5 note and since then the club members have competed annually for the Faldo Fiver.

The owner of Scarista House at that time, Alison Johnson, had written a book 'The House by the Shore' about their experience of converting this old Georgian manse into a small hotel. I had booked this stay for Mum a few weeks before, deliberately, because it was not in our grading scheme: I would have no report to write and I thought Mum would enjoy a birthday treat of staying where Prince Charles had once rested his head.

Unfortunately, I'd chosen the very night the Johnsons had off. Instead of the room with a view of the bay which I had booked, the main house was full, and we had been decanted to the annexe behind the house. The food was disappointing, quite bland for a place with such a good reputation; Scotch broth, a lamb casserole and diced root veg and mash, followed by a very basic apple crumble. Maybe all pre-cooked so that the staff only had to heat and serve it.

The only glimpse of the Johnsons we got was when Mr J. came running down the stairs carrying their black Labrador on its side with tongue lolling, Mrs J. ahead of him shouting 'Out of the way'. Their dog was obviously sick: a bit like I felt after the disappointing room and evening meal.

Delivering Training in South Africa

In 2001 South African Tourism had invited Tony, our Head of Department and Richard, the Chief QA to visit a range of their accommodation with a view to adopting our Hotel Grading Scheme. Their own one had been abandoned because of lack of support from the industry.

I flew off to South Africa for two weeks to conduct a hotel training programme and was met by their previous Chief Inspector at Johannesburg airport. We drove to Sun City where *WOW* kept running through my mind. I was allocated the superior suite looking out from the double balcony onto the estate and surrounding hills. The decor shouted Africa, with animal skin furnishings, rugs and bronze gazelle lamps, the most exotic hotel in which I have ever stayed.

Prince Charles in Scarista House? I slept in the room in which Mandela had stayed.

My host and I walked from the terrace into the dining room, the doors of which were large enough for an elephant to pass through. The kudu steak I had for dinner tasted like venison, gamey but much lighter in flavour and the glossy jus was smooth with great depth. I could have run my finger over the plate and licked it. I didn't.

I floated to my bedroom on a cushion of contentment after dinner, probably also influenced by the bottle of Boschendal Shiraz/Cabernet Sauvignon we shared.

Thankfully, on the way to my room, I didn't trip on crossing the steppingstones, looking down at the golden carp in the shallow pool below. A chambermaid was waiting outside my bedroom door and came in with me to see if everything was to my satisfaction. In my room the bedside lights were lit, the TV programme lay opened at the current evening's page. My nightdress was laid out on the bed, scattered with rose petals. I'd been *petalled* and thanked her with a tip.

In the bathroom, the wash basin had a floating candle burning along with a few more rose petals strewn on the hand-hot water. I slid down into the six inches of foam on my scented freshly drawn bath with candles flickering on the ledges and drifted off to sleep.

The impeccable timing of when to fill my bathtub must have been communicated from the dining room, while we had our digestifs with coffee. That night, after my long flight, it was like arriving in paradise.

The breakfast buffet was indeed world class too: every salad and fruit I recognised and some I didn't were there, with a cornucopia centrepiece overflowing with oranges, grapes, guavas, persimmons and nuts. The service at both meals was outstanding, unobtrusive and very attentive.

Most of the SA course attendees were ex-hotel inspectors from their old scheme. I detected an inspectorish culture, an I-know-best kind of arrogance in one or two but in others, a real willingness to embrace our system of measuring quality as well as facilities. I also hoped to put across the ethos of our consultative approach; building a supportive relationship which would hopefully encourage continuous improvement where needed and follow-up visits after the first initial incognito one.

The first training course was in the Rosebank hotel in Johannesburg, the second in the Victoria and Alfred on the Waterfront in Cape Town. I escaped on my own for an hour one evening and strolled along to the waterfront. It was buzzing with life in the warm evening sunshine; the bars, restaurants, music, impromptu dancing in the street and smiling people created a really joyous holiday atmosphere.

We'd been given the use of a large suite of rooms as our classroom. We discussed what contributed to being world class standard: Five Stars. There were 50 scoring areas needing to be justified; a minimum of 93% achieved overall. Housekeeping had to achieve a 10 out of 10, all service elements had to score 9 or 10 and no item could score less than and 8.

On a practical level, I set tests for checking housekeeping standard in both hotels. No-one picked up on any of the three things I'd planted. A pair of my shoes left under a bed, the high-quality soap beside the wash basin had been used, or that I'd placed a crumpled tissue in one of the pockets of a bathrobe, an indicator that housekeeping staff had not checked the bathrobes: they would not have been laundered. Any of those small housekeeping oversights could be objectionable to guests who've paid to experience the best. Appropriate questions to ask management would be, were they missed by an individual member of staff? Is a supervisor checking? Is this a training problem?

We were assessing the lunch and dining room services during a working lunch in the V&A. The restaurant was full and our lunch which was booked to be within a one-hour slot, overran by three-quarters of an hour. Where did the problem originate? Communications: between Front-of-House staff and Kitchen? Understaffed in kitchen or dining room?

Only one waiter placed our food correctly in front of us without having to ask who is having what? Was he trained here, or had he brought that skill from elsewhere?

We should have returned to the suite of rooms with all those questions prepared for the hotel manager to help him identify the source of the breakdown and offer solutions where appropriate.

All course attendees were white South Africans except for two, one in Johannesburg and one in Cape Town. With the new regard for equality in the post-apartheid Rainbow Nation and the Black Economic Empowerment policy, their tourist organisation was told this was not acceptable. Considering this, I was asked to return and conduct another week of training to correct the balance. We were already pushed to complete visits for the current year-end in Scotland so returning to SA was not possible.

I was invited to be one of the guest speakers at their forthcoming Annual Tourism Conference. However, the gentleman heading up the arrangements disappeared from office a few months later: we never learned why.

Promotion

A position as a Senior QA was advertised. I had useful transferable skills in training and supervision from my counselling years by this time and had already trained the six temporary QAs. In the tourist board job, I enjoyed the travelling, loved meeting interesting people, it was sometimes great fun and it offered an employee pension scheme to full-time employees only.

My part-time job as a trainer and supervisor in counselling felt rewarding, very useful and I worked with Meg and Mary, those amazing women. Having to focus on one job would be simpler to manage, so on balance, the pension swung the decision for me. I was interviewed by Tony and Richard and got the job.

Along with two other SQAs, I would now manage a team of ten QAs and would be based in the Inverness Office one week in three. I'd resolve membership queries and complaints, review and consider all upgrades and downgrades as the resident member of

ARC (Award Review Committee) for that week. I would also be the account manager for several hotel groups.

One of my first assignments was to read submissions, visit restaurants and choose three finalists in the Best Restaurant category for the Scottish Thistle Awards which recognised and celebrated excellence in Scottish Tourism. A real pleasure.

Thistle Award Ceremony

At the award ceremony at the Edinburgh Conference Centre, I co-hosted a table of finalists with my colleague and friend Colin. Always the attentive host, he made sure everyone's glasses were kept topped up. As he drew his arm back after replacing a bottle in its cooler, his elbow caught my full glass of red wine and tipped it down my gold silk top where it then puddled in my lap and seeped right through my full-length, silk evening skirt and onto the chair.

My white napkin was now pink but the lady journalist sitting to my left, with one corner of her false eyelashes coming loose, splashed her white wine over the puddle. 'That should help.' she smiled. She was a guest, so I smiled too.

In the ladies' room, stares, gasps and murmurs of sympathy didn't help. The door attendant got me a taxi and I sped home; the driver waited, while I shouted to the bemused John to fill a basin with cold water. The saturated clothes soaked there while I had the fastest shower ever then got back into the taxi. I arrived just in time to catch the laughter and applause at the end of Fred MacAulay's apparently highly entertaining presentation.

Colin was very apologetic, was glad to see me return to the celebrations and presented me with a bottle of champagne and a bouquet of flowers on Monday. The silk outfit recovered fully.

AUTUMN 2001 – 2003

The Journey to Achiltibuie

I had my second stop on the 230-mile drive from Edinburgh to Achiltibuie to have a stretch and walk about at the Commando Memorial, a mile or so north of Spean Bridge. Visitors drifted from buses and cars, took photographs and stood with hushed respectful voices, reading the tributes and stories of the Commando soldiers.

From here there was a view of the whole of the Nevis range, white topped with early snowfall and that day, the clouds had cleared off the top of Ben Nevis itself, Scotland's highest mountain. The information board told me that the location overlooks the expansive grounds where, in 1942 the Second World War British Commando Forces, who exclusively wore the famous green berets, trained from their depot at Achnacarry Castle.

A gentleman from Toronto who was also reading the board beside me told me that his father had served with that battalion and he'd promised himself a trip to Scotland just to be here.

I still had a three-hour drive ahead with a couple of visits on the way, so settled back in the driver's seat. This autumn in 2001 seemed more vivid than I could ever remember. The snow line had descended to tree level, covering the tops of the mountains. There was mile after mile of skeletal silvery white-barked birch, with their black crusted slashes, interspersed with the deep reds and oranges of the rowan and hawthorn berries. The grasses and mosses in citrus, mustard and golden hues, tall arching copper fronds of bracken were all highlighted in the low sun's rays.

I turned left off the A835 and saw Stac Polliadh from some way off. Its vast jagged ridges becoming more defined as I drove towards it. I stopped again there in the car park beside Loch Lurgainn and learned from another information board that the mountains deep gullies and crumbling columns had been bypassed as sheet ice smoothed out the lower rock during the last ice age. Lengthening shadows stretched away from the huge boulders which had halted in the massive tumble of scree from its long summit ridge. What beauty in this long drive?

There were two other parked cars there which might have belonged to the tiny figures I could just see descending. I leant my camera on my car roof to attempt to capture the colours and this scene, to share with John, but these rich earthy scents of the end of summer, he'd just have to imagine.

I caught a phone signal so called him. Waiting for him to answer, I heard the thin mew of a buzzard and looked straight up, focusing on a patch of blue as the shredded drifts of white were dispersing. Then I spotted it, just a small dark line, gliding high up in the air currents.

'Hi John, how are you? Had a good day?'

I could hear an urgency in his voice and sizzling in the background. 'Ah. Hi Reet. Fine. I'm just cooking a fry-up for myself. How are you? Where are you?'

'I'm okay. I'm looking straight on to Stac Polliadh now. Do you think we could walk up it, or would it be too hard for us? Is this not the one with the small high-level ridge to the summit, with sheer drops on either side?'

'Yes, we could walk up Stac Polliadh and no, you are thinking of Suilven. That's a bit further north. Remember the father we met when we stayed at Lochinver? He was walking with his son. The lady walker who was stuck on the ridge on her hands and knees with fright and they'd helped her off it? That was on Suilven.'

210

'Oh yes. I remember now. It's been a wonderful day up here, blue sky, edge to edge. Can you see it too?'

No, I'm seeing crusted dishes from this morning and my sausages about to burn in the pan. I'm rushing Reet. I'm out tonight, remember?'

'Oh yes. I just wanted to say hello.'

'Okay, sunshine. See you soon. Stay safe.'

'Bye love, enjoy your evening.' Most of my phone calls home were like that. I'm fine. You're fine. Everything's fine. That's fine get off the line. He was a busy person, but it was nice to hear his reassuring voice.

What A Shock

I reached over into the back seat and pulled out the notes about this B&B from my large blue postal bag. It apparently had a commanding view of Badentarbat Bay but there were two complaints about the owners' behaviour.

First one: June this year: Young French couple returned 4.00pm-ish from a wedding reception in the village hall - needed access to their room - their baby tired and screaming - Mr Burtingside was seen moving about inside - no response to doorbell - got pushchair out of car to see if the baby would fall asleep. Husband had discreet pee in the shrubbery. Mr B. was quick to come to the door then - shouted 'My garden is not a bloody gents' toilet.' - called the husband a filthy frog. He'd thrown them out and a kind neighbour had offered them a room.

Second one: Mr B's mother refused to serve a couple an evening meal because they'd arrived 45 minutes late - they'd had to make do with the biscuits and crisps they carried in the car as snacks because there was no restaurant in the vicinity or further afield.

I had booked dinner, but no specific time had been mentioned, so drove on just in case I was thought to be late; *my* biscuits had long been eaten.

211

I dipped my headlights to climb their steep driveway in second gear and jeez; a shock shot to my very fingertips. Growling pit-bull-ish dogs; one running towards my car was jerked to a stop by a chain. Another coming out of the darkness reached my car.

Their barks and growls were chilling. The free-range one jumped up on the car, leaving slobbers on my window and I could hear his claws on the paintwork. I gave two beeps to the car horn and waited. I was afraid. An elderly lady pulled aside full-length curtains at the patio doors, then closed them again. An outside light was switched on. Was that it?

I put my headlights on full beam; bloody hell, the gralloched carcass of a headless deer was hanging by its hind legs on the high metal crossbar of a child's swing. The dogs stopped their barking as I slowly reversed the car, parking alongside two Land Rovers. I was not getting out of the car without help. I beeped my horn again. This time a young girl opened the curtains, waved then turned her head as if to speak to someone over her shoulder.

The dog, which was running loose moved over to the carcass, sniffed it then licked at the dark blood-puddle. I heard someone whistle: it glanced back with a look which I interpreted as don't even think about it, then with some hesitation lumbered off around the corner of the house. The other one had lowered its back to crawl through the well-gnawed corner of the wooden outhouse door, dragging the chain behind it.

No-one was coming. Annoyed and still a little afraid, I clicked open the boot. *Blast. It sounded loud.* I closed it ever so quietly, lifted my case and hurried on the balls of my feet to the front door, catching a whiff of the sickly-warm stench of the carcass as I passed it. I'd carried my case for fear of the trundling noise disturbing the dogs again and it battered against my legs as I hurried. No one answered the bell quickly enough for my liking, so I let myself in.

I was in an open-plan living area full of people. A silver-haired lady came towards me, red-faced and flustered. 'Are you Mrs MacLennan?'

'Yes. Goodness, I got a fright with those dogs.' I smiled weakly.

'Oh. You're here then. You didn't confirm your phone booking, so didn't know if you were coming or not.'

'I remember you taking my booking. You said your daughter-in-law was out. But I don't remember being asked to confirm it. I also booked an evening meal with you.'

'Oh well, you are here now.' I followed her as she struggled, puffing and grunting to the top of the open-plan stairs. 'You're in here. She's put you in my room. Dinner is in 15 minutes. Your bathroom is opposite. You're sharing it with the Germans.'

I sat on the bed for a minute, kicked off my shoes and lay back to recover. That was another first, a pit-bull welcome. This was obviously her room, a pair of thick stockings holding the memory of her knees and heels, had been left on the radiator behind the bedroom door. I had an internet signal, so checked their website. There was no reference to deer stalking or gun sports or, worn stockings.

A quick freshen up, then I went downstairs. I counted seven adults and four children. They had signed my colleague Sheila's report to verify that they didn't take more than six guests, but I couldn't see any sign of equipment or fire regulation signs. since her visit.

Some adults stood around drinking wine and beers, others sat by the fire on the sofa and armchairs. I smiled and mouthed 'Hello' here and there, not wanting to interrupt them listening to the guy in mole-skin trousers and thick socks. He was sitting on the sofa talking in a loud voice about stalking.

A border collie was curled up beside him and he slapped its rump, dislodging it for me to sit down. He made no effort to acknowledge me otherwise. The ginger cat which had been sitting upright, toasting his back and watching the scene with narrowed eyes, lifted his paw ready to cuff the collie if he came too close.

I brushed some of the grit off the seat, but not wanting to make a thing of it, sat down. The collie circled, placed her chin on my knee with intense eye contact. I stroked her head thinking. *Your welcome is warmer than that of the family you live with.*

The children were playing with Pick-a-Stick on the floor and one of the young girls joined me. 'Were you frightened to get out of your car?'

'I was. Did you wave to me from the patio doors?'

She nodded. 'Yes, the dog in the shed keeps running away just now, Daddy says there is a bitch like, in heat, so he is chained up.'

'I see, and the other dog?'

She glanced at the man beside me, still talking. 'She's Daddy's dog too but she doesn't, like, run away. They're not allowed into the house. This one is Floss she is old. She's gentle and sleeps at the fire when Marmalade, that's my cat, allows her. Don't you Floss.'

She stroked Floss's head and then leaned her hands on the arm of the sofa, pointing highland fling steps in her slippers, looking at her feet.

'I'm Reta. What is your name?'

'Gillian, with a G, not a J.'

'Are you a highland dancer Gillian?'

'Yes, and my mum says I have to put my kilt on and do the Highland Fling after dinner.'

'That'll be nice.'

'No. Not really. Like. Nightmare. I was dancing at the Assynt Highland Games in the summer. I only got like, a bronze medal. One of my stockings slid down, so I lost a mark. There were so many people watching.' She dropped her voice to a whisper. 'I was like, so panicking, and am nervous again now.'

I dropped my voice too. 'I don't think anyone here will be able to get a bronze medal for dancing the Highland Fling, will they?' She shook her head.

'They'll love it.' I continued 'That lady whose finishing setting the table, is she your Grandma?'

'Yes'

'She told me the guests were from Germany?'

'Yes, they are, and you know they all speak English. She says they, like, get it from about primary two. They gave us German gingerbread biscuits with icing on top. They are people shaped. Would you like one?'

'That's kind of you. After dinner then.'

We were asked to be seated and Gillian got a signal from the kitchen door. 'That's my mum. I've got to go and help carry plates to the table.'

I hurried back upstairs to wash the dog-smell from my hands and joined them. The menfolk sat at one end of the table and women at the other and I took the empty chair between them. There was only one other chair left empty. We were one short and I guessed why when Grandma and Gillian's mother arrived carrying their own plates. Somehow, they managed to share the one remaining chair, with only fleeting smiles. Stress had joined us.

Part of my job was to gather anecdotal information. The German lady beside me did have excellent English. I learned that the men had been hunting wild boar in Normandy, then salmon fishing on the Tay before arriving here. The women had flown into Edinburgh four days before, had hired a car and they were all now moving on to the Isle of Skye together. The men were still enthusing about the day's hunting today, the women and children had visited castles and lochs and enjoyed shopping over the last few days. They loved Scotland and found us all so friendly. The men were driving home with the venison and the shopping and the women and children were flying home from Glasgow.

I took my chance when the mother and grandmother were in the kitchen to gather more information and the guest's reply confirmed that deer stalking was part of the B&B business. Some of those guests' friends had stayed last October and had to cancel this year, so they were lucky and took their place.

When the cafetières arrived after a very good home-cooked meal, I moved with the ladies to the soft seating. Gillian had changed into her highland dress and while her mother was fastening her waistcoat, I took the opportunity to compliment her on her delicious home-cooking. She glanced up from her task and muttered a thank you.

Her mother put the bagpipe music on the CD player. During the first eight bars, a blushing Gillian positioned her feet, lifted her arms, with her fingers perfectly splayed to represent the stags' antlers, raised herself onto her toes and was off. She delighted the guests who clapped in time as she held her back straight, head erect and a beautiful bow in her insteps throughout. The guests applauded with gusto and asked for an encore.

One father emptied his wine glass and stood beside Gillian, his legs flailing about doing his best to copy her. Everyone laughed, even Gillian's Mum and Grandma and cheered his efforts, clapping again in time to the music. She was a little star and afterwards took the other children over to their space guiding them through the steps while they wobbled in their efforts.

Mrs B. and Grandma cleared the table and probably continued washing up in the kitchen. Mr B continued to talk with the menfolk. I complimented Gillian, who fanning her face with both hands then gave me my biscuit from her box on the sideboard.

Back in Grandma's bedroom, the handwritten note blue-tacked to the back of the door said, 'Breakfast is between 8.00 and 9.00 am. Room MUST be vacated by 10.30am at the latest'. Some joker had added *Aye right!*, and another French occupant, *Trop de petite règles*. So, this was not the first time Grandma had vacated her own room. I settled in bed and read Sheila's report from a year past in Spring.

Sheila, a very experienced QA with a reliable eye for detail had written a thorough report. She had been there only on a day-visit, had obviously not been shown Grandma's room and it was not the season for deer stalking. There had been no complaints prior to her visit but how things had changed since then.

The house was still silent at 8.00 am it had been 1.00 am before the last heavy-footed guests climbed the stairs. Anyway, I was showered and dressed so headed downstairs, but before I reached the bottom, saw the table was still littered with bottles and glasses from last night's late drinking. I returned to my room.

At 8.45am I heard activity so went back down. Gillian in her nightdress was rushing to clear the table. Mrs B was bustling about, still in her dressing gown.

I said 'Good morning. Looks like a nice day.'

'Morning' she managed.

'Do you think it safe for me to go out to the car? Are the dogs tied up?'

Turning towards the kitchen with her hands full she sighed. 'Probably. My husband is away already, and the dogs are likely with him.' She then hurried off, probably embarrassed about not being dressed yet.

What an atmosphere and I didn't feel very reassured by *probably* and *likely* so checked, looking out of the French windows. The chain from the hut had no dog on the end of it, the carcass had been removed. A garden hose lay on the ground and a stiff long shafted brush beside it. The blood-puddle had been swept to the edge of the concrete and an armada of iridescent blue-bottles was rising and settling there now.

The morning air felt sea-fresh and soft. A heavy dew covered the grass and tiny glass-like beads hung in the delicate webbed hammocks stretching across the bracken fronds. I walked down the driveway and crossed the road to the shoreline of Badentarbat Bay where the free-range sheep were nibbling the salty grasses on the long stretch of machair. The sea was smooth and looked tideless, reflecting the landscape with only the tiniest of ripples playing at the edge. My shoes made a clacking, hollow knocking sound on the dry sea-tumbled stones until I reached the shingle. I picked up a few flat stones to skim while searching for a mobile signal and was thinking I was the odd one out last night. The one who didn't belong to the party booking.

The mother-in-law is living with Mrs B and I didn't detect any closeness between them. They all fell short on customer care. She hadn't managed to get breakfast organised and seemed work weary. Maybe sleeping more people than she should was a one off, maybe not. If they normally had deer-hunters who were single occupancy in each of the four rooms and used grandma's room as well, that would still be okay without a Fire Certificate. Maybe the current booking was a one-off. Then there were the two serious complaints: one about the husband and the other about the mother-in-law. It could be a tricky feedback time.

Success. I had a signal. Well above the tide line lay the beached remains of a clinker-built boat on its side, most of its aged ribs exposed and its name gone. I leaned against it filling my lungs with the lightness and brightness of the day while I phoned the office. It was now just after 9.00.

'Hi, Tracie. How are things?'

'Hi, Reet. Oh, the usual end of year flurry and beginning of the next. Where are you?'

'I'm in the Achiltibuie area and it's a perfect morning here. How is it in Inverness?'

Our admin support team had a lovely way of dispelling the distance between us with any news. Tracie told me that Isobel, one girl in my team had stopped to vacuum her car at a petrol station. She'd emptied the boot but forgot she'd left her laptop in its bag on the ground. She'd reversed over it. Later, that same day, she'd taken a corner on a country road, maybe a bit too fast and skidded out of control on a patch of cow slurry, landing in a ditch. The farmer got his tractor to haul her car out and it was drivable, apart from a lot of muck and a few scratches, it was fine. But of course, she needed to visit another petrol station, this time for a car wash. She was okay, although anxious about the consequence of wrecking the laptop.

I asked her if there was a visit I could pick up between here and home on Thursday night on my way south. There was one and she offered to book it for me as it was not so easy for me with poor mobile coverage.

I walked back on the tarmac road, passed the dry-stane walls of a new-looking fank where the crofters would work with the sheep. It was not assembled like some, from breeze blocks, field or shore stones, but each one had been hewn to a fit with the next. It was a work of art and I thought if we wanted to branch out, have a Country Crafts award scheme, this would be a good one. Not so daft; a suggestion had been put forward for public toilet inspections. I know which we'd rather look at.

The guests' children were now outside playing, one of them on the swing where the deer had been. Grandma was putting the finishing touches to the table, placing paper napkins on each side plate, so I sat down.

'A late breakfast has been requested this morning, so we won't be serving until everyone is ready.' She announced.

'How much later do you know?'

She just shrugged, 'I don't know, just when everyone is ready.

'I'm not sure I can wait much longer for breakfast. 'I added as she disappeared to the kitchen.

I moved to a chair by the fire and a few minutes later the mother appeared with a pot of coffee and tea and a tray of cups and saucers, offering me some. She also apologised for the breakfast situation.

I had a coffee and picked up a magazine. A thin finger of smoke rose from the embers as a few fresh logs began to catch on the remains of last night's fire. By 9.30 am. two couples had still to arrive. The coffee pot was being passed around, I had been able to smell the bacon cooking, so knocked on the kitchen door.

'I have a schedule to keep to. I really need to eat now if that's possible?'

'No. Sorry.' Grandma said again, her hand on the half-open door, shaking her head. 'We've been told the others won't be down for maybe another 15 minutes. We wait till everyone is down before we cook the eggs.'

'I felt anger rising. So, you're saying I can't have breakfast yet?'

'That's what I've just said,' She might as well have added *dummy*, judging by the look on her face.

'Well I am working; I need to push on. I would like you to take the cost of my breakfast off my bill, since I can't have any.'

Grandma shrugged, adding 'You just want to pay then?'

In all the years in this job, I'd never been denied breakfast in a B&B at 9.30ish. This intransigent attitude was so uncaring about my needs. I was a paying guest.

I was not going to be able to see the other rooms anyway while the guests were still here so decided to go. There was no sign of fire extinguishers or notices, so it would appear as if they were breaking the Fire Regulations. Welcome and Friendliness, (remembering the complaints too), Reception Efficiency and Breakfast Service were all going to be marked as poor, so they were going to fail anyway.

I'd already packed, left my case at the foot of the stairs and knocked again on the open kitchen door. On seeing it was me, Grandma sighed. I offered my cheque and bank card. She turned away to write down the card details and when she returned my card, I handed her my business card. It felt as if I was being vengeful, it was not what they wanted to hear at that moment, but I was really pissed off with their lack of care. 'I'm from the Scottish Tourist Board.'

She turned to look at Mrs B who, while working with frying pans at the cooker answered 'You can see how busy we are. I'm sorry. I just can't speak to you just now.'

'Yes, I can understand that. It doesn't look as if I would be able to see your rooms this morning anyway.'

'Yes, we are full.' Mrs B apologised, rubbing her forehead, still standing at the cooker.

'I could come back later in the day.'

'I'll be out shopping, that wouldn't suit me either. I'm up to my eyes in work just now. We are just too busy.'

'Could I ask you to tick the boxes to confirm if you have a Fire Certificate and Public Liability Insurance please and sign at the foot of the page?'

I glanced at the form as it was handed back to me. They had no Fire Certificate and had ticked the box which claimed, 'Sleep no more than 6 guests at any one time'.

'I can't confirm your award on this visit, but I will write to you.'

Grandma pursed her lips and gave me a look that could curdle the milk. 'It's like the Massacre of Glencoe, we give you your dinner and you stab us in the back in the morning,'

My colleague Colin once had this said to him years ago, perhaps word had travelled. The coastal drive to Lochinver, the friendly service with my carry-out BLT and a fresh squeezed orange juice restored my belief in humanity.

Soon after, I had the report completed, covering letter written and was trying to put it out of my mind and move on to the next visit's paperwork. John had learned from Fede, our young Italian friend, a sign Italians used: they'd throw a problem over your shoulder. I could imagine him just then, advising me to do the same.

A few weeks after they had received my letter with reasons why I was removing them from membership, a letter arrived from Mr B. He claimed there had been no deer carcass hanging on the frame of the child's swing. I must have been confusing their garden with somewhere else.

The other guests were not paying guests, but a German family who had brought their daughter over as part of a school exchange programme.

Was this true? The German lady had told me they had taken a friend's cancelled booking.

They claimed I did not sleep in their grandma's room; it was a single guest room.

Coincidentally, there was a supportive letter attached from very happy guests who stayed the week after my visit, praising their hospitality and kindness.

They asked for their membership to be reinstated and have me banned from visiting again.

They were also members of an organisation which advertised farm stays and we contacted them for their opinion. Mr. B *was* a deer stalker. They had no other farmhouse B&Bs in that area and made a plea to give them another chance; that organisation had received no complaints, but the organiser did add 'I could imagine the grandma's face when confronted.'

On reflection, although I'd had a bad experience, we had enjoyed a very good meal, they had entertained us, and the guests were happy

We did give them another chance. We wrote saying that we would reinstate their award only if they paid for and had another incognito visit. We didn't say when. We didn't say that we would send a couple next time to follow up. What we did do, was inform the local Fire Officer to keep an eye out for the number of cars parked outside and check how many guests were sleeping there.

What's My Line?

The visit Tracie found for me on Thursday night was a real treat. The owners had purchased this small Four-Star country-house hotel the previous Spring, but as awards are not transferable, they required an overnight visit to assess facilities and services under the new ownership.

Guests were served coffee and hand-made petit-fours in the lounge after dinner and I was joined by an interesting couple in their 30s who'd been entertaining themselves by imagining the lives of the other guests.

They'd been people-watching and had woven a story around me. I was thought to be a divorcee or widow, travelling alone and rich because my diamond engagement ring had caught their eye. They concluded I was a successful crime writer researching my next novel. *As if.*

I told them I had a husband at home, had been sleeping around Scotland on my own for more than a decade: they got the joke and laughed. They were also amused when I told them my ring was a reward for waiting several years for a replacement to all my jewellery which had been stolen in a burglary. The insurance money had been redirected towards a more urgent need at that time; a lead roof for the new garage.

After a few years of John joking that he could change gold and diamonds into lead, I didn't find it so funny. He'd bought me this beautiful replacement as a reward for my patience when his life-insurance policy matured.

If I had been playing their game, I could never have imagined their careers. He was an RAF helicopter instructor who trained pilots to manoeuvre in war zone conditions and fly in the low-level cloud along valleys. It was not long after the horrific September 11th attack on the Twin Towers of the World Trade Centre in New York and he was about to fly to Afghanistan to join the US ground force fighting there against the Taliban.

She was a psychopathologist studying the personality of serial killers and was currently interviewing those incarcerated in high security at the State Hospital in Carstairs. Because of the nature of her work, she would only do a few months at a time without a break. She told me that the character of Hannibal Lecter was not confined to the realms of fantasy and that the public never get to hear the details of some horrific murders.

They planned to marry in Scotland the following summer and were searching for a venue. I just hoped they both stayed safe enough and alive to be able to make that happen.

Reta MacLennan

Evangelina's Way

It is a little-known fact that in 1748 three Episcopal Church ministers when imprisoned in the Tolbooth, in Stonehaven were still baptising babies by pouring water onto their heads, out through the window of their cell. But the holy water would have been blown back onto their own heads on the Autumn day I was there.

Hurricane Olga (believe it) had formed out in the Atlantic basin and the tail of it was swirling around the buildings and rocking my car in Evangelina's car park. She was from Belarus.

I decided to manoeuvre and park nose-on to the gale. I was walking at a steep angle against the buffeting gusts, holding the skirt of my raincoat closed, my suitcase flipping about on its wheels. when she saw me arriving and signalled to go around to the south side of the house. I'm glad she did otherwise I could have been blown right through their glass vestibule door without opening it.

Mr. Mitchell, Evangelina's husband, had called to say his wife was disappointed in their three-star award and wanted to go into next year's advertising at Four Stars. She had read the report and believed she had implemented all the advice she'd been given, payed for a second incognito-overnight visit and that was why I was there. Naomi, who did the first visit was one of six new QAs I'd trained the previous Spring and this place was certainly a one-off in the bedrooms; one to test a new QA's ability to lay aside any subjective opinions.

Her liquid-tan was orange-ish, her lips scarlet, her skirt was thigh-high over fishnet tights, and she wore gold, embossed-hoop earrings the size of the lid on a marmalade jar.

I relaxed in the restful surroundings of her traditional cream and pastel-green lounge; Wedgewood plaques, pictures of local scenes on the walls, in front of an open fire. Watching spume being blown off the white horses out to sea, I felt amused at what I'd just found upstairs.

I had been offered tea and refreshments at four o'clock; blinis topped with sour cream and smoked salmon, delicious little honey cakes and strong black tea. Concerned that I needed warming up on such a chilly windy day she also poured us both tots of schnapps held in the glass by surface tension. I'd embarrassing memories from my first schnapps experience, but hey, this was work. I was duty bound. I carefully clinked with her offered glass and she toasted *Nozhtrovia*, to your health. and I responded with *Slainte Mhath*. Wow, after not being allowed to refuse a top up, I stayed well back from the candles.

I asked her when she'd first come to Scotland. She purred; 'I fell in love wiz my derling Scotzman five yearz ago ven I ceme in Glazgow. I still love 'eem like vee firzt met. Eezz a verrry good man for me.'

The decor upstairs was a contrast to downstairs. Scarlet walls, deep burgundy door frames and skirting boards. Tall branches of a silver birch were placed to one side of the archway bent to follow the curve, the twigs of its denuded branches entwined with looped ropes of silvery-pearl beads and chiffon drapes, tiny Venetian masks, a bunch of black plastic grapes and a stuffed jackdaw with one glass eye, glowing red. Subdued coloured light from the stained-glass window in the end wall was echoed in the jewel-coloured glass of a dragonfly tiffany lamp on the small side table. It might have been the entrance to a high-class brothel; not that I've been in one.

Having slept in so many bedrooms, they had merged into a sameness, this one made me smile. A deep gold satin-like quilted bedspread and sham pillow-covers, cream-coloured bed linen with burgundy bathrobe and towels. A print *of Reclining-nude Facing Right*, by Gustav Klimt, hung above the bed and on the opposite wall a pencil sketch of a ballet dancer, side on, folded over from the waist, tying the satin ribbons of one of her ballet shoes. Her tutu was flipped up like an Elizabethan collar, and if she was wearing tights, they were invisible. The tea tray on a side table had a couple of Tunnock's tea cakes and today, somehow, they also seemed very sensual.

There was a small bottle of massage oil placed with a huge black bath towel to protect the bed linen. Hand-cream, cotton buds and a nail file in a dish on the dressing table were usual accessories but the items in one of the bedside cabinet drawers were not; a copy of Forum, a selection of condoms and a pocket-size pack of tissues. The videotapes included two adult ones. What if elderly ladies of a delicate nature were here? Or a Free Presbyterian minister? It might send him onto his knees to pray for her soul.

There were five of us sat at one table for breakfast; the food, a fusion of Belarusian and Scottish. Multi-grain Bircher muesli, a basket with warmed croissants, slices of rye bread, as well as the usual toast. Hot potato dumplings with strips of crispy bacon and a fried egg, cold salami-type sausage slices, meats, and relishes, blueberry and apple smoothies, a choice of jams, local honey and marmalade. The freshly-ground Arabic coffee was so strong I could almost feel my hair curl. A variation on the usual Scottish breakfast and delicious.

I had to ask for hot water for my strong coffee, to which she answered when delivering a jug of hot water. 'Eet eez good to get zee heart going in ze morningz. No?' It certainly did, my heart was already banging away.

Evangelina, in an unobtrusive way, made sure we didn't want for anything: clearing our empty plates, checking the buffet serving platters and bowls to see if they needed replenishing. This was a very attentive breakfast service.

At feedback time I did mention the unexpected items in the bedside drawer, saying that I'd never come across those items before in a B&B.

'Eet eez normal no? Eet eez nice in zee bedroom, no?'

'Yes. It is a beautiful bedroom. But I see that the beds are zip-and-link so maybe, if say, you had to separate them to twin beds for a mother and daughter?'

'Eez theez a problem for zee tourist board? I 'ad two sisters who ztayed wiz me, very very old, faces with cracks. Vun 'ad a valking stick and she told me zey laugh about ze megezine.

You eez a married lady no? You never 'ave a beet of fun on 'oliday. No? You zink zee tourist board don' like people to 'ave fun in bed in my house, only 'otels? 'otels have sexy moviez on the TV, no?'

I was feeling like a right prude now and also didn't want to upset her. 'Your home is beautifully decramental.' *Wha-a-at? A new word.* I'd been thinking decorative or ornamental. She didn't notice.

I think if you show pictures of all your rooms, with close up shots of details they will see your style of interior design. People will then have a good idea of your B&B style. Perhaps use your judgement. If some intimate items would be better removed for some guests, just do that.'

'Okay I do zat. Zee tourist board vould like eet you think?'

Phew! 'Yes, I think your guests would too.'

Naomi's notes had shown great feedback and they'd agreed on recommendations for a higher award. Evangelina had adopted all of those suggestions since then, so I was able to award her the Four Stars. She was so pleased with the outcome, she leapt off her chair and kissed me on both cheeks, flooding my nostrils with her heavy perfume.

As I left the cleaner was vacuuming the hallway. I praised her for the high standard of housekeeping. Without stopping she laughed, took a sharp intake of breath, and shouted above the noise.

'Aye. *Oanystoor'n'amootwaethecloot.*' I had to think for a moment. Any dust and I'm out with the duster. It was easier to follow Evangelina's English.

Reta MacLennan

The Good Life

In the late Autumn of 2002, I had been driving around for several days with the cloud base touching the tarmac, misting my face, frizzing my hair and warping my notebook, but today there was a promise of watery sunshine.

Driving on the main road towards Tain, in the northeast, I was looking for a side road. My directions seemed vague but were actually all that was needed. 'There should be a new sign: Old Church House on the main road, look for a small break in the pine trees in a long straight stretch.'

Crawling at under 30 miles an hour on this busy road looking for the turnoff, I'd created a tailback; a caravan went swaying past, then a lorry almost on my bumper started tooting his horn. I spotted the small hand-written sign and an arrow, so swerved off onto the side road. Just then, in my peripheral vision I noticed something white moving by the roadside. I pulled over and walked back to the junction. A hen was stuck in the shallow fast-flowing ditch one wing trapped at a strange angle against the small steep bank.

This was not a happy hen. I couldn't just leave her there.

I tugged my feet into the yellow wellies, annoyed as I felt a toe burst through my tights. I pulled on my plastic mac too. Hen-poo on my suit would not make a good first impression.

Speaking softly, I set her down on the roadside to see what would happen. The poor bird had a red weal on her head, her wing seemed fine, but she was too weak to shake her soaked feathers and toppled forward, exhausted.

She crouched there in the footwell of my passenger seat putting up no resistance with her pale-red comb flat and flabby above one eye, blinking. Then she let her head droop while yesterday's Scotsman soaked up the ditch water. She looked past caring. I'd always wanted to keep hens, but John said while they lived on Harris, he'd had enough of them. He wouldn't have a choice if I took this one home with me. Yes, he would, he might draw her neck.

I told her 'You'll be fine now if I haven't scared you to death.' I recalled bringing an RSPCA officer out to have a look at a mallard with a very swollen gullet which the boys found at the foot of our garden. We put him in a cardboard box to rest in the quiet and dark. By the time the officer had arrived the duck was dead, and the officer was very angry; perhaps also because it was New Year's Day.

The Old Church House sign appeared. With the engine purring, I drove cautiously on the rough track over soft layers of fallen pine needles. I steered between the trees, trying to avoid skidding on raised tree roots. There was now a smell of wet hen and poo, so I rolled the window down and the sweet earthy scent of pine woodland poured in. The rough track, the remoteness and the misty atmosphere seemed right for a car creeping along with a body and a spade in the boot; a knackered hen in my footwell was the best I could do.

The track rose and after about 40 metres the belt of pines gave way to mature oak and beech canopies, with an orange and copper carpet of fallen leaves. We had left the low-level mist, my hen and I and now shards of sunlight were slicing through the grey-gauze day as the trees thinned. A clearing opened out and the converted old grey-granite church appeared; my home for the night.

Blousy red geraniums in terracotta pots stood by the wide double-doored entrance. A dreamcatcher hung just inside in front of the glass inner doors. A winter's worth of logs was neatly piled under a sloping roof of shingles against the side of the building.

Two tethered goats munched the grass well away from the entrance and the arrival of my car chased a family of long-tail tits from the bird feeders, playing catch-up-and-overtake heading for the trees.

I felt a thrill of anticipation: there were hens scratching the ground and white farmyard geese with their necks stretched forward honking my arrival. This place seemed glazed with magic as if a Disney-like Snow White was going to appear from the woods with the seven dwarfs Heigh-Ho-ing along behind her.

As I approached the entrance, a lady with a baby-bump appeared in faded dungarees, and a white t-shirt, pushing her arms into a multi-coloured Kaffe Fassett cardigan. Her husband, in jeans and an oversized thick-knit black jumper, gave me a wave. They were a couple who looked to be in their mid-to-late thirties. As I parked, he stood behind her, resting his chin on her shoulder and wrapped his arms around her somewhat shifted waistline.

They both had easy smiles which started from their eyes, a look which said life was good. 'You must be Mrs MacLennan. Did you find us okay? I'm Ken and this is Rachel and sproglet, patting her tummy. Our son Adam is about somewhere on his bike.'

And I'm Reta. A laugh rose in me as we shook hands. 'I'm pleased to meet you. Would you come and have a look at my passenger, please? I'm not quite sure what to do with her. I found her stuck in the ditch water just along the road.'

I remembered I was still wearing my yellow wellies, but they didn't seem to notice that it was a strange dress-sense with a business suit.

'Oh, my poor pet,' Rachel said. She lifted the hen and cradled her round to the back of the building to a hen hut in a penned area. 'Look at her. They must give the poor things fortified feed to produce this large breast meat. That is what the customers want. It's gross.'

Rachel set about preparing some straw bedding, checked the water and scattered more grain while Ken checked her wings and feet. He thought she was probably a deep-litter casualty; they are so restricted for space they peck each other. The windows are painted red to try and prevent them from seeing the blood.

Rachel and I walked to the old church conversion together while young Adam stood on his pedals, avoiding the geese and vroomed around. 'I am so relieved you could take her. I hadn't a clue what to do with her but couldn't leave her there.'

I opened the boot for my suitcase. Rachel saw my large blue postbag, a filing system of stationery and forms and asked if I was from the Tourist Board. I smiled, nodding. She'd called the office just a few days before wondering if they'd been forgotten and said the hesitancy in the girl's voice before reassuring her, made her think that my end-of-season booking might be that long-awaited visit.

'Ken will see to your suitcase. Come and have a cup of tea with us first? We just thought there was no point in pretending, it would just be awkward.'

'You are quite right, and a cup of tea would be lovely, thank you.' I replied showing my grubby hands. 'Where can I freshen up first?'

I joined her in their open-plan space, and she moved a pile of ironing from a sofa to the dining table so that I could sit down. They'd had no guests for days then just before I arrived a couple had turned up on spec, so I'd have company for breakfast.

I asked Ken about converting the church to become their home. They bought the land and this almost-derelict building from the Church of Scotland some six years ago and lived in a mobile home on-site through two winters while they tackled the restoration themselves. Adam was born in the house in the first week after they moved in.

'But we did it.' Rachel smiled. 'My mother stayed when Adam was born, trying to ignore the bags of cement and the sawdust. We were camping here, all together.' She spread her arms indicating the communal ground floor area. 'The bedrooms upstairs didn't even have walls then. The bath was temporarily in place but just stood upstairs in the open space. My mother had a permanently startled look.' They both laughed at the memory.

I could identify with that. Our home had needed total renovation too and I told them our similar story. I was 8 months pregnant at the time and our two boys were 6 and 4. We had spent six very cold weeks in January in our front garden in a caravan loaned to us by neighbours Margaret and Denis. Even with the Calor gas bottle and pipework all lagged, that little neck where the pipe came through the floor had frozen so we had no gas heating or hot water in the freezing mornings. The windows were frozen on the inside, like when I was a child.

We were thankful for other kind friends too; Eileen had given us their house key so that we could have hot showers, another friend Hilary offered baths, complete with a back-scrub and prosecco.

After a cold six weeks of this we moved into the house. I cooked on a two-ring camping gas stove beside the standpipe, with a bucket as a basin. 'Our dog was very confused, with the floors up and cement bags and timber around he couldn't tell if he was indoors or out, so you can imagine.' We all laughed, totally understanding each other.

I'd been so keen to share the similar experience that I thought I'd gone on just a bit too long about it. If they were bored, they didn't show it.

While Ken relaxed with me, Rachel had been listening, moving about in the open-plan kitchen, a gentle trail of steam rising from the kettle on the Rayburn. The walls were shelved to take dishes, mugs, pots and pans and recycled coffee jars for storing rice and other dried goods.

Out of the oven came scones she had been warming, scented with lavender. She topped them with fresh bramble compote and thick set natural yoghurt, all their own produce.

I admired the design of the interior. Heavy exposed oak beams were recessed into the deep walls and others supported the roof right to the apex, all walls were plastered and painted white. An open-tread oak staircase was cantilevered into one wall, with an almost invisible glass balustrade and a balcony running right across the width of the building. The upper floor was cut away in front of the original tall church windows so that their light reached the ground floor level. Ken explained that this was a deliberate design feature. I wondered about ventilation to the bedrooms and opening windows but said nothing. I'd wait to find out.

The sofas were sagging and stained, the coffee table was ring marked and Ken tidied the jigsaw and Lego away to make space for our tea. This was first and foremost a relaxed and happy family home.

My eyes followed the tall steel chimney which climbed through the roof from a log burning stove. Then I noticed the thick ropes from the centre-beam attached to a swing. The dining table and seating area were positioned so as not to get in the way of its arc. I'd love to have had a go.

Ken was an aircraft designer who worked from home, his drawing board, plan cabinet, desk and computer taking up one far corner of the area beneath the upper floor. Because he was close to a BT receiver, he had the internet and used computer-assisted drafting (CAD) for his design work. Working from home suited him and when he was required to attend meetings in London, he could fly from Inverness and be back the same evening.

Rachel was a weaver. I was interested to see her work, so she took me over to her space in the opposite corner to Ken's. Beside her spinning wheel stood a basket, her carding combs lying on top of the soft ochre coloured fleece; I was told this was the result of dyeing with onion skins. Huge jars of gathered lichen, dried berries and flower heads with which to dye her wool stood on sturdy shelves and soft pastel coloured skeins hung on a clothes rail. 'I'll show you pictures of some of my work later if you like, but I have to now go to a friend's house to collect my grocery delivery.' She explained. 'The van can't negotiate the way in here.'

'That's fine by me. I have some work to do now anyway. Is my room upstairs?'

'No, our B&B rooms are in a chalet, among the trees just across the clearing. I'll take you there.'

'Oh, I did notice a log cabin further off, is that it?'

'Yes. The guests have their own place over there and eat breakfast or dinner if they wish, here with us.'

233

The phone rang, Ken excused himself to answer it and I indicated that I would see myself over there. 'Your suitcase is in your room. Come back over any time after six o'clock whenever you like for the evening meal. Just join in.'

I got back into my wellies and picked my way across the grass area avoiding the droppings where the goats, hens and geese kept the grass short. Adam got on his tricycle again and accompanied me making vrooming and screeching noises then stopped at the wooden slatted walkway across a bogy-reedbed area. This was the access route to the cabin.

He said 'Look out for giant house spiders, just put them outside if you don't like them. Don't kill them.'

'Spiders. I'm not fussed about them, but in my bedroom I am. I crossed, holding onto the thick rope handrail looping between posts, chicken wire nailed onto the slippery boards to give a better foothold.

I admired their courage in making such lifestyle choices unhampered by the restraints of convention and I appreciated the standard of the building they'd created Although it was clear that the converted church was where the money had been spent. My accommodation was a weathered old pine log-cabin, moss grew on the roof, the decking and the doormat. This was a damp woodland setting and spiders' nests, two with occupants, lived in corners between the exterior logs at the door jamb. They were not the floor-running hunters. They were web-making, thread-hanging, prey-wrapping ones and the woodland was primarily their territory, not mine.

I entered into a kitchen-dining-living room. Two doors led off this area, my suitcase was already in one. The bedrooms were very basic, with a shared bathroom. The curtains and bedding were fresh and clean and there was a heavy torch in my bedroom for which I was grateful; it would light my way to and from the house after dinner.

Rachel was cooking and Ken assisting; he handed me a glass of white wine with a smile, along with the cutlery and placemats. 'Want to just muck-in? Make yourself at home.'

I was happy to.

They were self-schooling Adam and I could see their influence in his very creative artwork held in place on the fridge by magnets. Adam climbed onto his swing whooshing past my back with the confidence of a circus performer, shouting 'Watch me.'

I walked in the beam of the torch back to the cabin, noticed that those two spiders were still bunched up in their nests and closed the door. I checked the floor and walls for others inside and thankfully found none.

I wrote my report and once settled, read my book for a while, put the light out and was almost asleep when I heard the couple in the adjacent room returning. I had to sit up and look to convince myself they were not actually in my room; there was no deafening in the walls. I soon heard every whispered giggle, the rustle of clothing, the sighs, the quickening of breath and bed creak.

I felt a bit like a voyeur, just without a peephole. If I had even coughed initially, they would have realised I was next door, I lay awake in the darkness, afraid to move in case the bed creaked.

I heard the lightest tap right beside my ear on the pillow. A spider! I sat up fast, a loud shuddering sound of revulsion escaping from my throat. They must have heard that.

Leaping out of bed, I caught my foot in the tucked-in sheet and tripped, slamming into their wall. I scanned the darkness with one arm to locate the bedside cabinet, knocking over the lamp and my large bottle of water and heard the heavy torch hit the floor and roll away. *Oh, Help, help help.'*

In the total darkness, I felt along the wall and located the light switch by the door. An almighty grandad of a spider, almost crab size, stood high on its legs on my pillow, looking in my direction. I found the drinking glass and advanced towards it. It disappeared down the back of my pillow. I lifted the pillow and saw it scuttle between the mattress and the wooden bed frame, so had to lift the top end of the mattress to get at it. It dropped through the slats onto the floor. More noise as I pushed the bed aside. I saw it stand ready to sprint again.

Remembering our son Douglas had quoted me a statistic about the number of spiders we eat in our sleep, a chase began. I caught it under the glass, but I had trapped a leg. I eased the glass off. It was so big it just fitted into the glass and no more, but I won. It would be imprisoned there till daylight then I'd return it to the outdoors. Would it have enough oxygen? It might die a slow death during the night. Anyway, I was not opening the door to let it outside. It would just have to shallow breath.

From the other side of the wall was utter silence.

I lay there, thinking about the high chance of another insect, alert for the least sound of scuttling. I recalled my boss Richard's experience of finding two cockroaches running up his leg. He'd to resort to fetching his sleeping bag out of the car to ensure it didn't happen again. I'd no sleeping bag.

I tensed and relaxed my toes, legs, worked my way up to my jaw to calm my anxiety and was drifting off when snatched awake by the loud ticking of the rusted wall-mounted electric heater which now glowed red where it shouldn't. I was in a wooden cabin, in total darkness (except for the glow), the bedside lightbulb broken, no fire extinguisher and no fire blanket.

Richard had once noticed the lack of a Fire Notice in one guest house and the owner had responded with 'Oh I'll just shout loudly '*Everybody ooot*!' Poor me. Poor spider?

In the morning I was still alive. The spider was still alive, so I threw it outside. I told myself once again, most of the things I worry about never actually happen.

I heard the other guests getting up at 7.00, I saw them walk with their backpacks to the house and by the time I arrived for breakfast at 8.00 they had gone.

I had noticed a slight give in the flooring under the lino in front of the shower cubicle so pointed it out to Ken. He crawled under the cabin to discover that the waste pipe from the shower must have been leaking for some time: under the new linoleum, the wooden flooring was quite sodden, even coming away in his hands. he was dismayed, imagining the essential work and cost in time and money.

I really liked Ken and Rachel, they were relaxing to be with, but I imagined they might not like the award I was about to give them. The high quality of the church conversion and their excellent food was affected by the untidiness and well-used furnishings and the low quality in the cabin. Therefore, their award only amounted to Two Stars.

They took the news very well and as they intended to invest in improved heating, fire precautions, plaster boarding the internal chalet walls, adding insulation and deafening, we agreed on an Award Pending: the shower plumbing and damaged flooring now becoming a priority.

I told them about the late-night antics. I could see their concern, turning to smiles. They looked at each other and burst out laughing. The couple who'd just left had said they'd heard thumping and banging and wondered what the guest(s) next door were up to.

I asked them to let Adam know the spider was alive and outdoors now. As I left, I was presented with half a dozen of their free-range eggs and they told me they'd named my rescued hen after me. That was cool. Better than a rose.

Duke of Gordon Hotel

It was now the Autumn of 2002. I was working in the Cairngorm National Park where tourists can walk and cycle in the surrounding hills, the Rothiemurchus Forest or around Loch an Eilein and ski on the slopes of the Cairngorms. I met up with Neil in Kingussie and over a coffee break on his way to Inverness he conducted my annual review. He had been promoted to Chief in the previous March when Richard's career had taken a different route, so was now my boss.

Everything had gone well with my review and I stayed over at the imposing Victorian stone-built Duke of Gordon hotel owned and run by the Southcott family. It stands on the main street in Kingussie, with a backdrop of heather-clad hills.

In front of it, is a well-tended public garden where we stopped many years ago after collecting our first Jack Russell puppy, Ross. It was his first outing and autumn leaves were whirling on the grass then too, rising in little columns. At first, he wouldn't leave our feet, but after ten minutes was tumbling amongst them chasing them down.

The hotel hallway has original oak panelling. The open fire was well fuelled and a welcoming warmth and smell of the wood burning gave a real highland feel. I had time to take this in as I waited behind a gentleman at reception who was trying to get the best deal.

'Am I hearing right? B&B is £42 and £19 for dinner? I could have got it along the road for £26 and only £12 for dinner.' The potential guest protested.

'Well, that's a very good price, why didn't you take it? Drew asked him with a hint of a smile.

'I would have, but they were full.'

'Ah well' said Drew with his smile broadening, 'When we're full we could tell you we are only £12.50 for B&B and £9 for dinner if we liked.'

There was a pause, apparently, the gentleman laughed heartily then booked five nights for his wife and himself, shook hands on it and offered to buy Drew a drink later.

I'd arrived very late for my evening meal after most people had finished, but no one rushed me or limited my choice of food. A gentleman guest stopped as he passed my table, 'Enjoy your meal? It's just like home cooking and plenty of it. Oh yes.'

He was right. I felt satisfied and relaxed and noticed that those leaving the dining room seemed equally contented as they drifted towards the sound of live music. In the next room, the ceilidh was well attended; the sound of the music, singing and laughter drifting into the hallway and this on a Tuesday night too. I took my coffee through to listen and watch and was soon tapping my foot to the music.

A two-piece accordion and fiddle band was playing Scottish tunes and couples moved around the room dancing the Gay Gordons to the tune of Donald Where's Yer Troosers.

An elderly lady in a wheelchair was watching from her table beside the dance floor, clapping her hands and singing along. One of the staff delivered her drink to the table and said something to her. She nodded and the young gentleman waiter, put down his tray and wheeled her onto the floor. He guided her and her wheelchair through the motions of the dance and the others made space for them; forward, reverse, swivelled her chair to the right, then left and turned her around. She moved her hands about in time with the others and at the end, got a round of applause. The waiter bowed to her and she hugged him.

When I met with Phillip Southcott and his two sons, Richard and Drew next morning I was very impressed with the commitment to their philosophy; maximise revenue, minimise costs and look after your staff. This had resulted in an occupancy rate of 90% and allowed them to keep their high-quality trained staff, all year round; not easy when there is a high demand from other hotels. Staffing is one of the hotel industries highest outlays and this approach ensured them the most effective percentage on wages spend too.

Their second largest outlay was food and being able to rely on consistently high quality at the right price, had been difficult. They moved to buying from local producers, providing a steady stream of demand which also benefited the growers. The same applied to the quality and quantity of meat. They found local farmers who could guarantee the quality, then employed their own butchers; one full-time and two part-time and installed huge walk-in fridges and freezers.

Phillip reached for a file and flipped through it until he reached what he wanted. 'In the last year we have gone through 4 tons of beef, 3 tons of pork, 4 tons of venison, 4 tons of premium salmon, and 2 tons of trout. Buying in bulk and supporting the local producers we can ensure a constant supply all year round.'

The main thrust of their business was coach-party bookings from tourism operators. However, those companies, if they couldn't fill a coach would cancel at very short notice, leaving the Southcotts with empty rooms and no time to fill them.

They'd found a solution to this major problem too by buying their own coaches. They advertised in the press in the north of England and the Midlands, offering a pick-up and drop-off service for a three-night half-board stay, including excursions to the Highland Wildlife Park, top of the Ski-lift on the Cairngorms and live entertainment every evening. Within three days of advertising in local newspapers, they could fill the hotel.

They also had a high return rate in guests. Phillip told me 'Some of our guests visit so often they are like old friends. Two of our guests, Brian and Eileen, had been travelling up from Birmingham, coming four or five times a year since 1985. They then moved up here and now live only two hundred yards away, but still, come here for Christmas and New Year, Eileen pops home to do their washing. They also attend the entertainment on the nights they are not resident.'

I was very impressed by their enthusiasm and commitment which had resulted in a very successful business.

Bad Karma

This couple's impressive website showed me a new bungalow within the Cairngorm National Park and told me that they welcomed and were equipped to cater for families with babies and toddlers. They offered highchairs, cots, safe play areas, toys and a babysitting service. There was a photo of them in their well laid-out garden with plenty of equipment and space for children to play.

Angela had smiling eyes and an air of calmness about her when she answered the door to me amid chaos.

A young mum was breastfeeding a blanketed bundle, standing, swaying in front of the fireplace with a screaming toddler wrapped around one leg. Another girl of about three was lying under the coffee table amongst a scatter of plastic toys beside a good-natured golden retriever, lifting its ear and shouting into it. 'Give me back my Lego.' The father was kicking a softball around with a boy of about four or five. I was glad the children were all bedded down by 7.00 in the evening and the house was quiet.

I woke very early feeling pain, but not sure at first, from where? I put on the light. A wasp was on my bed. I'd been stung on the inside of my upper arm. I dispatched it with my rolled-up newspaper, picked it up by a wing and dropped it in the waste-bin.

I put the light out and thought in all my years of travelling, I'd never had to kill a spider until a few weeks ago, and now a wasp.

It took me a while to get back to sleep, then I wakened again, was stung on the neck this time and there were two more wasps on the bed. I was sore. I killed them too.

I then saw one fly out from the ensuite followed by two others buzzing around then heading for the curtains. There were more there. In the darkness they must have been attracted to the white bed linen, now to the first light of day.

The chorus of their buzzing scared me like a Hitchcock film. I pulled on trousers, tucked them into my socks, then put on a thick jumper.

I traced the source. It was the extractor vent above the shower: they must have had a bink up there. I tore off a sheet of toilet paper, climbed onto the edge of the bath, because I am not tall enough otherwise, and let it be sucked against the grill. That is how we checked if an extractor was working.

I became a vindictive killer: I pulled back the curtains and as they settled on the window I used my own full-proof system. They didn't see the clear A4 plastic folder coming towards them. I could see through it and squashed them with my thumb.

Being someone who hand-fed a blackbird at her back door and makes insect houses, I was shocked at my own commitment to kill. Maybe I could have just opened the window. I consoled myself with knowing they were in the slow lane at the end of their lives anyway and had saved them from a cold and starving death.

After a very quick shower, I heard children crying. There was movement in the house. My hair still wet, I found the owners in the kitchen and brought them to my room.

At first, they were very concerned that I'd been stung, that was before they saw the pile of little innocents. I'd scooped them up onto my newspaper, leaving it on the carpet.

The three of us stared at the carnage: it looked worse seeing them in a heap. They'd only been trying to get out to forage after all. I felt guilty now, heat rising to my face.

They looked with astonishment and horror from me to the neat pile of wasps; squashed, battered, some with legs still twitching.

I offered. 'I'd been stung. Twice. On my arm. Then my neck.'

They remained silent. Then I remembered. *Good grief! They are Buddhists.*

I tried again. 'They are sluggish at this time of year anyway. They're beginning to reach the end of their life.' It sounded a lame excuse when I heard myself say it.

They were just too polite to comment, but I could see the concern on their faces for what my bout of violence had done to my Karma.

Two Christines

On another staycation holiday, on a Sunday, John and I needed to cross the main road at the foot of the driveway to Crathie Kirk, on Royal Deeside just as a policeman stopped the traffic. Not for us, but for the Queen and Duke of Edinburgh: they were leaving the kirk in their mirror-finish polished Rolls Royce. I could see the reflection of the coats, trousers and shoes of the people cheering at the roadside as the car slowly passed by. Then other royal family members followed in the tiny cavalcade which drove them back to lunch at their Scottish residence, Balmoral Castle.

I heard an American lady say afterwards 'Geez. No horses, carriages. I told you we should have gone into the church, Martha. Lovely hats, waving gloves. Was that it?'

What she didn't know is that it is not possible to see the royal family during a service anyway, they have their own side entrance and they occupy their own pews, giving them privacy, to one side of the altar.

John and I were spending a week at the award-winning Crathie Courtyard Cottages on holiday with our friends from Sheffield; Christine and Conrad and her family. Christine did extremely well to find this place in Scotland where we could all be together; so comfortable and beautifully presented with facilities which were a great help for Conrad in caring for Christine, who had multiple sclerosis.

Dr Christine Barton was a pioneer in improving facilities for disabled people. With her logical and practical attitude, she'd helped many hoteliers with an accessible approach to their facilities. She'd wanted to hear the story of how this well-thought-out facility had come about. It was just not possible during our visit to speak with the other Christine, Mrs Sloan, the Rev. Sloan's wife who'd had the initial idea for this project, but I wrote to her afterwards, and she emailed me with the following attachment. Her story is worth telling.

A New Venture Begins - from Mrs Christine Sloan.

'In 1996 my husband became the new Minister for the Parish of Crathie and Braemar. We settled into the large rambling manse in April and soon discovered an extensive garden and beyond, on the banks of the River Dee, the manse stables; a reminder of the status and requirements of ministers in bygone days!

'Through years of neglect, those granite buildings had become dilapidated; broken doors, shattered windows, sagging roofs and was overgrown with weeds. During our first summer, we had picnics with friends on the bank of the Dee in front of the stables and weather permitting, got very wet playing in the shallows. I felt privileged, enjoying this unique private place.

'Ministers are said to be called to their new parish and wives are assumed to be willing companions! Looking at the stables, an idea took shape and I began to feel a definite call from God to pursue the idea of sharing the beauty and peace of this special corner of Deeside.

'As I made friendships with members of the congregation, I shared my wish and a small group of us eventually met regularly to talk about the possible restoration of the stables and how they might be adapted to benefit the wider community. The VisitScotland website showed very few self-catering properties with fully accessible facilities and even fewer where those with disabilities could share the space with their families. I held on to a conversation I had with a couple who both had cerebral palsy but lived independently in their own flat. "We don't need nursing care; we just need the right equipment to be provided and we can't find it."

'In 1997 these ideas took shape and the vision of such a holiday facility developed. Within the presbytery, we found a wonderful ally, our Property Convenor who happened to be an architect. He was excited about rescuing the buildings, and despite there being no funds, he agreed to draw up provisional plans and costings.

'Our enterprise was now a major challenge; actually, became an obsession. To provide evidence of the need for such a development, a questionnaire was sent out to gain an insight into their requirements: the Deeside Disability Action Forum and around 100 organisations which represented people with health issues or impairments,

'We needed to establish our project as a charity, fortunately, I already had experience of that, then our fundraising could commence. We made accurate costing, sought planning approval and put a business plan in place before embarking on the task of raising £600,000.

'Starting with a small donation of £250 from Crathie Church and no professional help we approached grant-giving bodies and completed numerous application forms. As "sorry to disappoint you" replies came trickling in, we realised that a small, unknown and untested charity could not compete with the well-established ones. We then embarked on a major publicity drive: photos and news updates in the Deeside Piper, fundraising events within our local communities, ceilidhs, coffee mornings, sponsored events, Burn's suppers, fun activity days and a charity shop which proved to be very successful. We applied to the National Lottery Community Fund for financial support and despite major disappointments and setbacks, our fourth attempt was successful, and we celebrated in June 2001, reaching our target of £600,000.

'We gave the go-ahead to our contractor and could hardly believe it when the diggers finally rolled down into the site and worked throughout the winter. They completed the rebuild and refurbishment for the opening in 2002. The pleasure and excitement of our first guests, The Scottish Disabled Ramblers made it all worthwhile.'

John and I relaxed on a picnic blanket outside the cottage by the river Dee with Conrad, Christine in her garden chair, laughing because I'd had to run after their golden Labrador Meg, her assistance dog, to retrieve one of my sandals. Meg loved chewing any footwear left lying about.

Christine told us of the time when she'd still been able to move the little joystick on her wheelchair and had come into the house from their garden. The conservatory door had blown shut behind her, leaving Meg outside. Christine's mobile phone was outside too, and it rang. Meg dutifully collected it, and not being able to give it to Christine, stood looking at her through the glass door, with a wrinkled forehead. When Conrad came home, she'd to tell him 'The mobile is buried in the rockery.'

245

Our dear friend, Christine had a severe form of multiple sclerosis. Only a slight movement of her head remained now and that was it. Despite this, she chaired the governing bodies of the General Social Care Council and the School for Social Care Research, was Trustee of Voluntary Action Sheffield and as she said, could still cause trouble on committees in the many other organisations she worked with. In 2000 she was honoured with an MBE for her services to disabled people.

Christine did bring two important advantages to this retirement phase of her life: firstly, she had the professional qualifications and experience to work at senior levels and to be listened to with respect by decision-makers. Secondly, although the level of physical impairment created by her MS was devastating, her brain and speech were largely unaffected. She used a voice recognition programme to write reports and emails and when going to London by train for meetings became too difficult, she set up video conferencing from home and carried on working.

This year, 2002 was also a significant year for them. They updated us on their current idea of a project; one of Christine's inspirations, a website called the www.accessible-property.org.uk which Conrad would run from their Sheffield home, advertising properties for wheelchair users.

They'd realised that when someone with disabilities plans to sell their home, they are generally advised by estate agents, to remove the special aids. However, those with mobility impairments are looking for just such homes. They were almost up and running and would eventually wish to have web-links with national estate agencies and were intending to add a section on holiday accommodation, including Crathie Cottages.

People who knew her remarked that she lived an extraordinary life. 'No,' she would say, 'I try to live an ordinary life – I just have to do it in an extraordinary way.' One of her last roles was as a lay reviewer assessing research bids for funding for the National Institute of Health Research. She worked right up until the week before she died, in March 2013.

In order to achieve their goals, those two Christines applied themselves with the same qualities: vision, determination, endless patience and a tenacity to make their dream became a reality.

Memories

Something about crossing even the shortest stretch of water on a ferry always gives me the feeling of reaching another land. Even the car ferry churning across the Corran Narrows on Loch Linnhe, just south of Fort William to Ardgour on the Ardnamurchan peninsula gave me one of those moments.

Now that it was 2003, I would be retiring in October. I was very conscious of the fact that I'd really miss driving through all those scenic parts of Scotland. I felt attached; my sense of my place had expanded from my house, my village, my cities to become my country. I was familiar with the places, the people behind their front door where I'd been invited in with a purpose. I would remember their kindnesses, their friendship, their experiences with guests, their personal stories and the ones I might one day write about.

Which Hotel?

Driving from the Corran ferry to Kilchoan, I passed places where memories rolled through my mind. In Strontian I arrived at my hotel; they'd no record of my booking, which was strange. Only after I'd sat on the bed, plumped up the pillows at my back, drank their complimentary tea, eaten the shortbread and used the loo, did I read the last QA's description of the bedrooms. There was no similarity. I went to the dressing table, looked at the room information and read the name of the hotel.

I returned to reception to confess, feeling deeply embarrassed about being in the wrong one.

The young chap on the desk couldn't give a toss. He leant on his folded arms, smiling at me. 'Did you use the shower or anything?'

I hadn't and told him what I had used.

Shaking his head, he continued 'So I'll have to change the pillowcases, the duvet cover, clean the loo, change a towel, refresh the tea tray. There's only me here too. No-one else to do it.'

I gave him a good tip, from my own money of course and wasn't that bothered whether he told anyone or not. But he amused me. Time to retire.

Checking into the right hotel which was a stones-throw away, I hoped they hadn't seen me leaving the other one. It was one of those hotels where the owners run it alone in the shoulder months and enjoy refreshing their skills in turning their hand to everything the staff take care of in the summer.

I felt a poignancy that evening, sitting alone looking out on the wind-driven rain falling into Loch Sunart. I would even miss that too.

Laura Ashley Land

Then on to Loch Sunart I recalled the time I parked alongside an empty beach on the shore and sat in the passenger seat wriggling into my black jeans and removing my shirt to pull on a thick black polo-necked sweater. As arranged, I saw the motorboat leaving the opposite bank and speed towards me. Something was missing. A box of Black Magic.

I laid my suit in the boot of the car and pulled on my yellow wellies, zipped the relevant documents into an attaché case and with it under my arm crunched my way across the stones on the shoreline, and waded out a little to the boat.

The owners of the guest house, on the other shore, had been watching for my car. The gentleman's offer to collect me saved me several miles of single-track road then a rough track to their house. That very hospitable couple lived in a house which afterwards I recalled as Laura Ashley Land; most of the wallpaper and soft furnishings had come from there. That was a very pleasant day-visit.

Breaking News

I drove passed another memory; a small private hotel nearer Kilchoan with a reputation for impeccable services including refreshing towels and a turn-down service while guests were dining. They were also renowned for their wonderful fresh local produce; venison and lamb from the hill and local lobster, crab and scallops from the sea in Loch Sunart.

They offered a glass of complimentary sherry in the lounge before dinner when guests gathered for the announcement of the evening's menu.

It was there I met a charming couple in their late forties from the home counties; Teddy and Arabella, she told me Bella for short. They were interesting and cultured people and I passed a very pleasant evening in their company. I hadn't been informed there was a BYOB arrangement for wine, but Teddy insisted I share their Malbec, walking round to my side of the very large dining table to pour. I noticed how he gave the bottle a practised little twist so as not to leave a drip on the highly polished mahogany surface.

I had left my radio on in the bedroom and picked up some surprising news when I visited my room for a comfort break after dinner.

It was the 9th of December 1992. I heard: *The Prime Minister John Major relayed an announcement from Buckingham Palace to the House of Commons: Prince Charles and Princess Diana are to separate.*

I returned to join my fellow guests in the lounge for coffee and home-made fudge in front of the soft glow of the fire and told them the sad news.

Teddy replaced his coffee-cup slowly to its saucer and looked thoughtful. Bella was blinking fast with her mouth open. Then Teddy announced 'Bella, dear, we'd better return straight home tomorrow Charles might need a bit of support.'

Christmas Shopping

In Kilchoan, I remembered meeting a leatherworker John Chapel. His wife and he had a self-catering apartment. He showed me his work and I ordered three pleated thick leather belts as gifts for John, Douglas and Steven and a handbag for myself. When they arrived, he had hand-stitched each of our initials on our items.

Many of my colleagues and I shopped for gifts, on our travels, buying from local craftspeople to help support their work.

Get Oot O' Ma Hoose

In those last months, still more memories returned as I drove past places where I'd worked. On my way to Mallaig, I visited the Morar Hotel with wonderful views towards the silver sands of Morar where some of the beach scenes in Local Hero were filmed.

The lady in her 70s who lived just across the road had run a B&B for years and since her husband had died, considered closing. The hoteliers knew she would miss the company so offered to take responsibility for her laundry and provide breakfast for her guests if she didn't feel up to it any morning. That was enough to persuade her to keep going. They said she was a kind, old-fashioned landlady who pampered her guests. However, one couple proved to be unsuitable. She'd sent them packing.

The gentleman had come to view the room and had returned to his wife, sitting in the car, to report that it was lovely accommodation. The wife came to see for herself, pulling back the duvet to examine the sheets.

The B&B lady asked, 'What are you doing?'

'I'm just checking if your sheets are clean.'

'Could you just lift your skirt for a minute?' she'd asked.

The tourist looked at her. 'Why would I do that?'

'I just want to check if your drawers are clean enough to get into my bed. Get oot o' ma hoose at once.'

Old Seafaring Host

The end of my long journey enhanced by mountain and sea views was an initial disappointment; the first impression of Mallaig was one of corrugated sheds and industrial buildings. However, driving further in, the traditional houses, the town centre and harbour with its fishing boats, the ferry port and yachting pontoons had real character.

I found the B&B I was looking for tucked behind a terrace of cottages. I had too many overnight stays to do in the Mallaig area so decided to see this gentleman's one-bedroom B&B on a day visit.

He settled himself heavily into his fireside chair and continued carving a piece of wood into a kind of Captain Birdseye character while we talked. He was a retired mariner, his leathery skin had deep expression lines probably etched there from continuous watching for a horizon. I couldn't see his mouth move: I only know his untamed moustache and beard moved when he spoke.

He told me that his tourists were entertained listening to his seafaring adventures around the world and he was not interested in my folderols. He had read none of our guidance booklets so was not informed in the least about our requirements and had no interest in knowing. We disagreed on so many areas.

Bedside light? He raised his eyebrows. 'No need. Why would they want that when they could be sitting with me by the fire? You go to bed to sleep.'

Remove personal items from the bathroom? 'My old loofa? I dove for that in the Caribbean and cleaned it up myself. I don't mind if they use it.'

What do you offer for breakfast? - 'The usual, but If I'm busy or am having a lie-in they cook it themselves. They manage the bacon and eggs fine in my wee galley kitchen.'

Supply an electric iron? (he only had a solid cast-iron one, the kind which sits on top of a stove to be heated). 'I'm not buying one just for them.'

Richard, had heard a more interesting answer than that from a self-catering owner. 'It was good enough for my Batman in Africa, so it's good enough for them.'

I really was wondering what to do about him.

He let out the heartiest of laughs, drumming his feet on the floor saying 'Oh I've got you going, haven't I. Drink your tea and get over it.'

There was vintage dust everywhere and leaning on his kitchen table, I felt my jacket sleeve peel away from the stickiness. However, he had been entertaining guests for around 5 years, had only applied to join us last March and the local TIC had never had one complaint. No award for him, but plenty of paperwork for me to explain why.

Knoydart

This was another time I'd had to find a quiet place in which to change my clothes in the car; jeans and warm jumper with waterproof anorak, it could be cold speeding across the water, even on this sunny warm September day. There was no road into Doune Bay Lodge in a wilderness area on the Knoydart peninsula.

With a practised turn, Andy slowed the engine and stopped to tie up at the foot of the metal ladder which dropped vertically into the water. I stepped down on the rungs with the seaweed and barnacles beside me on the harbour wall at Mallaig. We shook hands and he heaved empty canisters, bags and boxes onto the harbour and carefully manoeuvred full ones onto his boat, a couple of boxes of groceries were delivered, the engine idling and gurgling during this exercise, then we were off.

Once out of the harbour, the full throttle made the speedboat stand on its stern which was now almost level with the churning wake. Long streaks of foaming waves fanned out behind us. We were really shifting. I looked back at the receding site of the fish processing sheds, the backdrop of the hills, the cottages clustered close to the shoreline.

Around the late 1960s, early 70s, I am not clear which, the original owners, Alan and Mary Robinson had been sailing off Knoydart and were very drawn to this area. They spotted Doune Bay from the sea and after making enquiries and tramping over the hills to reach it, decided it was where they wanted to settle. They became excited about the idea of living and working there. Alan could visualise a boatyard where his skills would bring in a good living.

They survived the first winter in a tent pitched within the walls of one of the ruined cottages. In the rebuilding, every tumbled stone was found and built into place, and a roof erected. However, all new materials had to come in by sea.

Their vision, determination, enthusiasm and workload were shared with their teenage sons. After some years and much hardship, including a fire which destroyed their new workshop and the boat they'd almost completed refurbishing, they didn't give up, their stoicism saw them through. They still managed to open for business. Around 1992 they invited their friends Andy, my driver and his wife Liz Tibbett to join them.

Mary had already gained an amazing reputation for her home cooking using fresh local produce. Walkers and climbers, yachties and guests all gathered there, enjoying Mary's own bread rolls, locally caught langoustines, home-baked pies, roasts and puddings. Their pine-clad dining room had become the place to be for a good ceilidh.

My bedroom was one of three, rebuilt from the row of derelict cottages, each with its own door onto a veranda and the shoreline. Looking out at the sunset view from the front door, over the Sound of Sleat to the Isle of Skye, I thought myself so fortunate to have enjoyed moments like this while travelling Scotland. The rustling sound of the breeze in the grasses, the call of the seabirds, the evening sky casting rose and violet reflections on the water were ever changing. This was tranquillity.

After dinner, I was invited to join them for a bonfire and a drink on the shore as a farewell to one of their staff who was leaving the next morning. The smell of the burning wood, sparks flying up into the dark night sky, a myriad of stars above us, my hands cupped around a glass of Merlot was a special end to a special day.

Next morning Andy dropped me off at Inverie to see two self-catering cottages. Around late afternoon the local Mallaig ferry arrived. I sat on a bench outside the cafe/restaurant, but I wasn't the only one watching for that ferry. A white speckled hen came running up from the shore. She'd learned that the cafe served ice cream cones to the tourists after it docked. I took a photo of her eating the end of my cone with the last of my ice cream.

West Highland Way

Just before my retirement, John and I walked with friends on the West Highland Way, Scotland's first long-distance footpath: 155 kilometres and now part of the International Appalachian Trail. We were easily spotted, all wearing Otago tartan bonnets a gift from David and Isobel Halliday, two of the group.

By chance, we had a week of sunny skies also brightened by the changing colours in the Autumn leaves. A bonus too: there were no midges in October.

On our first night, we strolled into Balmaha and stayed with our friends Joe and Betty Twaddle in their very comfortable

Passfoot Cottage B&B. They were walking with us and still managed to produce a hearty breakfast the next morning.

Their garden is on the shore of Loch Lomond and that evening the boats in the small boatyard close by were mirrored in the stillness of the surface of the loch. We were still too, at the end of our first day of testing exercise, muscles relaxing in the comfort of Voltarol and alcohol.

On the loch-side section from Inversnaid to Inverarnan, we could hardly take our eyes off the ground; crossing rivulets and tree roots. At Bridge of Orchy, we had a photo shoot moment with the Hogwarts Express as it had stopped at the station for a while.

Our longest walking day was crossing Rannoch Moor. After passing the towering mass of Buachaille Etive Mor, *Great Shepherd of Etive* at the beginning of Glen Coe rising some 1011 metres on our left, the end of that day's walk was in sight. We were more than ready to ease off our boots outside the bar at King's House. I downed a half-pint lager shandy so fast that when I walked to the bar to get a second one, I heard lapping in my stomach.

We were transported on to Kinlochleven where we were to stay for two nights. Exhaustion hit us as we were required to form an orderly line unlacing our boots outside on the front path of the guest house.

'Right.' Our landlady announced, licking the top of her pencil. 'I'll take your supper order now.'

Most of us had a more urgent need after downing pints just an hour earlier.

'Choices are Mushroom Soup or Small Salad. Okay? Then Chicken Kiev or Beef Casserole. Then Sticky Toffee Pudding or Tiramisu?'

We dutifully made our choices and were grateful for the massaging foot bath she'd thoughtfully provided in each bedroom. Her generous evening meals, breakfasts and packed lunch portions would have fed two people, not just one.

I waited to see if this landlady recognised me, but she didn't of course. Many one-nighters pass through her house. I'd stayed with her two years before, in my official capacity. On that occasion, she'd shown me around the rooms in the morning, turned the key of one of the bedroom doors and announced in a loud voice, 'Don't get up Jimmie, it's just the woman from the tourist board to see the rooms.' The poor man was on nightshift having worked at the local smelter and had just got to sleep. Of course, I declined to disturb him further.

The West Highland Way showed off Scotland at its best. We walked by rugged, majestic mountains and lochs, crossed the sweep of wilderness moorlands, through shards of sunlight in the ancient forests, our cameras recording all of it.

Drenched

Glencoe's dark history, majestic mountains, high corries and the deep cleft of a valley running through, attracts experienced climbers, intrepid hikers and also car-park- tourists who stop at the water cascade, in awe of all this grandeur. Even in stormy weather when it looks foreboding, it has an awesome appeal all its own.

On the last Friday afternoon at the end of September 2003 when my retirement was only one week away, I was going to Fort William and had my last chance to entertain myself. To see if I could still coast in neutral gear from the top of Glencoe to sea level at Loch Leven without touching either the brake or accelerator pedals. It needed no traffic in front and careful judgement of speed to manoeuvre the bend at the waterfall without braking and still have enough speed left to cover the long level stretch before the next dip to the coast. I managed it once again and got a *YES* moment, a trivial sense of achievement.

In Fort William, I waited in torrential rain in the car park at the south end for the storm to abate, taking the opportunity to touch base with my team. They'd had a good week, happy staff and happy members and mostly good weather: except for one girl who was trapped on the Isle of Coll, the ferry being cancelled due to strong winds.

The prevailing westerlies were funnelling up the length of Loch Linnhe, driving rivets of unseasonal ice-cold rain onto my car. After my phone calls, I decided to move round to the passenger seat for more room and use the next half hour to tidy up documents on my laptop. I pushed against the wind to open the door but once I had stepped out, it was wrenched out of my hand and slammed shut, breaking two fingernails in the process. *Blast!*

The keys were in the ignition, my raincoat on the back seat and the bloody doors locked. I'd be drenched in no time so ran for cover to the tiny car park attendant's hut at the entrance.

He held the door open for me, handed me a paper towel and told me that this often happened in the wettest town in Scotland. He was smiling and said with confidence. 'I'll get you back in lass, no bother.' He also promised it would soon stop raining and enjoyed relating tales of hats flying over the loch, motorbikes tipping over, a flying fish-supper, small children blown over and people like me, locked out and sharing his Pan Drops. 'I've sheltered four in here' he proudly claimed, 'in my wee hut, but they were wee skinny Japanese' He grinned.

As he had predicted, after a few minutes the sky cleared, the wind dropped, and it was only the torrenting ribbons of silver water, etching their way down the hills behind Loch Linnhe which bore witness to the morning's mayhem.

True to his word, he took a length of rigid plastic tape which he carried inside the rim of his cap and bumping the window with his gloved fist, manoeuvred the glass till it slipped in and over the button. It popped up. Easy as that. A law-abiding break-in. Later that day I bought him another bag of Pan Drops.

Trust the Gut Feeling

I had a day-visit to do and now sat with a lady B&B owner who, after a bad experience had decided never to take single men again. Her husband worked away from home during the week and she was alone at home with her guests.

The TIC had phoned her offering a single gentleman for a one-night booking and as he had no car, she had driven down to collect him. She thought he was a bit scruffy and definitely hadn't showered recently. He had no suitcase, just a small backpack and was reluctant to chat once he was in her car. He just didn't fit with the usual holidaymaker or working man's profile.

He had showered and left the room after an hour, taking his backpack with him. She checked his room and noticed a lingering unfamiliar earthy-sweet smell. There was only his newspaper left behind.

She felt more than uncomfortable being in the house with him alone, almost afraid and decided she wanted him to leave. She phoned the local police station, described him and her concern and they followed him in an unmarked car. They watched him meet with two pupils, not far from the high school gates. It had been pre-arranged. They called for a second police car and picked up the boys as well as the man. He'd arrived in a yacht out of Dunstaffnage on which he'd offered to crew and was pushing marijuana.

Her instincts were right.

My Final Official visit

The long driveway was hidden from the hotel by dense wild rhododendrons. Perhaps the black wire I drove over on the tarmac driveway announced approaching cars because when the grand frontage of Inverlochy Castle and its lawns sloping away towards extensive views opened in front of me, the porter was already in the doorway waiting under the porte-cochère.

I pulled up at the door and it did feel world-class standard, Scottish style. I had valet parking, my registration details were already printed, I just had to sign my name as confirmation and was then escorted to my room, offered refreshments and had the facilities explained to me. This was how it should be. It felt poignant though: It was to be my very last visit before retirement.

In my room I read Ranald's detailed report from the previous year. He had worked in a five-star establishment before joining us and missed nothing. It was good to note that the visit had gone smoothly with all the attention to detail expected at this Five Star level. I hoped that my stay would be the same; a good one to finish on.

Coming down the grand staircase for my afternoon tea I had time to admire the ornate plaster ceiling, the swagged-and-tailed windows and massive crystal chandeliers. I settled in a red velvet winged armchair with a plumped-up cushion, a crackling log fire adding to my castle-ish experience.

Act One: Four young Russians had rearranged the furniture to create an enclave for themselves, monopolising the fireside area. There was quite a dynamic in the conversation between the boy sprawled on the floor in front of the fire and the girl in an armchair. He seemed arrogantly relaxed, one hand behind his head, the other holding a full champagne flute.

The girl had an empty glass and he had control of the champagne bottle standing on the carpet by his side. She held her glass out towards him. He murmured something under his breath. She heard it, got up and gave him a hard kick in the ribs. The unexpected attack made him spill his bubbly and knock the bottle over himself. The only Russian I understood from this exchange was *fuck*.

He jumped to his feet holding his side and kicked her in the shins, then called loudly to the waiter who had just left the room, 'Hey,' pointing to the mess and his empty glass as the wounded girl hobbled off crying.

The two other teenagers in the party shared a sofa. They were reading; the boy resting his head on a cushion at one end, his legs sprawled across the girl's lap with his boots on a cushion at the other end. They lifted their eyes from their books to watch but otherwise made no move to get involved.

Act two: Shortly thereafter a growling Brezhnev-like father arrived, the injured girl limping behind him. The champagne drenched boy received a hard slap to the back of his head and the other on the sofa quickly stood up and received his. Both boys were sent off, the girls attempted to clear up, but the staff swiftly intervened, tramping dry towels into the spilt champagne, rearranged the small table and furniture, finishing with plumping up the cushions again.

Job done. Or so I thought.

Act three: The father announced to the few of us who had witnessed the scene: 'Our children are like young animals. I apologise for their behaviour. My wife, she kisses them, and I hit them. That is my job.' He laughed from his belly.

Some guests acknowledged his concern with smiles and nods. He took the rearranged chair by the fire and picking up a Country Life magazine from the coffee table.

Act four: A heavy featured lady descended the staircase and crossed to join him. Her sudden stop made her ears lobes swing with the weight of the gold they carried. Gold bracelets climbed her arms. Rings the size of walnuts must have been hampering her hands. The father stood and lifted her hand as if to kiss it, but she held it in both of hers, bending his fingers back till his expression changed to a grimace. Leaning towards his ear she whispered something. The Country Life slid to the floor as she kept a firm hold on his hand.

They climbed the staircase, the lady leading the way. I noticed he was grinning as he slapped her bottom.

John was driving up from Glasgow to join me. In such grand establishments, under the guise of being a couple, I was less likely to be from Michelin, AA, Tourist Board or a food critic and I was looking forward to his company for the last time on one of those official visits. The last time we would enjoy such luxury and only have to pay for John's food and drink; the room charge being the same for either one or two occupants.

I'd showered and dressed for dinner and was sitting downstairs in the main lounge watching for John's arrival with a chilled glass of Cointreau, lime juice and soda cocktail. I'd requested dinner at 7.30, it was now 7.00 and just before I was thinking of phoning him, he arrived.

'Ha. Hello, sunshine.' He put his briefcase down and greeted me with open arms and that big genuine smile in his eyes. 'I'll just freshen up and be right down. I'd like a G&T, please. I feel so stupid. I've left my overnight bag in the Glasgow office, but the concierge says they can give me a shaving kit and anything else I need. I'll have a speedy shower and join you.'

'It's a good job we put your weekend clothes in my car then, isn't it? I smiled. 'They're hanging upstairs ready for you.'

Ah well, that tested the hotel services. One I'd not planned.

I watched him twizzle the stick, chasing the cucumber in his misted glass and closing his eyes, savouring the Hendricks and tonic. He gave a satisfactory exhale: I imagined he was letting the working week and the long drive fade away.

'I've got great news. My visit to London yesterday? I was handed a thirty million contract over lunch at Le Gavroche. Didn't even have to bid for it. We're to provide all the engineering design services for the new Radisson Blu on Argyle Street in Glasgow. Looking around, he added, this is a wonderful place in which to celebrate. Cheers, my darling.'

'My goodness. That's fabulous. Well done John. Was it a surprise? Unexpected?'

'Yes. Totally. He told me he liked working with me, trusted me. Gave me the job. Amazing.'

John who abhorred any kind of bragging, had allowed himself that moment of pure joy. His smile widened as he looked around then reached for some olives.

I whispered. 'This is the hotel where Roger, you've met him, arrived late after his guest was already sitting with a drink and a dish of olives in front of him. Remember?'

'No, I don't.'

'He joined his guest, ordered his drink and threw back some nuts into his mouth. But they weren't nuts; they were his guest's olive stones.'

John nodded, quietly laughing He'd remembered then. 'What a mistake. He'll never forget that one.'

'At that year's Christmas party, he was awarded Gaff-of-the-Year, and if my memory serves me, a prize of an olive dish with a separate area for the stones.'

John looked around for the staff. 'I am hungry. I missed lunch.'

His gin was hitting an empty stomach. I was wary. My gentle-natured John, after a glass or two loved life even more than usual. I saw the signs: the combination of that gratifying euphoria, contentment, tiredness and alcohol, he could increasingly lose a grip on his usual social filters. So, could I, of course.

I mentioned that the standards here had to be no less than world-class and he'd to remember I was working, and he was to be very discreet with comments on the meal and services.

'No need to remind me. I know, I know. Relax. This is your very last, final, official, never-to-be-repeated, visit.'

'I will relax when I know you remember the usual rules. You mustn't compromise my feedback tomorrow.'

'Would I do that?'

'Yes. Unwittingly of course.'

Every dish on the menu enticed us. John was smiling. 'You call this work! You are going to miss this lifestyle.'

'Don't I know it. But I need to stay alert. Matthew Gray is Executive Chef. He has worked his way up here since 1996; Pastry Chef, then Second Chef then in 2001 became the Executive

Chef keeping the one Michelin star, three AA rosettes and he has five Red Stars.'

'So, you've done your homework then.' John smiled.

I ordered my main course; Pan Fried Roe Deer marinated in gin, with a pomegranate and star anise sauce, roasted baby leeks with crumbled walnuts and potato and celeriac dauphinoise. John's choice was Breast and Confit of Wild Mallard with Duck Pate Pithivier, sweet red wine jus, red cabbage with cox's orange pippin, roasted garlic and caramelised pearl onions.

The sommelier asked, 'Have you decided on your wines?'

At Five Star standard, I'd have expected him to be already informed on our food choices and be introducing a small range of complementary wines across a price range.

We chose a half bottle of a crisp dry Austrian Riesling to accompany John's starter of a Hot Salmon Mousse and my Cream of Celeriac Soup with Chorizo Samosa and Truffle Oil. And to go with our main courses, a half bottle of a rich red from Cahors.

Two staff came to the lounge when our table was ready, one to collect our drinks and seat us, the other to clear the table and again, plump up the cushions. I didn't want to be fussing John or spoil his euphoria, but his celebratory mood made me nervous.

Out of the corner of my eye, I saw the sommelier approach his side table with our half bottle of white. He didn't taste our wine. I whispered. 'The sommelier's coming over with it now. If he comes to you first, ask him if he's tasted it.

'What's that?' John asked.

'Would you like to taste the wine sir?'

'Oh! Perhaps my wife would prefer to taste it.'

He hesitated, then came around and poured a little into my glass.

'She's the expert.' John explained. 'Or she thinks she is!'

The sommelier smiled.

When he left, I whispered again. 'It's okay. You could have tasted it yourself.'

The Austrian wine was fruity at first then had an aftertaste of fresh air. A light condensation was gathering on the outside of the glass and a few bubbles just breaking on the surface. A perfect choice for our starters.

'Remember I told you to just nod and say, thank you if you are asked for an opinion on the food.'

He laughed. 'I won't do that. I've always thought that's a stupid reply. I can't just sit here like a dummy. I have the right to my opinion. It will be perfectly okay.'

'You think everything is perfectly okay.' I murmured, in case the staff were watching.

In fact, after all these years he still says 'perfectly and okay in the same sentence. His *perfectly* and *okay* come from a well-trained Free Presbyterian tolerance, sense of security and well-grounded childhood on the Northton croft in Harris; there was no electricity or running water and the toilet was in the byre. That had to be perfectly okay for him then.

He signalled for the waiter. 'Could I have some more butter please?'

'I was going to say, don't ask, see if he notices we need more first, but what was the point now. I gave him that look which he understands.

'Relax Reet. Just enjoy it. You are not going to downgrade it anyway.'

'What! If they don't make Five Stars on this visit, I can't confirm Five Stars. They can request another incognito visit and …'

'Oh, come on, when did Gleneagles, Turnberry, Inverlochy, what else, the Balmoral or the Caledonian ever lose their Five Stars? It is not going to happen. Just enjoy it. R-e-lax'.

'As I was going to say; if they don't make the grade, they will want to sort things out. They would have a second incognito visit just like any other member. But we wouldn't ask them to take down their plaque for a few months. Hotels must train new staff to a high standard; they can make mistakes. It is the management and training systems I am considering. Consistency of service.'

I really didn't want to be snippy with him. Why was I bothering with an explanation of what he already knew? I didn't want this evening to deteriorate into bickering, so stroked his hand. He understood.

I suggested we swap courses halfway through so that we could taste each other's choices. We were not disappointed. Both the main courses were cooked medium rare as requested, the subtle depth of richness in the jus with my roe deer and John's brambly sauce with the mallard was superb.

One kitchen error which must have escaped notice at the pass. The stack of dauphinoise was burnt to dark brown on the underside. Matthew Gray would want to know.

The red wine had been decanted. It had very little aroma, although it was at room temperature, and I didn't like the taste. There was a brownish tinge to the reddish-purple and it was rather cloudy. Some unfiltered wines are left to be cloudy, but something might be wrong. Perhaps it was oxidised. I wasn't sure. I could embarrass myself if I was wrong.

I signalled to the sommelier. 'I'm not sure if there is something wrong with this wine, but it is not as I remember it.' *What a story.* 'Would you mind tasting it for me please?'

The Maître D' returned to apologise, saying that the sommelier was off that night and the waiter was in training, but he confirmed that the wine had oxidised. *Phew.*

He told us that because there is limited demand for half bottles, this small vineyard opens full bottles and decants them into halves: W*as this true?* During this process, oxidation can happen. This allowed me to see how they handled mistakes. We enjoyed the more expensive replacement at no extra cost and in the circumstances, the situation was recovered beautifully.

The dining room had been fairly quiet, enough soft furnishings absorbing the murmur of conversations until a group of loud-voiced guests were led to the round table in the centre of the room.

Reta MacLennan

The host, a rotund gentleman in tartan trews, wine coloured velvet jacket with a satin roll collar who looked to be a septuagenarian, was heard saying 'I'm usually here with my mother.' Then directing his guests where to sit pulled out the chair beside his own. 'You sit next to me Clary I want to hear about your cruise.'

One of the other elderly gentlemen guests was an Alan Bennett look-alike, except his blond-ish toupee perhaps once matched the colour of his silvering hair. His raspberry-coloured linen jacket drooped well beyond his shoulders.

Clary was a bleached-straw blond with an eight-inch cleavage, a Diana Dors type with lipstick applied well beyond her narrow lip-line maybe imagining it made them look plump. The other really elderly blond lady was skinny as a French-fry. The third lady didn't seem to fit with the group. She looked studious, her hair looked as if she'd cut it herself in the dark, she wore no makeup and her peach-coloured crimplene suit was from the 1970s.

The gentleman beside her was hidden from my view, but I did hear him laugh on the intake of his breath and often trumpet into his handkerchief. If it had been August and we had been in Edinburgh I would have believed we were at a Fringe show.

If only I'd been able to master eavesdropping on more than two simultaneous conversations but occasionally a raised voice would break through the babble, surface like a synchronized swimmer before sinking back into the ripple of murmurs and occasional laughter.

'It is really hard to divorce one when he's so ill.'

'People might think …. and he was so unreasonable.'

'I said now darling, there's no need to bring up minor motoring offences.'

'Thank you darling. I knew you'd understand; you've been put through the mill too.'

'I think your lectures are outstanding, everyone should hear them.'

'Isn't he the one who hanged himself?'

'Didn't he represent you at one time?'

'I said to the driver just take me to the nearest Casino.'

'He was a bit bent and always looked like a travelling salesman.'

'I thought I saw him once and said to him "Is that you?" to which he answered "No it's not. I'm escaping." He never paid his debts you know.'

I had set my alarm for 2.00 am which would not have been an unusual time for a jet-lagged tourist to want fed. While waiting for the food to arrive I wondered about the explanation regarding the oxidised wine. I'd need advice on that.

I heard a gentle knock 'Room Service' and a plate of hot scrambled eggs and smoked salmon was delivered with crisp brown toast and Earl Grey tea. Thank goodness this was the last time I'd have to taste food in the middle of the night and flush it down the toilet.

Next morning, I called our son Douglas's friend Jamie who is now a renowned sommelier. He confirmed that where small wineries can perhaps only afford a standard size bottling run, they do decant from larger bottles into the half-sized ones.

Matthew, the head chef, had reputedly a gentle nature was not a shouter or a bully with his brigade, like some chefs. He ran an orderly and quiet kitchen. He found it hard to believe that the dauphinoise had a burnt bottom and set off to find out why. He was back in five minutes with the explanation. The young kitchen trainee who was cleaning up had moved the oven-tray with the potatoes onto a hot plate by mistake, submitting it to fierce bottom heat. 'He was mildly annoyed, but now that he knows, I would bet that wouldn't happen again.'

Regarding the half-bottle episode, the Maître D' was glad we'd drawn it to his attention and would in future do the tasting himself when the sommelier was off. Problem removed.

Having experienced all the service elements, also observing the service at other tables we'd indeed had a Five Star stay and I was confident in confirming their award

Retirement arrived

After eleven years with the Tourist Board, it felt like the right time to go. I loved my job, I'd felt useful. It had been rich in experiences; the thrill of a successful retraining programme for hotel inspectors in South Africa. The unexpected: being physically threatened by Scrook in North Harris. The warm feeling of belonging in getting to know people in the island communities. So many interesting memories. I felt an acute loss.

My colleagues and I had indeed removed the rascals, the poor-quality places from advertising with us, influenced our accommodation providers in Scotland and standards had risen. I'd miss contact with amazing people in the industry, my gregarious colleagues, our post-meeting suppers followed by banter and dancing together like one of the Wild Things in Johnny Foxes' pub on the banks of the Ness.

Being paid to drive into the farthest corners of Scotland's spectacular countryside was wonderful. I'd have to part with my leased petrol-blue BMW with cruise control too, which filled the gap after my Opel Manta finally retired.

I was going to lose my identity. Who would I be now? When meeting new people, work would inevitably come up in conversation 'I used to work for the Scottish Tourist Board. I managed a team of Quality Advisors.' But there was something about 'I used to … which seemed a bit sad at the moment, as if life had just stopped.

I needed to be with people and was glad that six months previously, I had thought about opening a B&B in our home. I had so much experience of high standards now, so much information on Scotland to share, I ought to be able to do what I'd encouraged others to do. I could still get my people-fix and have an identity. Why did I need one? Why could I not just, be?

I delivered my leased car to the Edinburgh office and got the train to Inverness for the last time. I attended my last departmental meeting; it was a strange feeling, listening to the discussion and decisions in which I'd play no further part. Keeping quiet was difficult for me.

That evening, Friday 3rd October 2003 at my retiral party, a buffet of hot and cold food soon disappeared from our plates and we laughed at Mark's sketch; Laura, Catherine and Mark in silly clothes, flipping the pages of their scripts while looking at a makeshift bed, caricaturing the problems of the worst B&B ever.

Colin made a farewell speech, backed by a slide show, clicking through photographic memories of milestone events we'd all shared and Christmas party revelries. I was delighted with my unexpected retirement gift. A fine gold necklace and matching bracelet.

Back home, Monday 6th October was the start of our retirement project. Builders were knocking through the walls of our 200-year-old cottage disturbing ancient plaster dust, truly as fine as face powder. John had designed a reconfiguration of our home to incorporate ensuite shower rooms.

We were open for business as a B&B with guests in residence for Edinburgh's Hogmanay and a new lifestyle had begun.

This book has been self-published on Amazon, Kindle Direct Publishing. As an indie author, I need good reviews to be able to promote it.

If you have enjoyed travelling with me through my stories, I would be very grateful if you would place a really enticing, complimentary and a *you-must-buy-this-book* review on Amazon please.

If you could persuade your friends and family to buy a copy and review it too, that would be fantastic. I will be ever so grateful. They can do so by searching Reta MacLennan, or One Yellow Welly in Amazon in France, Spain, Italy, Germany, Japan, Canada and USA.

Please tell me what you think about my book.

 retamaclennan.writer@gmail.com

   @oneyellowwelly